congress and the classroom

congress and the classroom

From the Cold War to *"No Child Left Behind"*

LEE W. ANDERSON

THE PENNSYLVANIA STATE UNIVERSITY PRESS | UNIVERSITY PARK, PENNSYLVANIA

Library of Congress Cataloging-in-Publication Data

Anderson, Lee, 1961–
Congress and the classroom : from the cold war to No Child Left Behind/
Lee W. Anderson
p.   cm.
Includes bibliographical references and index.
ISBN–13: 978-0-271-03223-8 (cloth : alk. paper)
1. United States. No Child Left Behind Act of 2001.
2. Educational accountability—United States.
3. Federal aid to education—United States.
4. Educational law and legislation—United States.
I. Title

LC89.A78 2007
379.73—dc22
2007017105

The Pennsylvania State University Press is a member
of the Association of American University Presses.

It is the policy of
The Pennsylvania State University Press to
use acid-free paper. This book is printed on
Nature's Natural, containing 50% post-consumer waste,
and meets the minimum requirements of American
National Standard for Information Sciences—
Permanence of Paper for Printed Library Material,
ANSI Z39.48–1992.

contents

tables

acknowledgments

This book grows indirectly out of my two decades of federal education policy analysis, evaluation, and research at Stanford University and SRI International. It stems more directly from my 1990s dissertation research at Stanford's School of Education. Subsequent events have refuted my main argument in that work, namely, that a law like No Child Left Behind could never be enacted in the United States. So much for predictions.

Many people helped me refine the ideas in this book. I am grateful to my original dissertation committee and examiners at Stanford University's School of Education: Professors Michael W. Kirst, Denis C. Phillips, Milbrey W. McLaughlin, and Professor Emeritus David B. Tyack. Political Science Professor Barry Weingast taught me about Congress and showed me some handy uses for "ADA Scores." Political Science Professor Emeritus Charles Drekmeier taught me a great deal about political theory and ideology. In my Stanford career, I also learned important lessons from Education Professors Arturo Pacheco (now at the University of Texas at El Paso) and Henry M. Levin (now at Teachers College, Columbia University) and from Professor Emerita Nel Noddings.

I spent more than ten years as an education policy analyst at SRI International in Menlo Park, California, and benefited from collaborations with numerous colleagues on topics as diverse as charter schools, math and science education, and schooling for children of poverty. Several of my SRI friends made important contributions to my thinking about federal education policy: Daniel Humphrey, Nancy Adelman, Patrick Shields, and Kara Finnigan (now at the University of Rochester).

Several people at, or enlisted by, Penn State University Press provided invaluable assistance to me. Director Sandy Thatcher shepherded the project through the review stage with professionalism, wisdom, and encouragement. Kenneth Wong and Andrew Rudalevige helped me refine my argument and made a number of helpful suggestions. Manuscript editor Peggy Hoover improved the book in countless ways. Cherene Holland, Kristin Peterson, Laura Reed-Morrisson, and Tony Sanfilippo have also been very helpful and efficient. To everyone at the Press: Thank you.

My immediate and extended families have always inspired me. Many of my family members are distinguished educators, writers, and community leaders. Most are past or present consumers of public education. There are even a few school board members and public university leaders.

My wife, Anne, is my best friend and supporter. She is also my critic and editor of first resort. Our daughters, Kendall and Brooke, may hope that some of their own complaints about school make it into the book. They will be disappointed, but I know they will benefit from the commitment their teachers have to quality education. All children deserve this benefit.

introduction

Conservatives and Liberals Go to School

All significant policy prescriptions presuppose a theory, a political theory, of the proper role of government in education. When the theory remains implicit, we cannot adequately judge its principles or the policy prescriptions that flow from them. . . . We do not collectively know good educational policy when we see it; we cannot make good educational policy by avoiding political controversy; nor can we make principled educational policy without exposing our principles and investigating their implications.

—AMY GUTMANN, *DEMOCRATIC EDUCATION* (1999)

Beginning with "Dame schools" and the one-room schoolhouse, education in the United States has been a local matter, and the operation and oversight of public schools has typically been the responsibility of states and local communities. Throughout most of the nation's history, the federal government was not expected to play a major role regulating or directly financing schools. Even though important types of federal support for schools and for the principle of education date to the beginning of the Republic, there has been little agreement about what educational role, if any, the founders intended the national government to play. Today, most politicians and citizens accept federal involvement in schools, but how extensive that role ought to be is still subject to lively debate. The ongoing ideological tension between proponents of an expanded federal role in schools and advocates of a limited role is the subtext of most twentieth and twenty-first-century education proposals before the U.S. Congress.

Before the late 1950s and early 1960s, it seemed unlikely that the federal role would grow beyond collecting information about the nation's schools and administering a few specialized programs (Munger and Fenno 1962). A conservative coalition of Republicans and Southern Democrats in Congress effectively opposed most new education initiatives. These foes of federal involvement reinforced one another's fears of desegregation, federal aid to parochial schools, and centralized control of education (which might entail a national curriculum).

Two pieces of legislation reversed the fortunes of federal-aid opponents. Supporters of the National Defense Education Act of 1958 (NDEA) and the Elementary and Secondary Education Act of 1965 (ESEA) rediscovered a strategy that had worked for education proposals in earlier eras. These laws established programs for specific purposes that supplemented the regular school program. Since then, the federal role has continued to expand. The Education for All Handicapped Children Act of 1975 (Public Law 94-142) was passed almost unanimously, the U.S. Department of Education was established, and the No Child Left Behind Act of 2001 (NCLB) was enacted. Moreover, President Ronald Reagan's conservative agenda for education was rebuffed in the 1980s.

At present, the No Child Left Behind Act is the most visible federal education policy. The polarizing law has attracted attention because of the sweeping new requirements it imposes on schools, school districts, and states. Indeed, the legislation is difficult to understand in the context of earlier limits on federal involvement in the nation's schools. It extends certain federal-aid precedents established by earlier policies, but it also departs from those precedents in important ways.

What happened to the conservative opponents of federal involvement in schools after the early 1960s and—especially—after the 1990s? Answering this question requires a close study of federal education laws over the past five decades and of the thinking and actions of the lawmakers that enacted them. In this book, I analyze the ideological and political factors that underlie the increased level of federal involvement in education since 1958. Most of the ideological and political precedents for No Child Left Behind occurred between 1958 and 1996, along with a gradual expansion of the federal role that NCLB has greatly accelerated. Under the 2001 law, the federal government has placed itself at the center of a high-stakes accountability system for all schools.

The weakening of ideological positions on federal involvement in education over time is the key explanation for increases in the federal role and for the passage of No Child Left Behind. Conservatives, in particular, are now embracing types of federal action that they had a long tradition of opposing. For example, most conservatives in the U.S. Senate and House of Representatives have now accommodated themselves to levels of federal support and intervention they would have decried as a federal "takeover" of schools in earlier eras. While recognizing that the difference between liberal and conservative positions on federal involvement has narrowed over the past several decades, it is also important to acknowledge that liberals and conservatives have retained some of their traditional commitments: equality of educational opportunity in the case of liberals, and fiscal restraint and fiscal accountability in the case of conservatives.

Conceptual Approach

The analysis of federal support and regulation of schools in this book draws on the disciplines of political science, political philosophy, and history. The main focuses of the book are federal involvement in education, school-related deliberations in Congress, and ideology. I also treat these issues over time by looking at the long parade of federal education policies.

Why Congress? In a nation of laws, Congress is the place where national laws are made. Its two chambers, the Senate and the House of Representatives, provide the most visible and representative forums for studying the ideology and politics of federal legislation. As members of the legislative branch of the federal government, senators and representatives consider their own proposals as well as those submitted by the executive branch (that is, the president). The laws passed by Congress affect the state and local constituencies that legislators represent. Congress is also an arena where the concerns of constituents are aired through the testimony of legislators and committee witnesses. In addition, Congress provides an ample database of proposals and votes on an endless variety of topics. Finally, members of Congress tend to rely on earlier laws and debates when they consider new legislation. This makes Congress a good place to go to understand federal policy-making over time.

The deliberative nature of Congress makes it an especially fruitful venue for analyzing national education policies. Philosophers and political theorists from Plato to John Rawls have expressed great fondness for enlightened debate and education. In particular, Amy Gutmann (1999) persuasively posits a normative relationship between deliberation, democracy, and education. "A guiding principle of deliberative democracy is reciprocity among free and equal individuals," she says. "Citizens and their accountable representatives owe one another justifications for the laws that collectively bind them" (xii). Moreover, "deliberative democracy underscores the importance of publicly supported education that develops the capacity to deliberate among all children as future free and equal citizens" (ibid.).

Therefore, "a primary aim of publicly mandated schooling is . . . to cultivate the skills and virtues of deliberation" (ibid., xiii).

Regardless of one's perspective on the conceptual relationship between deliberative democracy and schooling, congressional rhetoric and argument about education policies enacted in the last fifty years helps explain why federal assistance has increased and why effective opposition to it has decreased during this period. Committee and subcommittee hearings, committee reports, floor debates in each house of Congress, and the final laws all reveal "legislative intent." Over time, education debates in Congress document the evolution of ideological beliefs about appropriate and inappropriate types of federal involvement. The debates also show how different ideological positions influence one another and how the interactions between them define which education policies are acceptable at different times.

Because it focuses on the arguments made by legislators of varying ideological stripes, this study is about political rhetoric rather than political behavior. I am more concerned with what politicians say about federal aid to schools than with what they do about it. Although some may disagree, I assume that there is some relationship between the thoughts, words, and actions of legislators. I also assume that the philosophical dispositions of different legislative factions are reflected in their arguments for and against proposals to expand the federal role in education. Of course, there are cases in which a group's rhetoric is contradicted by its political strategies, tactics, and maneuvers (for example, the "strategic voting" scenario described in Chapter 1). Yet, it is reasonable to assume that politicians mean what they say and that they argue for and vote their political preferences. This assumption opens up a "philosophical space" consisting of arguments and underlying values that roughly parallels the "policy space" of possible legislative actions and outcomes. (Giandomenico Majone [1989, 158–59] develops a similar notion of "policy space" to denote the relationships among several policy areas.) Put another way, I view arguments for and against different positions on federal aid to education as epiphenomena (or by-products) of politics.

Each of the laws I analyze was built on a foundation of earlier laws. They also served, or will serve, as precedents for later laws. Policies evolve as years and decades pass, along with ideological beliefs and values about specific laws and overall policy domains. The "issue evolution" framework of Edward C. Carmines and James A. Stimson (1989) demonstrates the dynamic, evolutionary character of policies, ideologies, and political parties. With respect to civil rights (which Carmines and Stimson also call "racial policies"), for example, Democrats in Congress became more liberal after the elections of 1958 and 1964, while Republicans became more conservative. Indeed, between 1945 and 1980, Democrats and Republicans "had reversed their positions" on racial issues (163). The transformation of conservative views on federal aid to education may not be as dramatic as the shifts on race described by these authors, but the expansion of federal authority for schools under No Child Left Behind and conservative support for it are phenomena that can be understood only in historical context. Both the policies and the attitudes about them have evolved over time.

There are other avenues for studying federal education policy besides deliberations in Congress, and analytical lenses other than ideology. Ideology, by itself, is insufficient as an explanation for (or as a cause of) political phenomena. Nevertheless, I believe that a close study of ideological perspectives on federal aid to education is necessary to understand how No Child Left Behind and earlier laws affect public schools. The earlier laws and congressional debates laid the ideological and political groundwork for NCLB and federal involvement in education today. The federal role has changed in surprising ways since the 1950s, in part because the values and beliefs of conservative and liberal legislators have also changed. The fact that many state and local policy-makers and educators are objecting to the expansion of federal authority on ideological grounds makes it especially important to understand the ideological changes that have occurred at the federal level. Because No Child Left Behind is permanently altering the relationship between the federal government, states, and school districts, we need to know why, how, and when this transformation happened.

The philosophical and ideological arguments underlying the politics of federal aid to education are rich. Most of them have long histories, like the popular and partly idealized tradition of local control and the alleged unconstitutionality of federal assistance to schools. Supporters of proposals for extending the federal role must confront these long-standing claims by showing either that new actions are consistent with old beliefs or that they are justifiable departures from them. Congressional rhetoric is a necessary supplement to political explanations for the growth of the federal role. That is, I believe that the rhetoric and arguments in congressional deliberations about education expose the ideological motivations for political action.

In sum, education debates in the U.S. Congress are the primary source of information for my analysis of the federal role in schools as it has evolved since the late 1950s. The debates reveal the ideological values and beliefs that underlie federal education laws, and the arguments for and against these proposals help explain why federal authority for education expanded in the ways that it has over the past five decades. The ideological content of education debates in Congress also sheds light on the kinds of federal education policies we may see in the future.

"The Federal Role" and Other Definitions

In the United States, there is a strong tradition of local, democratic control in the rhetoric and practice of public schooling. The role of state governments in local education varies, but local boards and district administrators can typically be counted on to monitor school practices closely and to implement state and local policies on curriculum and instruction, student assessment, and staffing. States and school districts welcome direct and indirect subsidies from the federal government. However, educators and administrators also regard the national government's interest in schooling with suspicion, especially when federal regulatory presence in schools increases. Local educators and administrators often believe that federal regulations outweigh federal resources: Why, they ask, does the federal government impose requirements and then not provide funding to help for states and school districts to meet them?

Charges of regulatory interference and "unfunded mandates" by the federal government have been commonplace since the 1970s. Yet ambivalence about the federal role in education is almost as old as the federal role itself. The national government has supported education since the beginning of the Republic, and there have always been different ideological perspectives on the appropriateness of federal involvement in general and with regard to specific programs. The constitutionality of federal assistance to schools has been challenged and defended at different times, for example, but the fact remains that K-12 schooling is a permanent concern of Washington policy-makers.

By "federal role" I mean actions taken by the federal government to influence state and local education practices. This role consists of many activities: providing money and technical assistance, gathering statistics and conducting research, implementing and enforcing legislation and court decisions, and exerting national leadership around an overarching vision of schools and schooling. The federal role in education, therefore, consists of money, rules, and leadership, all of which have been dispensed in increasing amounts by Washington policy-makers since the 1950s.

Resources and regulations are tangible markers of the expansion of the federal role, but the rhetoric associated with broader federal visions of education is critical for understanding how and why this growth has occurred.

The federal government can constrain as well as provide opportunities to state and local education agencies; an observer's perception of how this scale tips is a good indicator of his or her position on a given federal-aid proposal. For example, enforcing equality of access to schooling has become part of the moral vision endorsed by the federal government since the Supreme Court's *Brown v. Board of Education* decision on school desegregation in 1954. Yet this stance was also viewed with alarm by opponents of federal aid (and integrated schools) because it encroached on states' rights and local control. Hence, the same federal policy can entail different and even contradictory definitions of federal involvement. Moreover, as the federal vision of schooling evolves, new opponents and proponents are activated. Conservatives balked at policies promoting equality of educational opportunity in the 1960s, for example, but came to embrace them as a rationale for high-stakes accountability by 2001. After working hard to increase federal support for education in the 1950s and 1960s, many liberals lamented the threat of federal domination of schools during the 1970s debate about establishing the U.S. Department of Education and during consideration of No Child Left Behind two decades later.

There are several definitions of the federal role in education. These definitions should be analyzed carefully to break apart the tangled and conflicting ideological terminology of the federal role. I have attempted to develop a federal role construct that recognizes different perspectives and opinions over time. The concepts and definitions I combine to form the federal role construct enable me to analyze related arguments and rhetoric. This approach is necessary because of my focus on the beliefs of factions for and against federal involvement.

Limited federal involvement is a baseline that characterizes the history of the national government's role in education from 1785 until the late 1950s. Opponents of federal involvement were vocal during more than half of this period and successfully blocked most attempts to expand it. To federal-aid proponents, the pre-1950s status quo meant that an important source of revenue for the schools was not being tapped. Moreover, in their view the federal government was wrongly excusing itself from tough questions about the adequacy and equity of school resources. "Limited federal involvement" remains an important rhetorical principle for both opponents and supporters of expanded federal assistance, although it is getting harder to square this traditional value with the magnitude of the federal role under No Child Left Behind.

General aid, or unrestricted financial assistance to schools, is occasionally demanded by federal-aid advocates who ignore or explain away the local-control status quo. Some general-aid proponents call for as much as one-third of education revenues to come from federal sources (Halperin 1978, 62; Senator Christopher Dodd [D-CT] [*Congressional Record* 2001, 6017]). Arguments in favor of this type of support refer to the large federal tax base, unequal state and local fiscal capacity for supporting public education, and the national consequences of uneven education quality in different states and regions. Examples of general aid are the Ordinance of 1785, the Northwest Ordinance of 1787, and Goals 2000, especially after the 1996 amendments. Some commentators viewed the Elementary and Secondary Education Act of 1965 as general aid when it was enacted.

Many opponents of federal involvement in schools tend not to make sharp distinctions between general aid and more restricted, special-purpose programs. They believe that any form of federal-aid risks federal interference in, or outright control of, local school systems. On occasion, however, conservatives seem to favor general aid as relief from tightly circumscribed programs. The problem for some critics is that general aid costs money and may take deregulation too far.

Categorical aid, unlike general aid, consists of federal funds supplied to states and school systems for specific purposes or for the needs of specific categories of students. Categorical aid is a type of federal involvement that reflects nineteenth- and early twentieth-century efforts to reconcile the concept of a limited federal role with increasing levels of federal support for schools. Even though the idea predates the Elementary and Secondary Education Act by more than a century, Title I of that 1965 act is a good example of a categorical program; vocational education, bilingual education, and special education are others. Federal-aid proponents in the 1950s and 1960s relied on the categorical-aid rationale to increase the federal share of school spending while sidestepping the thornier issues of general aid and the federal-control threat. Many federal-aid opponents were not convinced. To them, categorical aid to them was a Trojan horse for federal control.

"Federal control" accurately characterizes the misgivings of federal-aid opponents generally and of critics of specific proposals. To these individuals, federal assistance to schools means federal control. All federal education programs lead in this direction, according to many conservatives (and

some liberals), because government is inherently regulatory—or worse. Opponents and proponents of federal involvement detest federal control, but they disagree about its inevitability once federal funds flow to schools. To opponents, the American principle of local control of schools is necessarily compromised by any degree of federal involvement. Although the extent of federal interference varies over time and by program, the distinctively undesirable feature of the federal role is that it occurs at all. In this view, the best way to circumvent federal control of community school systems is to resist all efforts to expand the federal education mission.

Proponents of federal assistance rarely concede the unseemly control implications of these proposals. It does not seem possible for an American politician to defend federal control of education per se. Instead, the federal government is portrayed as a friendly giant with deeper pockets and more consistently refined ethical principles than the rest of the country. Certain needs, such as those of educationally disadvantaged students and students with disabilities, can be satisfied only by federal action. Governmental oversight, necessary to prevent "waste, fraud, and abuse" in the use of federal funds, is not equivalent to outright federal control. Moreover, each proposal for assistance includes painstaking assurances that federal control will not result if it is enacted.

The preceding definitions make up the federal role construct for this book. In places, the elements overlap. There may also be gaps and inconsistencies. I do not use this construct as a rigid framework for sorting all federal actions in education. Rather, the construct orients my analysis of the rhetoric and arguments about federal involvement in the following chapters. This brief rendering of the federal role helps illustrate different viewpoints at different times.

I also rely on several other definitions.

Opponents. There are several kinds of "opponent": (1) Opponents of all or most types of federal aid. This faction was strongest before the mid-1960s and consisted of conservative Republicans and conservative Southern Democrats. Today, few legislators oppose the general principle of federal involvement in schools. (2) Opponents of particular programs who may or may not oppose other programs. Several liberal Democrats, for example, with records supporting education, opposed President Jimmy Carter's proposal to form the Department of Education. (3) Opponents (or, more precisely, critics) of existing or proposed educational strategies or policies. For example, politically motivated formulas for distributing Title I funds under the Elementary and Secondary Education Act have been criticized throughout the law's history (for example, Commission on Chapter 1, 1992).

Several legislators criticized the assessment and accountability provision of No Child Left Behind while not necessarily voting against the final bill. All these opponents are driven by ideology to some degree; some are driven further than others to oppose federal involvement.

Proponents. Those who favor federal support and regulation of schools and who can generally be counted on to support the expansion of one or both of these types of involvement. I count as a proponent any legislator or other citizen who believes that federal action on behalf of students and schools is legitimate and desirable. Supporters of federal aid include different types of legislators at different times. Proponents have always tended to be more liberal than opponents, although widespread conservative support for the expansion of federal authority under No Child Left Behind is an important development. Note that proponents are not necessarily the opposite of opponents, although I try to minimize the overlap between the two in my use of the terms.

Arguments. For my purposes, "arguments" are the cases made by the opponents and proponents of federal aid that clarify and bear the content of their positions for or against particular proposals. Legislators make arguments to defend their own positions, to convince others of the worthiness of those positions (Majone 1989, 2), and to establish public records on behalf of those positions. "Reasons," "rhetoric," "rationales," and "justifications" are included in this definition. Arguments in this sense are the logical correlates of political action and, in this study, are distilled from systematic analyses of political debates. Note that this is not the definition of a formal "argument" in logic or philosophy. However, the definition does anticipate the need for the arguments made by different factions and individuals to be situated in political context.

Even with this explicit definition of "argument," an important tension persists between political and philosophical standards for judging arguments, reasons, and justifications. Philosophers eschew inconsistent or ambiguous premises in framing their arguments. Politicians, on the other hand, use ambiguity and inconsistency to great advantage in forging political compromises or evading controversial charges. This was certainly true when the Elementary and Secondary Education Act passed in 1965. Hence, this book is a study of the logic of political argumentation and of the evolution of the rhetoric associated with federal involvement in elementary and secondary education.

Ideology. I define ideology as a system of beliefs about society and government. In my use of the concept, ideologies refer to beliefs, values, and ideas, and they are invoked to defend or attack particular political actions.

These beliefs are "normative"; a person's ideology is a set of "first princi-ples" that expresses desires for how the world should be organized, as well as a system for interpreting reality in light of desired ends. If I subscribe to a collectivist ideology, for example, then I might object to market systems that force individuals to compete against one another for social goods.

The concept of ideology has a complex philosophical history and pejorative connotations. Karl Marx is partly responsible for both these legacies. Marx has elaborate discussions of ideology in several of his writings, usually in the context of class interests, economics, and "false consciousness." Ideology is a bourgeois concept in Marx's writings; the class that controls the means of production controls ideology as well. The arguments about ideology in the work of Marx and his successors is not my concern here, however. Indeed, I do not draw on Marxian complexities in my under-standing of ideology.

My definition of ideology assumes that anyone who interprets informa-tion about society and politics has an ideology, whether or not it forms the basis of political action taken by that individual. This approach differentiates my view from pejorative definitions that emphasize the irrationality or intensity of ideological beliefs. I do not assume that one's ideology auto-matically impairs one's ability to interpret political and social information from different points of view. Nor does subscribing to an ideology always mean that a person's political behavior, actions, or opinions are determined by it. It simply means that people are disposed to interpret political reality in certain ways—and may take certain actions—because of their beliefs.

Individual ideologies are difficult to describe because they include beliefs that may remain private, unexamined, or iconoclastic. For example, a liberal or a conservative may subscribe to a different set of values than those suggested by the label. Because ideologies are private beliefs that might be unconscious or unexamined, those beliefs probably resist change, although it is impossible to draw definitive conclusions about them. And because they are, or refer to, philosophical first principles, ideologies are unfalsifiable. That is, people usually do not part with ideologies because they are proven wrong by social reality or by counterarguments. Indeed, most theories of mental activity suggest that the situation is reversed: people's beliefs and assumptions—and ideologies—are tools that help them interpret the world.

I also assume that ideological politics can be differentiated and analyzed apart from other forms of politics. In reality, however, ideological politics, interest-group politics, party politics, and constituency politics are frequently intertwined. Even though I refer to the difference between ideology and politics throughout this study, I appreciate that in Congress various kinds of politics interact simultaneously. However, it is important to analyze ideologies, because they represent the fundamental values and beliefs that underlie other forms of political negotiation (Peterson 1976, 49). The specific ways in which ideological politics help explain policy outcomes vary by legislative episode.

The ideologies that I am most interested in exploring are liberal and conservative outlooks on federal aid to education. There are other ideologies as well, but the division between liberal and conservative is useful and important for my study. The liberal-conservative distinction (or, more accurately, continuum) captures most of the range of opinions expressed about federal school aid between the 1950s and the new millennium. I also find liberal and conservative labels to be ideologically more precise than the party labels "Democrat" and "Republican." Finally, questions about national education policy often divide liberals and conservatives into opposing camps.

As with ideologies generally, there are limitations to the use of the liberal-conservative continuum. Many beliefs and values are ideological without fitting into these categories or discriminating between them. For example, warnings about federal control are made by liberals as well as conservatives in Congress. Fiscal restraint is usually advocated by both sides as well. As I show in later chapters, race and special education are problematic ideological issues that do not divide legislators according to liberal and conservative labels. These limitations remind me to apply these labels with care and to look past them as I describe and analyze federal education debates.

My concentration on ideology provides a needed supplement to existing political explanations of the transformation of federal education policy since the 1950s. The ideologies that help motivate political action are important because the values and beliefs they convey recur in successive debates and evolve over time. I believe that ideologies and the rhetoric and arguments that best represent them are worth studying closely, even in cases where political calculations seem to overshadow them (for example, the nearly unanimous passage of P.L.94-142 in 1975). In no case do I believe that an ideology, by itself, has caused a particular outcome. The fact that ideologies are invoked to interpret political and social reality and to justify action or inaction does not mean that actions are taken solely on the basis of ideological arguments.

Politics. Politics and political maneuvers are conceptually distinct from ideology, although in reality there is considerable overlap between politics and ideology. I am interested in the ideological beliefs and values that underlie political action, but it is not always possible to disentangle the two. By "politics," I mean the existence, influence, and interplay of party positions, constituencies, interest groups, tactical maneuvers, and the votes of individual legislators. Of course, ideological first principles regularly enter into political action, so the two domains cannot be understood in isolation from each other. I believe that existing accounts of the politics of federal aid to education tend to overlook the ideological content of these policies. My study of ideology is intended to supplement and enrich our political understanding of federal involvement in schools over time.

Liberals and conservatives: I use the terms "liberal" and "conservative" to give more precise meaning to legislators' ideological dispositions. Party affiliation (that is, Democrat, Republican) does not do as good a job as the ideological terms "liberal" and "conservative" in determining whether legislators are likely to support or oppose education proposals in Congress. For example, Southern Democrats tended to oppose federal education proposals in the 1950s and 1960s even though Democrats from other regions supported them. Similarly, recall that there was a liberal tradition in the Republican Party on race and civil rights until the late 1950s and early 1960s (Carmines and Stimson 1989, 62–63, 163).

Again, the ideological shorthand of "liberal" and "conservative" can be misleading. The labels do not necessarily correspond to all the actions and opinions of liberal and conservative legislators, especially since 2001. Nevertheless, the distinction works well as a reference point for describing the range of ideological opinion on federal education policy over time. When there is a division between liberals and conservatives, it is usually because different beliefs, values, and assumptions make up their respective world views.

Because of the dynamic and interrelated nature of liberal and conservative viewpoints over time, it is a challenge to apply unitary definitions of these terms. Liberals tend to see the federal government as an entity that can help meet needs that states and school systems are unable or unwilling to meet themselves, such as equality of educational opportunity for special populations. For their part, conservatives are more likely to prefer state, local, and private initiatives for meeting legitimate educational needs. Both liberals and conservatives are wary of the federal-control threat and both have embraced the need for schools to be accountable for the public moneys they receive and for student achievement results.

I have much more to say about liberal and conservative labels and opinions in the episodes I treat in the following chapters. I shall also describe my method for applying ADA scores—"liberal quotients" from the interest group Americans for Democratic Action (ADA)—in the methods section of this chapter. I conclude the present discussion with an eloquent description of ideology in action. The writer is former Secretary of Education William J. Bennett, a conservative who claims to have once been a liberal.

> From what I have observed, the liberal elite proceed from a certain social and political predisposition. The predisposition tends to be an adopted orientation, not a condition based on evidence and argument. When you sift through the arguments, you will often find that modern-day academics and intellectuals (which many elites fancy themselves to be, or long to be) have arrived at their position not, ironically, through intellect, through open-ended, disinterested thinking and inquiry, but through disposition, sentiment, bias, and ideology. Many intellectuals are predisposed to accept certain premises and arguments—a preconceived reality. They search for facts to sustain their political position. The approach is (as philosopher Karl Jaspers said of Marx's writings) "one of vindication, not investigation." Serious public debate is therefore a casualty, since they are not likely to change their minds on the basis of compelling empirical arguments. Their starting point is not evidence but ideology. They are undeterred by what Thomas Huxley called "the tragedy of a fact killing a theory." (Bennett 1992, 27)

Notice that Bennett uses ideology in the pejorative sense that I avoid. He impugns the integrity of his liberal opponents without acknowledging the "social and political predisposition[s]" that shape his own "disinterested thinking and inquiry" as a conservative.

Methods

My purpose in this book is to identify and analyze the ideological factors that account for the expansion of federal involvement in education under the No Child Left Behind Act of 2001 and earlier statutes. I use the arguments and recorded votes of congressional factions for and against federal action at different times. In my analysis of these arguments and votes, I document the ideological evolution of attitudes about the federal role in schools.

The book focuses on the interval between 1957 (Sputnik and the National Defense Education Act of 1958) and the passage and early implementation of the No Child Left Behind Act of 2001. Legislative episodes within this period are sampled selectively, concentrating on congressional action directed at elementary and secondary education. This interval encompasses the early baseline of stable, limited federal involvement, the key debates and laws whereby that role expanded, and current actions that apparently confirm one of the worst fears of opponents of federal involvement: national testing requirements under No Child Left Behind. I also survey the history of federal aid to education before the 1950s in order to understand the origin of arguments and rhetoric for and against the federal role.

As already indicated, the U.S. Congress is the principal institution for my study of the rhetoric of federal education policy-making. I am aware that important events in federal education policy occur outside Congress, most notably in the courts. Although I refer to some of these actions, I do not conduct a comprehensive legal study of the federal role. Although I pay more attention to the role of the executive branch and different presidential administrations than to the courts, my main interest is congressional proposals and actions with respect to elementary and secondary education.

I use one main method in this study: systematic identification and analysis of arguments for and against federal involvement in K-12 education. This is the core of the study and the source of its key findings. I also employ a second method on a smaller scale: description and analysis of congressional voting blocs on education bills. The existing database of House and Senate votes is used to confirm the existence of factions in Congress that hold different positions on the federal role.

The primary sources for my analyses are House and Senate floor debates, testimony presented to different congressional committees and subcommittees, and documents from Congress and the executive branch (for example, proposed and enacted legislation, committee reports, presidential messages). Secondary sources are also used to help understand and analyze the arguments from sources inside and outside the government.

The debates I analyze culminated in a new law, an incremental reauthorization of an earlier law (the Improving America's Schools Act of 1994), or a vast overhaul of an earlier law (No Child Left Behind). All the resulting laws were shaped by the interaction between different belief systems. In addition, the debates reveal important ideological components of the federal government's role in schools. Certain legislative proposals were out-of-bounds ideologically and tended not to be enacted. Usually these proposals (for example, private-school vouchers) were elements of larger bills that did pass (such as No Child Left Behind), so it is possible to differentiate between ideologically acceptable and unacceptable policies within the same debate. (On the other hand, certain proposals—such as school construction aid in the 1960s and tuition tax credits in the 1970s and 1980s—were stand-alone bills that were defeated. These kinds of proposals are not treated in detail.)

Because of my concentration on Congress as the crossroads for federal education policy, I examine arguments leveled at particular proposals before that body. However, I also treat the general proposition of federal aid. This is an important distinction, because attitudes about the general principle of federal involvement are usually embedded in opinions expressed about specific proposals. I analyze the evolution and expansion of the federal role over time, so the general idea of this role needs to be distilled from arguments made about individual policies.

A mainstay of arguments against federal involvement is that all or most education policies lead to federal control of schools. This charge was first leveled in the mid-nineteenth century and is currently taken seriously as a charge against No Child Left Behind. According to this argument, federal tentacles strangle state and local educational autonomy through program regulations and such covert political agendas as integration and private-school choice. Federal-aid opponents sometimes apply this argument inconsistently. Conservative foes of federal aid manipulated racial politics with great success during the 1940s and 1950s, even though the desegregation directives they advocated—for whatever reasons—embodied the very same threat of federal interference that they strongly opposed (Smith 1982, 107–10). A similar technique was employed in arguments and debates in the 1930s and 1940s: asserting that a functional equivalent of federal control should be a precondition of federal aid. In the 1930s, former U.S. Commissioner of Education (and federal-aid opponent) J. J. Tigert believed that federal education funds would be wasted unless mandatory attendance requirements were imposed first (Tigert 1934, 132).

Below is an extract from a 1948 Senate education debate. Senator Raymond E. Baldwin (R-CT) simultaneously argues for the necessity and unacceptability of what he would define as federal control. The legislation in question is S.472, the proposed Educational Finance Act of 1947. This exchange illustrates the type of rhetoric I analyze in this study, as well as a core dispute between supporters and foes of federal education programs.

Sen. Baldwin: Suppose a state were to put the money [earmarked for education] into its highway fund. Could the Federal Government stop that, under this bill?

Sen. [Dennis] Chavez [D-NM]: I think so.

Baldwin: It seems to me absolutely necessary that it must be able to stop it. Right there we have Federal control, do we not?

Chavez: We have Federal control, because we are here proposing to enact legislation to help public-school education. That means that the money cannot be used for public highways or anything else except the purposes for which it was authorized.

Baldwin: Suppose a State using these Federal funds had the most impossible, inefficient, ineffective, profligate system of education. Is the Federal Government going to tax the other States that have good systems of education in order to maintain that kind of an educational system in one of the States whose income is low?

Chavez: No; I agree with the Senator from Connecticut that if we are appropriating public funds for a specific purpose, it will be up to the Federal Government to see to it that the money is used for that specific purpose.

Baldwin: If my distinguished friend will concede that, then he concedes the argument that . . . the Federal Government of necessity must have control. And once the camel gets his head under the tent, there will be Federal control of education.

Chavez: No; there will not be Federal control of education, because the business of the Federal Government will end when it sees that the money is spent for the particular purpose for which it was authorized.

Baldwin: My point is that the very act of the Federal Government in seeing that the money is spent for the particular purpose for which it was appropriated is in itself Federal control. That must be so, and it cannot be avoided.

Chavez: I fully agree with the Senator from Connecticut, and I think it is a sound proposition. When the Congress appropriates $300 million a year to help the . . . States in respect to their educational systems, I still think it is up to the Federal Government to see to it that that money is spent for the purposes for which it was appropriated.

Baldwin: If that is so, the provision about no Federal control, as contained in section 2, is an empty provision and means nothing. (*Congressional Record* 1948, 3927–28)

Senator Baldwin's argument took the following form: Federal aid without safeguards is a violation of the public trust, so safeguards—including the power to withhold funds—are necessary to ensure that these funds are spent responsibly. However, these safeguards are tantamount to federal control. Therefore, federal aid inevitably leads to federal control. Baldwin claimed that it was impossible to deny the federal-control implications of school aid while simultaneously enforcing fiscal safeguards.

I am not concerned whether arguments like this conform to rigorous standards of formal logic. Taking liberties with facts, logic, and semantics has a rich tradition in politics. It is worth noting that Senator Barry Goldwater (R-AZ) clarified this dispute in his 1960 book, *The Conscience of a Conservative*. This quotation is a generic statement, but it was part of a discussion about federal education policy. "Congress will always feel impelled to establish conditions under which people's money is to be spent, and while some controls may be wise we are not guaranteed against unwise controls any more than we are guaranteed against unwise Congressmen. *The mistake is not the controls but appropriating the money that requires controls*" (Goldwater 1960, 81–82; emphasis added).

The issues raised in the exchange between Senators Baldwin and Chavez recurred in almost every episode covered in this book. However, what was originally posed as an irresolvable conflict between the need for fidelity to the purposes of the school-aid laws and the risk of federal control eventually defined the middle ground for politically and ideologically acceptable policy. No Child Left Behind has challenged this middle ground by imposing regulations that would look very much like federal control to observers from the mid-twentieth century.

I also use congressional voting data to confirm the existence of voting blocs on education and to demonstrate that these blocs typically behave according to the arguments and beliefs that identify them and their positions. This is a comparatively minor part of my overall research strategy, but it is important to show that the rhetoric I am studying is connected to actual political events and ideological moods in Congress. These events and moods reflect the evolution and expansion of federal aid since the 1950s.

I perform simple arithmetic on a number of education votes in order to describe margins of victory and party alignment. I also use "liberal quotients" from the liberal interest group Americans for Democratic Action (also known as "ADA scores") as a proxy for liberal and conservative orientations of representatives and senators. ADA scores between 0 (conservative extreme) and 100 (liberal extreme) are assigned to each legislator every year. These scores are generated by matching voting records with a roster of approximately twenty key votes selected each year by an Americans for Democratic Action committee. These votes are chosen because they make clear distinctions between liberal and conservative positions (Sharp 1988, xii). A legislator's liberal quotient is the percentage of his or her votes that match the position of Americans for Democratic Action. For example, Senator Goldwater's 1960 ADA score was 0. Senator Raymond E. Baldwin (R-CT), a participant in the 1948 debate excerpt above, had a 1948 ADA score of 31, and his interlocutor, Senator Dennis Chavez (D-NM), had a 1948 ADA score of 63 (ADA scores in this paragraph are from Sharp 1988). ADA scores are well suited to this study because they, like many education votes, divide the House and Senate membership into liberal and conservative camps.

There are three important cautions about the use of ADA scores. First, ADA scores cannot be validly compared from year to year, so lower or higher aggregate or individual "liberal quotients" in different years do not indicate, by themselves, increasing or decreasing conservatism. Second, no comparisons can be made between the House and the Senate in the same or different years, because ADA scores for the different chambers are based on separate samples of votes. Third, ADA scores should be obtained for the year before or after the votes in question to ensure that these votes were not used in the calculation of ADA scores for that year.

I illustrate my use of descriptive voting statistics with the 1984 Senate vote on a proposed constitutional amendment to allow school prayer. School prayer was one of President Reagan's education policy goals, and the administration submitted its proposal to the Senate in 1983. Senators voted on the measure in 1984 (Table 1). Even though President Reagan's party controlled the Senate at the time of the vote, the measure was defeated. (It did not receive a two-thirds majority vote.) The first three rows of the table show the total votes and vote breakdowns by party. The remaining nine rows display ADA score analyses by party and voting position.

I do not use congressional votes as empirical tests for any hypotheses about the decline in opposition to federal school aid. Nor do I ever define liberal and conservative solely on the basis of ADA scores. In addition, the votes included in my analyses are restricted to final votes on measures that became laws, rather than votes on earlier bills or amendments. The voting data aid me in documenting the relationship between growth of the federal role and the rhetoric and arguments that help account for it. The voting blocs in the House and Senate are systematic indicators of the political and ideological factions revealed in congressional deliberations. The arguments and rhetoric of the different factions are my main focus

Table 1   1984 School Prayer Vote with 1983 ADA Statistics

1984 Senate vote on Senate Joint Resolution 73 to propose a constitutional amendment to permit school prayer (March 20, 1984). Such proposals require a two-thirds majority, so the resolution was defeated.

Final vote on S.J.Res.73	56–44 (56% "yes")
Democrats	19–26 (42.2% "yes")
Republicans	37–18 (67.3% "yes")

ADA Score Analyses

Mean ADA score of "yes" voters	25.3 (n=56)
Mean ADA score of "no" voters	65.8 (n=44)
Mean ADA score of Democrat "yes" voters	50.5 (n=19)
Mean ADA score of Republican "yes" voters	12.3 (n=37)
Mean ADA score of Democrat "no" voters	81.3 (n=26)
Mean ADA score of Republican "no" voters	43.3 (n=18)
Mean Democrat ADA score	68.3 (n=45)
Mean Republican ADA score	22.4 (n=55)
Mean ADA score of whole chamber (1983)	43.1 (n=100)

NOTE: ADA = Americans for Democratic Action; n = the number of senators in each cell with 1983 ADA scores. The 1985 ADA score was used for one senator who did not have a 1983 ADA score.
SOURCES: Congressional Quarterly Inc. 1985, 9-S, for the vote on S.J.Res.73 and Americans for Democratic Action website for 1983 ADA scores. (1983 scores downloaded October 29, 2005, from http://www.adaction.org/1983VotingRecord.pdf.) 1985 ADA score from Sharp 1988.

in this study. The analysis of the sample of congressional votes is a secondary strategy that reinforces the findings from my analysis of the arguments made for and against federal aid.

Overview of Federal Education Laws and Issues

Federal interest in education dates from the end of the eighteenth century, and the principle of limited federal involvement in schools is also more than one hundred years old. Because No Child Left Behind grows directly out of the laws enacted since the late 1950s, the book's systematic analyses begin then. The following overview is not exhaustive, but it provides sufficient detail to help the reader place No Child Left Behind in appropriate historical context. The lessons to take from the federal laws described in this section are as follows:

- In Congress, constellations of acceptable and unacceptable education policies change over time.

- Congressional interest in schooling, combined with the widespread belief that the federal role in education ought to be limited, exerts opposite ideological pressures.
- The gradual expansion of federal assistance to schools laid the foundation for No Child Left Behind, grounding the apparently revolutionary aspects of the law in an evolutionary process.

Several federal education laws stand out as precedents for the No Child Left Behind Act. These precursors are the National Defense Education Act of 1958, the Elementary and Secondary Education Act of 1965, the Education for All Handicapped Children Act of 1975 (P.L.94-142), the 1979 Department of Education Organization Act, the Goals 2000: Educate America Act of 1994, and the Improving America's Schools Act of 1994. These laws are important because they expose contrasting ideological and political views about federal involvement in education. In addition to being the key precedents for No Child Left Behind, these laws also provided opportunities for legislators to renew their debate about the federal role.

I begin with a survey of federal aid to education from 1785 to the 1950s in Chapter 1. This history shows that the principle and practice of federal assistance to schools was stable and long-standing before it started to expand with the National Defense Education Act. The early episodes also demonstrate that federal involvement was constrained by ideological opposition to the principle. This tension circumscribed the accepted range of federal activity, permitting federal subsidies through land-grant revenues, direct grants for specialized purposes like vocational education, and research and dissemination. It is also clear that the idea of limited federal involvement in schools was established as a rhetorical truism by the middle of the nineteenth century.

The National Defense Education Act of 1958 (Chapter 2) delivered—by dint of a single statute—categorical aid to elementary and secondary schools and to colleges. It also overcame the forces that had successfully opposed earlier proposals for increased federal assistance. Proponents passed this legislation by capitalizing on Cold War concerns about U.S. competitiveness, Soviet Sputnik launches, and existing momentum favoring expanded federal aid to schools. They exploited anticommunism as an argument for a decidedly liberal idea. Citing the threat of federal control, opponents registered their customary ideological objections. They also disputed the need for the specific programs authorized by the act.

One reason the National Defense Education Act succeeded was that its proponents respected the rhetoric and reality of limited federal involvement in schools. The supporters of the law advocated an incremental expansion of federal involvement, rather than a vast new program or bureaucracy. The National Defense Education Act is an important precedent for No Child Left Behind because it provided the winning strategy—categorical aid—that was later exploited by the first Elementary and Secondary Education Act in 1965. (No Child Left Behind is the eighth reauthorization of the Elementary and Secondary Education Act.) To conservatives in the 1950s, however, No Child Left Behind would have looked like a strong form of federal interference. Indeed, according to the foes of federal aid in the 1950s, 1960s, and 1970s, the threat of federal control was insidious because it was being imposed incrementally. What makes No Child Left Behind especially interesting vis-à-vis the federal-control threat is that the expansion of federal involvement embodied in the 2001 law was advocated by a conservative president and strongly supported by conservative legislators. The expansion of federal involvement occurred so gradually that many of those who opposed the principle in earlier debates came to embrace it by 2001.

The Elementary and Secondary Education Act of 1965 (Chapter 3) authorized federal education aid to help fight the War on Poverty. As in the case of the National Defense Education Act, its supporters used the mechanism of categorical aid as a strategy for overcoming the opponents of federal assistance. Elementary and Secondary Education Act managers also had to grapple with aid to parochial schools and, for the sake of southern votes, the politics of race. Despite their crafting a winning legislative formula, proponents of federal aid still faced ideological objections from remaining conservative opponents.

The No Child Left Behind Act retains the ostensible antipoverty focus of the first Elementary and Secondary Education Act. Yet, several things changed in the thirty-seven years that separated the two statutes. For one, the objections that had to be overcome were different in the two eras. In 1965, the use of education as an antipoverty strategy was a new, untested, and controversial idea. By 2001, no one challenged the antipoverty rationale of No Child Left Behind. Instead, its controversial elements were accountability, private-school choice, and the adequacy of the funds authorized by the act. (The consideration of the Improving America's Schools Act—the 1994 reauthorization of the Elementary and Secondary Education Act—portended many of the controversies of the 2001 reauthorization.)

In addition to being remarkably durable, the original Elementary and Secondary Education Act is noteworthy because of the extent to which the bill's supporters mollified "potential opponents" to federal-school aid.

Opponents could be outvoted only if the bill included aid to parochial schools and disproportionately large payments to the South, where policy-makers were sensitive about desegregation. Potential opponents were also present in the 2001 debate over No Child Left Behind. Many Democrats might have abandoned the bill if President George W. Bush and the bill's Republican managers had not retracted the private-school voucher proposal.

A final feature of the Elementary and Secondary Education Act helps today's readers understand the meaning of No Child Left Behind. It is what I call the "federal-control paradox," and it was a component of the arguments made against the Elementary and Secondary Education Act in 1965 and in earlier education proposals. Opponents reiterated familiar claims that federal control would automatically be the result of any attempt at federal regulation. Senator Absalom W. Robertson (D-VA) voiced the inevitability and paradox of federal control during the 1965 Senate floor debate: "Not only does Federal control follow Federal funds, but it is the constitutional duty of a Congress which appropriates Federal money to supervise its expenditure" (*Congressional Record* 1965, 7523). The situation is paradoxical because federal control (which is abhorred by all legislators and educators) is a logical consequence of the responsibility the national government must assume to ensure that education dollars are used for the purposes intended by Congress. The situation is simul-taneously contradictory and inevitable, according to some legislators, and it begins the moment federal funds are spent on schools. At the time, many conservatives believed that this paradox could be avoided only by defeating the ESEA bill. By the time the No Child Left Behind debate occurred, conservatives were less squeamish about exerting strong federal influence over schools. Hence, the federal-control paradox of earlier debates was replaced by a less paradoxical but still respectably conservative principle: "After spending $125 billion of Title I money over 25 years, we have virtually nothing to show for it" (Senator William Frist [R-TN], quoting Education Secretary Roderick Paige in *Congressional Record* 2001, 6354).

The Education for All Handicapped Children Act of 1975 (Chapter 4) was a milestone for children with disabilities, civil rights, and the federal regulatory presence in education. The legislation spelled out detailed due process and administrative requirements for educating children with disabilities. The protections provided by the law were overdue, given the number of children with disabilities who received little or no schooling in the mid-1970s. At the same time, the federal government took bold new steps into the nation's schools and classrooms. The tension between the principle of educational opportunity for students with disabilities, the enumeration and enforcement of these rights by the federal government, and the cost of providing them has been continuous in the three decades since this law passed.

When the Education for All Handicapped Children Act (P.L.94-142) passed, it was an anomaly in at least three ways. Its high level of federal prescriptiveness was unprecedented, as was the nearly unanimous support it received in both chambers of Congress. The law has also become the classic "unfunded mandate" in education, thereby fulfilling scattered but prescient concerns in the original debate about who would pay for the high costs of implementing the law. It is interesting that the original debate ignored the most anomalous feature of all: the law's momentous implications for federal interference with state and local school systems.

Several of these unusual features are present in No Child Left Behind: widespread belief that it imposes unfunded mandates on states and school systems, especially in connection with testing; a highly prescriptive approach that departs in many ways from past federal practice; and overwhelming support in Congress when the law was first enacted. The lesson from both episodes is that political pressure, on occasion, overturns the ideological status quo of federal education policy. How could a legislator oppose the education of handicapped children in 1975 or leave even one child behind in 2001? Finally, recall that children with disabilities make up one of the subgroups for which adequate yearly progress must be reported under No Child Left Behind. Supporters of the new law have portrayed its subgroup accountability requirements as a continuation of the federal role in protecting the civil rights of children with disabilities, English-language learners, and disadvantaged students. P.L.94-142 and the Elementary and Secondary Education Act set the federal civil rights enforcement precedents for No Child Left Behind.

By the late 1970s, the number and total size of federal education programs had grown to such a degree that some policy-makers contended that these activities should be consolidated in a cabinet-level department of education. A U.S. Department of Education (Chapter 5) was also a 1976 campaign promise by Jimmy Carter to the National Education Association in exchange for its endorsement. Despite its ostensibly nonideological reorganization rationale, the proposal to create the department generated political and ideological controversy. Supporters of certain education programs did not want to alter existing relationships in the federal bureaucracy. Others feared that the government was positioning itself to take control of the schools. The 1970s Department of Education debate turned into a thoroughgoing reexamination of the federal role as it had evolved to that point.

Traditional differences between liberals and conservatives were discernible during the debate over creating the Department of Education, but they were not as clear-cut as they had been during the 1950s and 1960s. Numerous liberal Democrats, such as Senator Daniel Patrick Moynihan (D-NY), opposed the measure, which they saw as a scheme to centralize federal education authority. Many conservatives shared this view. Many liberals also worried that the federal commitment to civil rights would be compromised by locating enforcement activities in an agency controlled by professional educators. Some conservatives—namely, Senator Strom Thurmond (R-SC)—were vocal supporters of the reorganization plan.

What does the decision to establish the Department of Education tell us about the historical context of No Child Left Behind? The relationship between the two episodes is less obvious than between, say, the Elementary and Secondary Education Act and No Child Left Behind. Nevertheless, the connections are important. First, No Child Left Behind measure received strong bipartisan support. Indeed, the original NCLB debate generated less ideological and political controversy than the debate about the Department of Education, making No Child Left Behind resemble the strongly supported P.L.94-142. Second, the relatively unpredictable behavior of congressional liberals and conservatives during the Department of Education debate signaled the possibility that conservatives could become supporters of certain kinds of federal education policies. No Child Left Behind was pushed forward by a conservative president with strong, bipartisan support. Without the long track record of expanding federal involvement and the softening of traditional ideological positions during the same period, No Child Left Behind might not have been possible.

The Goals 2000: Educate America Act of 1994 and the Improving America's Schools Act of 1994 (Chapter 6) introduced systemic-reform and standards-based reform strategies to the federal role. The 1993–94 deliberations also had characteristics of past debates. The imperative for international competitiveness, prominent in the National Defense Education Act of 1958, was invoked again as an argument for Goals 2000. Opinions about the Goals 2000 law were sharply divided along liberal and conservative lines, a division that recalled the sharp ideological contrasts on the National Defense Education Act of 1958 and the Elementary and Secondary Education Act. The aftermath of Goals 2000 was especially interesting. A conservative backlash against it forced the Clinton administration and Congress to retreat from several of the law's key provisions. After 1996, the program allowed wide spending discretion, like the National Defense Education Act and the Reagan-era educational block grant.

Although the main focus of Chapter 6 is Goals 2000, the text includes a brief account of the Improving America's Schools Act. The Improving America's Schools Act was the 1994 reauthorization of the Elementary and Secondary Education Act and was designed to conform to the Goals 2000 school-reform framework. Goals 2000 and the Improving America's Schools Act are important precedents for No Child Left Behind because they introduced many of the same legislative and educational objectives as the 2001 law. Unlike Goals 2000, conservatives have embraced No Child Left Behind. However, it is possible that the same political and ideological controversies that gutted Goals 2000 may also pose problems for the full implementation of No Child Left Behind. For example, the adequacy of resource levels for schools was contentious during both debates. Under Goals 2000, "opportunity-to-learn standards or strategies" were controversial because they would supposedly be used to determine the adequacy of state and local support for education. During the No Child Left Behind debate, many liberals criticized what they believed to be inadequate funding for Title I and other programs, such as special education. Liberal (and conservative) criticism of the funding levels has persisted since it was enacted.

In most of these episodes, supporters of federal aid to education in Congress were typically liberals and Democrats. Opponents of federal aid were usually—but not always—conservatives, Republicans, and Southern Democrats. Liberals frequently defended school aid as a necessary and appropriate role for the federal government. Conservatives (and others) were often concerned about the threat of federal control of schools when they opposed these proposals. In several of the laws and debates that predate No Child Left Behind, ideologically and politically acceptable modes of federal involvement were developed through the interaction of conservative and liberal values and beliefs. The constructive tension between supporters and opponents of federal involvement kept the federal government from playing too big or too small a role in the nation's schools. Hence, federal subsidies for schools serving disadvantaged youth have been acceptable for the past four decades, whereas unrestricted payments to private schools are usually out-of-bounds.

Enter President George W. Bush and the No Child Left Behind Act (Chapter 7). No Child Left Behind was debated and passed by Congress in 2001 and signed by the president on January 8, 2002. The law reauthorized (and renamed) the Elementary and Secondary Education Act. Although the new law retains the long-standing emphasis of the Elementary and Secondary Education Act on improving the academic performance of disadvantaged (that is, poor) students, it adds significant accountability requirements for all schools and school districts that receive federal funds, not just those schools with high concentrations of poor children. When the law is fully implemented, schools, districts, and states will have to meet "adequate yearly progress" criteria for student performance and all teachers will have to be "highly qualified" in the subjects they teach.

The No Child Left Behind Act is a relatively new law. It has attracted much attention, but it is not yet fully implemented. Hence, it is not yet possible to determine whether the new law is a coming to pass of earlier warnings of federal control. Nevertheless, the debate and passage of No Child Left Behind is an important chapter in the politics and ideology of federal education policy. The strong support from conservatives for No Child Left Behind appears to signal the end of the long era when conservatives could be counted on to oppose proposals to expand federal interference in schools.

This book is a comprehensive study of the relationship between No Child Left Behind and the patterns of federal involvement established by earlier laws. Because NCLB both builds on and departs from the precedents established in the long history of federal support for schools, it is important to clearly understand the law and its post–World War II precursors. Over the past five decades, conservatives in Congress have softened their objections to the principle of federal aid to schools, and liberals have allayed conservative fears about the unintended consequences of increased federal involvement. Long-standing agreement that federal involvement in education ought to be limited has been replaced by the presumption by many legislators that past federal investments justify imposing high-stakes accountability requirements on schools.

The implications of this new orientation for the future of federal education policy are explored in the book's conclusion (Chapter 8). As the boundaries between acceptable and unacceptable education policies have changed, it is possible to imagine a variety of new directions that future policies may take. The following possibilities are discussed:

- Continued emphasis on high-stakes accountability
- Additional federal funds for assessments and corrective actions (including private-school vouchers)
- Additional federal funds for operations in schools identified for improvement (for example, increasing teacher salaries and upgrading school facilities)
- Eroding political support for public schools identified as failing under No Child Left Behind

When federal education laws have been perceived as doing too much too fast (for example, Goals 2000), they are sometimes modified or overturned by later Congresses. Consequently, I also contemplate the possibility of Congress retreating from the controversial aspects of No Child Left Behind. I also discuss the ways in which the federal government has done too little for public education and the ways in which it has done too much. To the extent that federal aid was intended to address the inequality of education spending between poor and wealthier school districts, I argue that the federal government has not done enough. By spreading funds widely—including to those schools and districts that do not need extra support—I suggest that the government has done too much.

1

how the camel's nose got in the tent

Historical Precedents for Federal Aid to Education

Exclusion of the federal government from either direct activity or any form
of control over local educational policy was a principle established quite
early in American history. . . . The history of government and education
in the United States is, in great part, a history of the development of federal
stimulatory activities with the simultaneous limitation of the possibilities
for federal control.

—DANIEL J. ELAZAR, *THE AMERICAN PARTNERSHIP* (1962)

The precedents for federal support of education date to the beginning of
U.S. history. Likewise, opposition to the federal role is also long-standing,
starting in the middle of the nineteenth century. The federal stake in an
educated citizenry exists in the American context of a limited national
government, leading to a recurring ideological debate about what form
federal action should take. Federal interest in schooling, and the opposition
to certain methods of advancing that interest, exert opposite ideological
pressures. These pressures are still present.

This chapter is a historical summary of federal education policy before
the National Defense Education Act of 1958. This history illuminates the
ideological roots of issues, arguments, and strategies that have continued
to influence federal education policy in the last half-century and establishes
the precedents for a limited federal role in state and local school policy-
making. At the same time, the origins of direct and indirect subsidies from
the national government for schools and colleges will be documented.

The history of federal involvement to the late 1950s also suggests that
there was an ideological distinction between acceptable and unacceptable
education policies. Subsidies of various kinds were acceptable, especially
for institutions of higher education and vocational education. The use
of education to advance other national purposes, such as international

competition or "manifest destiny," was also widely seen as legitimate. A nationalized school system or federal control of local schools was unacceptable, along with certain kinds of direct grants from the Treasury, such as those tied to equalizing state expenditures for elementary and secondary education.

The first national laws to address education were the Ordinance of 1785 and the Northwest Ordinance of 1787. To encourage territorial and community support for education and westward migration, the Confederation Congress directed that new territories be divided into townships of thirty-six square miles and subdivided into square-mile lots numbered 1 to 36. Lot number 16 in each township was reserved for educational purposes (Clark 1930, 66–68). In 1848, the Oregon Organization Act added a second lot, number 36, to be set aside for education. Until the mid-1820s, these lands were rented and the proceeds were devoted to education. After that, the lands could be sold to generate funds for schools (Kaestle 1983, 183).

These eighteenth-century ordinances are forerunners of all federal education subsidies, and they reflect early beliefs that supporting schools was a legitimate national purpose. At least one commentator believes that the land-grant measures reflected the deep commitment of early American legislators to "nationalize" education (Clark 1930, chap. 2). Others dismiss this episode—or ignore it altogether—as a curious but irrelevant nonprecedent to federal involvement in education (for example, Smith 1982, 14). I consider the ordinances a genuine, albeit indirect, subsidy for education during an era when the land-rich, cash-poor nation was encouraging westward expansion. These laws signal the beginning of a remarkably consistent, limited federal role over time: encouraging and stimulating the educational impulses of states and communities by providing resources at the margins. This role was reinforced by the educational provisions in state enabling acts, requirements that probably exerted more influence than the early land grants (Tyack, James, and Benavot 1987, 22).

It is interesting to see, in retrospect, how later opponents of federal aid interpret these ordinances. Some strict constructionists, those who view the Constitution as originally written as the final authority for permissible federal activities, oppose all federal involvement in education on the basis of their narrow reading of the general-welfare clause. Moreover, the words "education" and "schooling" do not appear in the Constitution. Strict constructionists also believe that the Constitution (specifically the Tenth Amendment) leaves education as the exclusive province of the states. Hence, in this view, the early land grants, viewed as subsidies, were unconstitutional

(Elazar 1962, 143). In vetoing later education legislation, President Franklin Pierce denied that the Northwest Ordinance counted as a federal-aid precedent, because the land grants were made merely to encourage settlement and sale of public lands. No federal education policy (or subsidy) can be inferred from these land grants, and therefore land grants are not a precedent for federal aid according to this argument (Clark 1930, 159). Similarly, opponents of direct federal payments to states for educational purposes (which were proposed for the first time in the late nineteenth century) denied that land grants were a precedent for fiscal transfers. In their view, cheap and plentiful land is a source of support for schools that has a low cost-basis for everyone (federal government, states, and citizens) and is therefore not the same thing as monetary tax revenues (Lee 1949, 150–51).

The land-grant principle was the basis of the Morrill Act of 1862, the most visible education legislation enacted in the nineteenth century. This measure was designed to help states establish agricultural and mechanical colleges by making land grants of thirty-thousand acres for each U.S. representative and senator in the state (Clark 1930, 198). Proceeds from the sale of these lands were placed in permanent accounts to generate interest for the support of higher education. By the mid-1870s, thirty-one colleges were established with these funds, fifty by 1916 (Holt 1922, 1–2). Unlike the eighteenth-century land ordinances, the Morrill Act covered all states. Earlier versions of this legislation were defeated or vetoed; the Morrill Act was finally passed during the Civil War, while southern opponents were busy with the Confederacy (Elazar 1962, 222–23; Lee 1949, 14).

One of Representative Justin S. Morrill's (R-VT) reasons for introducing this legislation was the unequal distribution of existing educational resources across states and regions (James 1910, 30). The same rationale for federal aid was invoked during federal-aid debates of the 1930s, and 1940s. The law also set another important precedent. According to historian Gordon Canfield Lee, the idea of categorical aid—funds for specific purposes— was first used in the Morrill Act (Lee 1949, 17).

As with the earlier land grants, the actual relevance of education in the Morrill Act is disputed. Lee (paraphrasing I. L. Kandel) suggests that the law was directed not so much at higher education per se as at western farmers and their representatives. In exchange for this educational windfall, it was hoped that westerners would continue to support the high tariffs that benefited eastern manufacturing interests. There was also widespread misuse of grants made under both the Morrill Act (ibid., 16–17) and the land ordinances of the Confederation Congress (Kaestle 1983, 183; Swift

1931, chap. 3). However, by the end of the nineteenth century, many states—particularly those in the west—were receiving more than 10 percent of their education revenues from land-grant income (Tyack, James, and Benavot 1987, 22).

More than a century later, during consideration of the Elementary and Secondary Education Act in 1965, Senator Wayne L. Morse (D-OR) interpreted the Morrill Act as an important precedent both for federal aid to higher education and for arguments against it:

> [I]t would be wise to have a footnote added at this point, that the Morrill Act of 1862 was signed by Abraham Lincoln. Buchanan in the preceding administration had vetoed it. Buchanan, as far as my research shows, was the first prominent official to bring forward what I consider to be a very unsound and fallacious argument. It is an argument incidentally which did not bother Abraham Lincoln. Buchanan was concerned that the Morrill Act might lead to Federal domination of education, but Abraham Lincoln pointed out that Congress would not abdicate its functions and obligations in the event that the executive branch of Government attempted any such Federal control. So Lincoln had no hesitancy in signing what was, in a real sense, through direct aid, the first great Federal aid for higher education bill ever passed by the Congress and signed by a President. (U.S. Senate 1965a, 83)

Opponents of federal assistance to education, including President James Buchanan, were first activated by the legislative process leading to the Morrill Act. As a newly "crystallized" faction against federal encroachment on state and local school systems (Lee 1949, 28), they scored an early victory a few years later. In 1867, a modest Department of Education was established to gather statistics and disseminate information about the nation's schools. The action was controversial, however, and opponents managed to downgrade the department the following year (see Chapter 5). The same functions would be performed in the Bureau of Education within the Department of the Interior. In the nineteenth century an education department with a place in the president's cabinet was not acceptable; the threat to local control of schools was perceived to be too great.

Opponents were further galvanized by an 1870 proposal to dramatically increase the potential for federal control of schooling. The Hoar bill proposed to require all states to establish common school systems, and if any states failed to do so, a "nationally controlled and administered system of local schools" would be imposed on them. By introducing this bill, Representative George F. Hoar (R-MA) believed that states would be shamed into doing their duty and that federal action would not be necessary. Speaking in defense of his bill, Hoar remarked: "Nobody proposes not to permit the States of this Union to educate their people. But what is proposed is not to permit them not to do it" (Lee 1949, chap. 3; quotations from 51 and 55).

Despite Representative Hoar's assurances, the bill failed. Opponents acted decisively against this brazen threat of federal control and invoked the memory of it in future struggles. Education proposals during the remainder of the nineteenth century were not as prescriptive as the Hoar bill, but they too failed to pass. The charge regarding federal control has been made against education proposals in Congress ever since. The claim that federal aid is unconstitutional also seems to have originated in the case against the Hoar bill.

The next significant congressional debate about federal aid occurred in the late nineteenth century. The Blair bill, named for Senator Henry W. Blair (R-NH), was a proposal to make direct grants to states on a phased-in matching basis according to illiteracy rates and numbers of school-age children. The bill passed in the Senate several times in the 1880s but was never considered in the House of Representatives. To receive grants, states would have been required to operate schools for all school-age children without excluding anyone, although racially segregated schools would have been permitted. Familiar arguments questioning the constitutionality of and need for federal aid were leveled by critics. They also raised the threat of outright federal control and charged that northern states were being bribed with grants they did not need in exchange for approving funds for the South, still struggling after the Civil War and reconstruction. Opponents of the bill also claimed that states would become dependent on national subsidies, an "artificial stimulant," once the payments began (ibid., chaps. 5 and 6).

Few of the arguments against the Blair bill were new, but the new delivery system for federal aid (direct payments to states, as opposed to land grants from the public domain) invited close scrutiny and criticism of the bill's fiscal justification and funding mechanisms. Unequal treatment of states was debated during earlier land-grant legislation, and attempts were made in the Morrill Act and the Blair bill to spread benefits nationwide, although not equally. The Blair bill was structured to give a disproportionate share of federal aid to southern states. The fact that only "common schools" (that is, public schools) and not parochial schools were to receive assistance elicited strong opposition from the Catholic church. The "artificial stimulant" charge was a new argument that probably stemmed from the bill's departure from land grants. (Arguments over how land grants compared with direct payments were also common in this period. Critics charged that land grants and revenues generated through taxes were not equivalent and that to give rebates to states in the form of monetary grants was inefficient. Why not just let states keep the taxes in the first place?) (ibid.)

The Smith-Hughes Act of 1917 was another high-water mark in the history of federal aid to education. Passed just before the United States entered World War I, this legislation authorized financial support for public secondary school vocational programs in home economics, agriculture, and industrial arts. This legislation was recommended by the federal Commission on National Aid to Vocational Education, established a few years earlier. The Smith-Hughes Act demonstrated the power of two factors that are present in many successful twentieth-century federal education initiatives: (1) a powerful lobby (the American Vocational Association, its organizational predecessors, and other groups in the case of Smith-Hughes and its several reauthorizations) and (2) the use of education for international economic competitiveness as a rationale for federal involvement (Kantor 1982, 35; Cuban 1982, 59–60; and Holt 1922, 1–4). More recently, interest-group support has been important for sustaining the federal role in special-education and compensatory-education programs. Despite mixed reviews of the effectiveness of the Smith-Hughes Act in increasing vocational placements for students in participating programs, congressional support for vocational education has always been strong.

Federal activity in several spheres of public life increased during World War I and the Depression, most notably economic relief and banking. Many educators assumed that their field, hard hit by unemployment and evaporating public expenditures, would become a relief project of its own. Direct financial aid for schools was not enacted during the 1930s, although education did benefit from economic relief programs. The Public Works Administration built schools, and the Federal Emergency Relief Administration kept teachers employed as teachers. The Civilian Conservation Corps had a piecemeal education component for corps members. Administered by the Army, the activities consisted of literacy training and elementary and high school courses. The National Youth Administration, a unit of the Works Progress Administration, provided part-time employment and stipends to participating high school and college students. These programs were controversial at the time—and their significance as examples of federal education policy is still debated—because they mostly bypassed (or disrupted) existing education agencies in favor of new bureaucracies. The new agencies were viewed with suspicion and were usually perceived to be under tight federal control (Smith 1982, prologue and chap. 1).

In general, education was a minor agenda item of the New Deal (Kantor and Lowe 1995, 5–6). However, the 1930s were not without important developments in the federal-aid story. There were two Supreme Court decisions at mid-decade that apparently resolved lingering questions about the constitutionality of federal involvement in education while also explicitly defining limits to government control. In *United States v. Butler* (1936), the court ruled that it is permissible for the federal government to provide financial assistance to schools but that it was not allowed to enforce specific content or doctrines. In the *Helvering v. Davis* decision the following year, the high court ruled that Congress could determine what constitutes "general welfare" under the Constitution's general-welfare clause. By precluding an automatically narrow reading of the general-welfare clause, this decision stripped federal-aid opponents of a strong and reliable weapon used in past battles. At the same time, *Helvering v. Davis* fueled their concern that federal aid could jeopardize local control if Congress chose to include education in its definition of the general welfare (Smith 1982, 50–51).

From the 1930s to the 1950s, several education bills were introduced, but few passed. Those that did pass owed their success directly or indirectly to the national mobilizations during the Depression and World War II. Several acts provided funds to compensate local school systems for expenses incurred by serving tax-exempt federal installations, such as military bases. These funds, known as "impact aid," were appropriated without controversy (*Congressional Record* 1950, 10093–94). Federal-aid advocates and opponents alike recognized the unusual circumstances that made these grants necessary. Impact aid is still a popular program.

Notwithstanding the popularity of certain specialized programs, such as the Servicemen's Readjustment Act of 1944 (better known as the G.I. Bill), federal-aid opponents remained strong through most of the 1950s. A noteworthy performance by this faction in 1956 is highlighted as a textbook example of "strategic voting" (Riker 1986, chap. 11). Democrats proposed a school construction aid package for public schools. Lingering effects of the Depression and World War II had deferred school construction while simultaneously packing classrooms with baby boomers. According to the bill's supporters, temporary federal aid was necessary to help local school systems meet these needs. There was significant bipartisan support for the measure, suggesting that legislators saw a bona fide need and a legitimate federal role in meeting it. Another promising sign was that the House of Representatives in the Eighty-Fourth Congress was controlled by Democrats, a party that was then generally receptive to the idea of federal involvement in education.

Despite a favorable political climate, the bill, H.R.7535, was defeated. The reason was an amendment by Representative Adam Clayton Powell (D-NY) to deny federal school construction funds to states with racially segregated schools. Sensing the opportunity to kill the aid bill altogether, most Republicans voted for the amendment, knowing that they and a large number of Southern Democrats would vote against the amended bill. An unamended bill had the votes to pass, but House procedures precluded such a vote. Ironically, the impoverished South, the intended beneficiary of federal largesse under numerous proposals in the nineteenth and twentieth centuries, was eventually maneuvered into opposing federal-aid initiatives as possible threats to racial segregation. For more than a decade after the *Brown v. Board of Education* decision (1954), the South was a solidly unified opponent to federal education legislation and civil rights. This stance made Southern Democrats strategic allies of conservative Republicans. Strategic voting on the race discrimination issue had also occurred on a 1943 education bill (Smith 1982, 106–10; Riker 1986, chap. 11).

This overview of federal education policy before 1958 does not completely portend the expansion that began with the National Defense Education Act that year. More to the point, it fails to anticipate the dramatic expansion of federal authority that commenced with passage of the No Child Left Behind Act of 2001. However, the long experience of federal involvement before 1958 included many of the political strategies and rhetorical building blocks that were later used to justify increasing the scale and reach of the federal role.

The historical record also reveals a long-standing confrontation between supporters and foes of new federal programs for schools. The ideological foundations of these factions are deeply rooted in beliefs and values about the appropriate role of the federal government in American society. The interplay between shifting ideological factions defined the boundary between acceptable and unacceptable federal education policies for more than two hundred years. I refer to the early history of federal involvement in later chapters, where I examine the slowly—and then rapidly—expanding federal role in education in more detail. That narrative will help us understand what happened during the interval between the federal government's tightly circumscribed role in the late 1950s and the dramatic expansion of that role by the time No Child Left Behind was enacted more than forty years later.

2

was it really about sputnik?

The National Defense Education Act of 1958

Federal aid to education, which today shows up on the floor of the House in
a space suit will appear tomorrow in a surgeon's gown, next year in a
professor's robes, and the year after that in an engineer's tweed suit. There
is no end to disguises available and likewise no end to the spending
possibilities of this masquerade. The taxpayers are not amused.

—U.S. REPRESENTATIVE CHARLES B. BROWNSON (R-IN) (1958)

The 1950s marked the beginning of several decades of increased federal
activism in education. In 1954 the U.S. Supreme Court ruled against
segregated school systems in *Brown v. Board of Education,* injecting a new
federal priority into state and local school policy-making. Four years later,
Congress passed the National Defense Education Act (NDEA), ostensibly
in reaction to Soviet accomplishments during the Cold War. Even though
ample precedent for federal school aid existed before the 1950s, that decade
marked an important shift in the perception of schools as legitimate avenues
for solving national problems.

The National Defense Education Act of 1958 is significant because it
combined and expanded earlier federal-aid precedents while respecting
local-control rhetoric and practices. By financing specific activities rather
than unrestricted expenditures, the 1958 law was a categorical program
like the Smith-Hughes Act of 1917 supporting vocational education. It
provided funds to all levels of the education system—elementary through
graduate school—something that federal programs, taken together, were
already doing. Charges of federal control were overcome (but not silenced)
by offering schools and colleges wide spending latitude within broad topics.
The novelty of the National Defense Education Act was that it aided all
levels of the educational system through one statute. Moreover, virtually
every public and private education institution in the nation at these different

levels was eligible, in theory, for federal assistance. Finally, backers of the legislation exploited a specific international incident—the launch of Sputnik—and the Cold War generally to simultaneously blame and energize the education system in the name of national defense.

The National Defense Education Act is important because it passed—an unusual distinction for 1950s education legislation. It revived the categorical-aid strategy, which would govern the design of most future federal education programs. The NDEA episode also demonstrates how ideological and political arguments helped shape the allowable scope of federal involvement in education, a phenomenon that is important for understanding later legislation.

Provisions of the National Defense Education Act

The National Defense Education Act authorized a $1 billion four-year program of federal financial assistance in several areas, even though it is best remembered as a math and science program. The legislation provided funds for loans to college students, fellowships for graduate students, and the strengthening of elementary and secondary science, mathematics, and foreign-language instruction. The latter objective was to be achieved by supporting laboratory equipment purchases (on a matching basis with states) and professional-development opportunities for teachers (Carlson 1959, 4–18).

The statute was organized as follows. Title I enumerated general provisions and definitions. A federal loan program for "worthy and needy students" in institutions of higher education was established in Title II. Title III provided funds for laboratory equipment and teacher supervision in elementary and secondary schools. Funds for graduate-student fellowships were authorized by Title IV. Title V supported state and local programs for guidance counseling, testing, and identification of promising students. Training institutes on these topics were suggested as state activities. Title VI was intended to advance foreign-language development by underwriting research and training. Title VII sought to exploit the educational potential of television, radio, motion pictures, and other media by supporting activities in these areas. Existing vocational education laws were modified in Title VIII to establish regional vocational education programs for technicians in defense-related fields. Title IX directed the new National Science Foundation to establish a Science Information Service and a Science Information Council to track and disseminate information on international developments in science and technical fields. Title X provided funds to state departments of education to improve their statistics gathering and reporting capacities. It also included the act's administrative provisions, namely, that the bureaucratic home of the National Defense Education Act would be the tiny U.S. Office of Education in the Department of Health, Education, and Welfare (ibid., 3–27).

From the point of view of K-12 educators, the most appealing part of this legislation was Title III, in which Congress authorized funds ($70 million in fiscal year 1959) to help elementary and secondary schools purchase equipment for science and foreign-language laboratories (ibid., 3). Part of this law's attractiveness was the enormous latitude that states and school districts had regarding admissible purchases; the only firm rule was that federal funds be matched from other sources (Marsh and Gortner 1963, 27 and 41). This flexibility also appealed to legislators because it helped protect the program from charges that it would lead to federal interference with state and local school activities.

The Historical Context of the Cold War and Sputnik

It is important to differentiate the lineage of the National Defense Education Act from the agitation that surrounded Sputnik. According to several views of federal education policy, the NDEA was enacted because of Sputnik—three earth-orbiting satellites launched by the Soviet Union in October and November 1957 and in May 1958 (Clowse 1981, 6, 14, 112). However, other factors also explain this legislation. Throughout the 1950s, many educators and commentators called for greater pedagogical rigor in schools while casting doubt on what they saw as the excesses of progressive education (ibid., 33–34; Jennings 1967, 95–96). The pressure for greater emphasis on mathematics and science was heightened by the furor over Sputnik, but the pressure also predated these events. Carl Kaestle and Marshall Smith (1982, 395) argue that the National Defense Education Act was part of a "hard, empirical, technical" trend in federal education policy, dating especially to the Smith-Hughes Act of 1917, which authorized support for vocational education. (The Smith-Hughes Act of 1917 is also the most visible twentieth-century categorical-aid precedent for the NDEA [ibid., 389; Sufrin 1963, 8–9]. The Morrill Act of 1862 was also a categorical program.) "On reflection, it would appear that the NDEA may have been enacted under the pressures which the Congress felt from the Russian success in space, but the contents of NDEA represent both traditional activities of the federal government with respect to the educational programs and establishments of states, and substantive considerations which professional educators and public officials had been considering for some time. Sputnik was a proximate cause in a process which was developing quite independently" (Sufrin 1963, 11).

Nor was it a new idea to propose educational responses to international rivalries. The Smith-Hughes Act did this in the context of World War I. Sputnik revived the debate about international competition at the height of the Cold War. Many politicians and educators believed that the Soviets' success in space was due to a superior education system. The United States needed to improve its schools as a strategic response to the Soviet challenge. Persistent controversies about the principle of federal aid to education (for example, federal control) were overshadowed by Cold War rhetoric and sidestepped by reintroducing categorical aid as the delivery system for NDEA funds. It was not Sputnik per se that led to the National Defense Education Act. The legislation was shaped by the larger context of the Cold War (Kaestle and Smith 1982, 393).

Soviet space probes and the Cold War played well as rhetorical devices during committee hearings and floor testimony. The quotation from Representative Charles Brownson (R-IN; 1957 ADA score: 11) at the beginning of this chapter shows that he was skeptical of this strategy, but most of his colleagues cited Soviet progress in space and other technical fields as a necessary and sufficient condition for immediate federal action. Sputnik, a visible marker of the complex struggle between the Soviet Union and the United States, clearly contributed to the content and timing of the statute. These factors certainly were responsible for the votes of some legislators. Compare this episode with the ill-fated 1956 proposal for federal school construction aid in Chapter 1. The earlier bill failed because, among other reasons, it lacked a catalyzing event that would be perceived as an emergency.

In making this comparison, however, it is easy to confound Cold War rhetoric and the Sputnik "crisis." The Cold War was affecting political discourse—including talk of the appropriate federal role in education—before the Sputnik launches. Indeed, the Cold War influenced many domestic policies that seemed "quite remote from the zones of tensions between the superpowers" (Scott 1997, 11). This rhetoric added drama to domestic policy debates, as it did in the case of federal aid for highway construction (Rose 1979, chaps. 6 and 7), but other developments in education, politics, and national life suggest that Congress was ready to pass new legislation to benefit elementary and secondary schools.

The Case for the National Defense Education Act

As noted above, the National Defense Education Act debate in Congress was rife with Cold War rhetoric, so it is important to understand the content and role of these arguments. Moreover, it is helpful to see that other arguments in favor of federal aid were also considered. Equally important are arguments against the NDEA because they illuminate the loss handed to opponents of federal aid during this episode. The ideological violation that strong opponents of federal aid felt was acute, because they believed that all the arguments in favor of federal aid in general and of the NDEA in particular were wrong, deceptive, and dangerous.

Arguments about the need for an educational response to Soviet technical achievements were made in Congress even before the first Sputnik launch in October 1957. (House subcommittee hearings on some of these bills began in August 1957.) After Sputnik, the generic argument was: Sputnik is evidence of Soviet technical dominance over the United States. This superiority is due, in part, to superior schools. U.S. schools in general, and technical fields in particular, have suffered from decades of neglect and misbegotten reforms—namely, progressive education. The dual threat of Soviet technical prowess and global communism makes the continued neglect of American education a national problem. Correcting it demands federal action. Under most conditions, schools do not need federal assistance, but this is an emergency.

Representative of the Cold War argument is a statement by Representative Carl A. Elliott (D-AL; 1957 ADA score: 78), member of the House Committee on Education and Labor and chair of its Subcommittee on Special Education. Presiding over an NDEA field hearing in Eau Claire, Wisconsin, on October 28, 1957, three weeks after the first Sputnik launch, Elliott said:

> Our very survival depends, I believe, in maintaining the technical superiority of the free world over that of the Communist world, and maintaining that superiority depends largely upon our having enough scientific, engineering, and other technical and professional people with enough training of sufficient quality to outthink and outproduce the Russians. Some have termed this struggle between communism and the free world as the war of the classroom. Some have called it the war of the laboratory. It may be known to history by one of those terms. (U.S. House of Representatives 1958b, 143)

The House committee report, which recommended passage of the NDEA to the full chamber, began with similar warnings:

> America is confronted with a serious and continuing challenge in many fields. The challenge—in science, industry, government, military strength, international relations—stems from the forces of totalitarianism. This challenge, as well as our own goal of enlargement of life for each individual, requires the fullest possible development of the talents of our young people. American education, therefore, bears a grave responsibility in our times.
>
> It is no exaggeration to say that America's progress in many fields of endeavor in the years ahead—in fact, the very survival of our free country—may depend in large part upon the education we provide for our young people now. (U.S. House of Representatives 1958a, 2)

Several legislators and others mentioned the effect this competition had on the national consciousness. During rocket scientist Wernher von Braun's appearance before the House subcommittee, Representative Edith S. Green (D-OR; 1957 ADA score: 67) commented on the numerous comparisons between Soviet and American society being made and observed: "Five years ago, especially a politician, if he made a statement that the Communists or the Russians are doing it and it is good, and therefore we must do it, he would probably be investigated by the House Un-American Activities Committee" (U.S. House of Representatives 1958b, 1319).

The Cold War contributed to the timing, content, and popularity of the National Defense Education Act, but opinions about the Soviet threat were not unanimous. Nor were they the only arguments used by those who favored the NDEA. It is clear that other arguments in favor of federal action were virtually eclipsed by the alarmed comparisons between U.S. and Soviet schools and society. Nevertheless, the other arguments were part of the case for federal aid that grew steadily throughout the middle of the twentieth century. The justifications that follow also sustained the expansion of federal aid much longer than the momentary educational fixation on the Soviets during the Cold War.

The first argument was that the migratory population of the United States made the quality of education a national concern because the ability to finance education varied by state. This reason was used frequently in the 1930s and 1940s (Aly 1934; Muller 1934; Nichols 1948). The idea of the federal government's acting to help equalize educational opportunity dates at least to the 1880s (Lee 1949, 160). Migration came up briefly during NDEA deliberations. Edward D. Hollander, director of the liberal group Americans for Democratic Action, answered Senator Gordon L. Allott's (R-CO; 1957 ADA score: 67) questions about the rationale for federal interest in the equalization of interstate education spending levels. He made the following remarks during hearings before the Senate Committee on Labor and Public Welfare:

> The justification, I would think, sir, is that education is a matter of national interest. If there are children poorly educated in the rural schools or in the schools of a city or State that does not maintain a good school system, they migrate all over the country and they become the citizens and the workers of other States. They become not only taxpayers but tax consumers in other States.
>
> The extent of migration in this country alone, it seems to me, would make that a national interest, even if there were no question of the national defense or the fiscal problem. (U.S. Senate 1958b, 867)

Senator Wayne L. Morse (D-OR; 1957 ADA score: 75) envisioned the equalizing federal role as a theological corrective: "I have said this before, and repeat this morning, we cannot let the educational opportunities of American boys and girls be dependent upon an act of God. The place of birth of an American girl or boy is an act of God" (ibid., 1143).

Proponents of the National Defense Education Act cited the interconnected nature of postwar national life as an argument for increased federal involvement in education. They also sought to associate education with other national, regional, state, and local causes that merited federal action. This theme was expressed eloquently by Daniel Kerr of Huron College during a field hearing of the House subcommittee in Sioux Falls, South Dakota: "I am very much convinced, sir, that, if the Federal Government or any government, has the right to appropriate funds for the extermination or the control of bugs in the cottonfields of Texas, it has an equal and a greater responsibility to the controlling of bugs in the minds of young people, to either eradicate the bugs or possibly to put good bugs in their places" (U.S. House of Representatives 1958b, 348).

Finally, some proponents of federal aid, such as Representative George S. McGovern (D-SD; 1957 ADA score: 44), saw the need for federal assistance in school construction. Classroom shortages were well documented (and vigorously disputed) during the 1950s as children born after World War II started school. This rationale was more persuasive to McGovern than competition with the Soviets (ibid., 288). Even though school construction bills were defeated throughout the 1950s, McGovern made no apologies for continuing to press this case during the NDEA hearings.

None of these subsidiary arguments was a major rhetorical force in the NDEA debate. In fact, they were almost completely supplanted in the 1957–58 deliberations by international and technical concerns. Yet the larger case made in these arguments—regional disparities in education spending, precedents for federal action, and facilities needs—was also established by federal-aid advocates during earlier episodes. The willingness of legislators to act on behalf of schools was explained partly by their growing awareness that schools needed and deserved federal assistance for a variety of reasons, not just competition with the Soviets.

Before reviewing the case against the National Defense Education Act and federal school aid in the next section, it is important to be aware of the views of individuals who were critical of the educational approach proposed by the legislation. These critics were not opponents of federal aid; indeed, a persistent flaw in the NDEA identified by some legislators and educators was that the $1 billion four-year program was too small and restricted. (The adequacy of the funds authorized by No Child Left Behind years later was also questioned by federal-aid advocates, as was the overall design of the 2001 law.) Even though the categorical-aid strategy may have converted opponents of unrestricted, general aid, it invited criticism from other quarters.

Numerous legislators and committee witnesses expressed concern, skepticism, or outright opposition to the narrow focus on math, science, and foreign language in Title III, the K-12 equipment program that received the lion's share of NDEA appropriations. During House subcommittee hearings, Representative McGovern (and several others) cautioned against the narrow "defense studies" emphasis in some of the proposed programs: "Accepting the Soviet challenge in education, we must never forget the basic principles of democracy that we are seeking to defend. Likewise, we must remember that our goal is not scientific supremacy alone; rather, we seek education of the whole man. There is a desperate need for scientific and technical training, but we seek above all the well-balanced, educated citizen, who is aware also of his cultural, social, and moral responsibilities in a democratic society" (ibid., 289).

To be on the safe side, McGovern added an anti-Soviet rationale to his concern about the narrow range of subject areas: "[T]he American people are perhaps more concerned about the challenge of Soviet science and the Sputnik than they are some other challenges, but tomorrow it may be the challenge of Soviet missionaries that are operating in the economic field, or the ideological field, or even in the field of fine arts" (ibid., 680).

Robert Francis Goheen, classics scholar and president of Princeton University, expressed concern that higher education might be "stampeded" into meeting math and science needs at the expense of the rest of the curriculum and other areas of knowledge: "[A]s I look outward from America, it seems to me very likely that the contest to win the allegiance of the millions of peoples in the uncommitted nations of this world will turn in the end more upon our moral and cultural posture, on our ability to make live and to transmit our democratic humane ideals than upon our military and technological posture" (ibid., 1083).

Concerns about unbalanced curriculums had to be expressed carefully to avoid the appearance of advocating general aid, a label that killed other proposals to assist elementary and secondary education before and after the National Defense Education Act. Very few in Congress openly supported general aid or unrestricted aid. Outside witnesses had to tread softly, as well, lest they be accused of seeking, in the words of Senator Allott, "gifts to education without any strings attached to them" (U.S. Senate 1958b, 453). On the other hand, unrestricted aid was attractive to educators. Reviewing published articles on the National Defense Education Act during its early implementation, Sidney Sufrin found that most of the criticism it received came from those who felt that it did not cover a broad enough range of subject areas (Sufrin 1963, 42). This put legislators wooing the education lobby in a contradictory position. It was not possible to openly advocate what educators wanted most—general aid—because it was only possible to pass a categorical-aid program.

The Case Against the National Defense Education Act and Federal Aid

The National Defense Education Act was a setback for opponents of federal involvement in schools. The earlier success of these politicians in blocking many elementary and secondary education bills makes it important to understand their loss in 1958. The best way to understand the shifting fortunes of the different sides of the federal-aid debate is to analyze their arguments at different times. This analysis will not be sufficient to explain everything that happened, but it illuminates the ideological factors at work during this and other episodes in the expansion of federal assistance to schools.

Some participants in the debate disagreed with the most visible rationale for the National Defense Education Act: technical competition with the Soviet Union. House subcommittee witness F. L. Partlo, president of the South Dakota School of Mines and Technology, noted: "We talk about the threats to our way of life by our adversaries of communistic persuasion, but I submit to you that I would prefer that we go down to defeat in opposing communism and all that it implies, rather than to attempt to defeat it by embracing it, for then we would be absorbed by it" (U.S. House of Representatives 1958b, 322). According to this view, it does not matter what threats face the United States or its education system; we surrender our national principles if we allow federal involvement in schools.

The best statement of personal consternation over the desire to emulate Soviet accomplishments was made during the House floor debate on the National Defense Education Act by Representative Clare E. Hoffman (R-MI, 1957 ADA score: 0) in response to a colleague, Representative Wright Patman (D-TX; 1957 ADA score: 33). The quotation is self-explanatory.

> Mr. Speaker, it is always pleasant to listen to the gentleman from Texas [Patman]. Listening to him a few moments ago I just wondered why it is that we do not call top Russians over here to run our Government. We are always told how much further ahead of us Russia is, in every field and the progress they have made. If that is true, what is the use of fighting communism all the time? What is the use of spending our billions in an attempt to defeat it? Why not let their scientists and those others who have been educated up to the limit lay out our whole program? They are, according to those who have been attempting to frighten us into additional excessive and ruinous spending, doing pretty well. They are fooling us into spending ourselves into bankruptcy, and that as all know means disaster. The Texas gentleman just told us they have more scientists, more people qualified for many necessary activities than we—one group we do have—too many spenders. (*Congressional Record* 1958, 19576)

Representative Hoffman's remarks conclude with a note of fiscal conservatism, a theme taken up by K. Brantley Watson and John Miles of the U.S. Chamber of Commerce Education Department. They opposed the new government spending entailed by the National Defense Education Act and urged that the legislation be defeated. In response to their testimony before a joint hearing of the House General Education and Special Education Subcommittees, Representative Elliott decried the evasiveness of their objection:

> You are opposed to the Federal Government doing anything about [problems in American education]. On the State level, there are forces, strong, powerful forces, even as powerful as you, and in many instances your counterparts who are also opposed to doing much about it at the state level.
>
> Then when you get down to the local level, you have got powerful people again and powerful groups and organizations who are so oftentimes opposed to doing anything about it. . . . Are we going to say it is nobody's business and the result is that finally our school system decays to such a point that it is not able to discharge the function that a school system must discharge in a democratic society such as we have? (U.S. House of Representatives 1958b, 1526)

Whereas some federal-aid supporters questioned the narrow focus of the NDEA proposal, certain opponents declared that nothing in the proposal was justified. These foes were responding to the proponents' arguments about the need for federal action and the consequences of doing nothing. Some opponents apparently felt obliged to address these claims explicitly rather than simply reiterate their opposition in principle to an increased federal role. This happened in the "Minority Views" section of the House committee report. (Committee reports can include "minority," "dissenting," and "supplemental" views in addition to the main report, which represents the views of the committee majority.) The minority section was signed by Representatives Ralph W. Gwinn (R-NY; 1957 ADA score: 0), Clare E. Hoffman (R-MI), and Donald W. Nicholson (R-MA; 1957 ADA score: 11). They objected to the premises of the bill, asserting that there was no need for such a program. They claimed that there were plenty of funds to support national priorities but that existing funds were misspent on a "hodgepodge" of subjects, such as "junior homemaking for boys" and "square dancing," unrelated to the core mission of schooling (which they did not define). Moreover, they also averred that scholarship aid and loans were widely available for talented but needy college students and that the presumed shortage of personnel in science and engineering could not be documented with media and government labor market statistics (U.S. House of Representatives 1958a, 42–46).

Senator Strom Thurmond (then D-SC; 1957 ADA score: 17) offered a theological reason for opposing all national efforts to equalize educational expenditures, including those he saw in the NDEA bills. In the "Minority Views" section of the Senate committee report, Thurmond objected to assumptions of racial equality as well. He said that equality of opportunity can be legislated at the state and local levels but that "equality of ability or knowledge through education [cannot be]; for the Creator, in His great wisdom, made no two men alike, either physically or mentally. We must, therefore, return to a recognition of individuality in the application of the educational process, rather than continuing to attempt to use a common mold for all students" (U.S. Senate 1958a, 53).

Senator Thurmond also disputed the legislation's national-defense rationale. He believed that the national-security rhetoric surrounding the bill masked its true identity: general aid. Thurmond wanted the bill to require loan and fellowship recipients to actually study defense-related subjects and work in the national-defense interest after graduation, "at least for some minimum period" (ibid., 51–52). A hawkish observer would agree with Thurmond's criticism. Even though the legislation was based on national-security rhetoric, only a few titles had subject-specific provisions. To be eligible for student loans or graduate fellowships, no particular course of study was required, although institutions were directed to give preference to "academically superior" future teachers and professors and, for Title II loans, "math, science, engineering, or modern foreign language majors," in devising award criteria (Carlson 1959, 5). Thurmond wanted to see results that clearly benefited national defense because national defense was invoked as the main reason for passing the law.

Strom Thurmond sounded numerous warnings about federal control of education throughout his long political career. This particular argument against the National Defense Education Act is noteworthy because in it he advocated greater federal control, as defined by conservatives, in order to keep the bill's sponsors true to their national-defense intentions. The same dynamic was exposed in the House subcommittee by Representative Stewart L. Udall (D-AZ; 1957 ADA score: 100), in response to remarks by Representative Gwinn (R-NY). "The gentleman from New York is essentially saying if we do not [set up standards and guidelines but] simply give them money we are being irresponsible. On the other hand, if we propose to set up standards, the gentleman is talking about controls. So, we lose the argument with him either way. On one hand we are irresponsible and on the other hand we want to control the local people" (U.S. House of Representatives 1958b, 935).

Disingenuous as the tactic may have seemed to Representative Udall, it worked well until 1958 and is even reflected to some degree in the National Defense Education Act. The flexible and sometimes vague provisions of the NDEA reflected the compromises necessary to enact a bill that would not be seen by too many legislators as a federal-control threat. "The money provided for school use had no intrinsic rigor, nor could Congress make it an instrument of discipline. What the program had was magnitude and flexibility, but there could have been no program if its proponents had insisted on course standards as well. In order to pass in Congress, the Act had to be carefully and explicitly worded to deprive the federal government of means of control of the funds the Title would disburse" (Marsh and Gortner 1963, 87).

Charges of federal control were made and evaded by all sides during deliberations on the National Defense Education Act. Congressional proponents of the legislation tried to assure their colleagues that it preserved state and local control of schools and that "states and institutions of higher education retain basic responsibility for planning and administering the programs authorized in the bill" (U.S. House of Representatives 1958a, 4). The same theme was expressed by Senator Lister Hill (D-AL; 1957 ADA score: 58), chair of the Senate Committee on Labor and Public Welfare, as he opened the committee hearings. "The particular task of this committee is to consider how best to stimulate and strengthen science and education for the defense of our country and at the same time preserve the traditional principle, in which we all believe, that primary responsibility and control of education belongs and must remain with the States, local communities, and private institutions" (U.S. Senate 1958b, 2).

These assurances did not convince the hard-core opponents of federal aid to support the National Defense Education Act. Assurances about state and local responsibility for education, along with formal language to this effect in education laws, are obligatory but typically fruitless in getting ideological foes to let down their guard. In fact, the federal-control threat is the mainstay of arguments against most new national education programs. (The conspicuous exception is the Education for All Handicapped Children Act of 1975.) Warnings about federal control have been so rhetorically and politically potent that federal-aid advocates must also denounce federal control in their arguments. As shown below, NDEA proponents leveled the charge of federal control at aspects of the legislation they did not favor. The specter of nationalized schools has haunted federal education proposals from the mid-nineteenth century until the end of the twentieth. It remains the burden of federal-aid advocates to refute the charge.

To conservative federal-aid opponents in the 1950s and early 1960s, the federal-control threat took the following form: any law that gives the federal government authority for education will lead to federal control. The American principle of local control of schools is necessarily compromised by any degree of federal involvement because unchecked national governments are inherently tyrannical. Although the extent of federal involvement—and perceived violations of local control—varies over time and by program, the most undesirable feature of federal involvement is that it occurs at all. The best way to circumvent federal control of community school systems is to resist all efforts to extend the reach of the national government. (Were conservative opponents of the National Defense Education Act able to foresee No Child Left Behind, they would have been disappointed but not surprised, according to this logic.)

Senator Thurmond, national-security enforcer and federal-aid foe, warned about the deferred threat of federal control in the NDEA proposal. "There is little Federal control in the bill as proposed; but its ineffectiveness, assured by a fallacious approach, will be the excuse for imposition of Federal regulation by future legislative acts" (U.S. Senate 1958a, 54). The threat of excessive federal regulation will lie dormant until the consequences of the bill are realized in the future. By then, it will be too late to correct the problem. Ernest Wilkinson, president of Brigham Young University, used an erosion metaphor to characterize the creeping threat of federal control. "I am afraid of the disintegrating erosion of particular exceptions, and by that I mean that we legislate one day and say 'We will do this, but we will have no Federal control. Another day we will do this and we will have no Federal control.' Ultimately, it mounts up so much that there has been so much erosion that we do have Federal control" (U.S. House of Representatives 1958b, 449).

According to this view, the safest approach to protect local communities from federal interference was to prevent the government from establishing a foothold. Conservatives were correct in their conviction that it is difficult to reverse federal programs—or even stem their expansion—once they begin. Of course, in the view of federal-aid advocates, political compromises can also blunt the effectiveness of education programs once they are enacted and implemented. In the case of the National Defense Education Act, the protections against federal control diminished the intent of the bills' sponsors to have a more substantial effect on the quality and rigor of math and science instruction (Marsh and Gortner 1963, 88).

So odious was the charge of federal control that federal-aid proponents also use it as a weapon. As noted above, Representative McGovern was opposed to what he saw as a subject area imbalance in the National Defense Education Act. A vocal federal-aid advocate, McGovern regarded this emphasis as a form of federal control because the government was pressuring state and local educators to favor certain disciplines. He believed it was hypocritical to oppose federal control per se while supporting the subject-area restrictions of the bill. (McGovern also acknowledged the strategic necessity of linking the education bill to math and science education.) "Some of the people who opposed . . . the education bill in the last session of the 85th Congress did so because they felt it would be an opening wedge that might enable the Federal Government to put pressure on the administration of our school programs. When we enter into an area where we say Congress will determine what field will be supported, aren't we in effect aggravating the danger that our colleagues were concerned about?" (U.S. House of Representatives 1958b, 690).

Representative McGovern represented the views of many educators, who would have preferred unrestricted aid to earmarked, categorical funds. In their own way, educators also opposed federal influence over the use of federal funds in the field. The best safeguard against such influence was to get money that was free of any guidelines whatsoever. Even the National Defense Education Act's requirement for state and local matching funds under certain titles was seen by some educators as federal control, because it mandated how nonfederal education funds were to be spent (Sufrin 1963, 47).

The resulting legislation was clearly a compromise between the different factions. The act's supporters brokered a large federal program for schools and colleges that was less targeted than earlier federal programs, such as vocational education and impact aid. Substantial resources would flow to every level of education and to more institutions than ever before. Opponents of the bill, whom I call "conservative," lost on their objections, but their concerns were not completely overruled. Their fears of federal control were partially addressed by keeping the actual provisions of the act quite vague. The threat of federal control was always on the table, and it influenced the design of the National Defense Education Act and most other federal education policies.

Table 2   1958 NDEA votes with 1957 ADA Statistics

1958 NDEA votes with 1957 ADA scores	House August 23, 1958	Senate August 22, 1958
Final vote on H.R.13247 NDEA	212–85	66–15
(i.e., conference report)	(71.4% "yes")	(81.5% "yes")
Democrats	140–30	37–7
	(82.4% "yes")	(84.1% "yes")
Republicans	72–55	29–8
	(56.7% "yes")	(78.4% "yes")
ADA Score Analyses		
Mean ADA score of "yes" voters	61.5 (n=212)	55.5 (n=66)
Mean ADA score of "no" voters	21.6 (n=85)	14.0 (n=15)
Mean ADA score of Democrat "yes" voters	65.1 (n=140)	58.9 (n=37)
Mean ADA score of Republican "yes" voters	54.5 (n=72)	51.1 (n=29)
Mean ADA score of Democrat "no" voters	12.5 (n=30)	16.9 (n=7)
Mean ADA score of Republican "no" voters	26.6 (n=55)	11.5 (n=8)
Mean Democrat ADA score (whole chamber)	52.8 (n=232)	48.9 (n=49)
Mean Republican ADA score (whole chamber)	39.8 (n=197)	41.3 (n=47)
Mean ADA score of whole chamber (1957)	46.9 (n=429)	45.2 (n=96)

NOTE: NDEA = National Defense Education Act; ADA = Americans for Democratic Action; n = the number of legislators in each cell with 1957 ADA scores. ADA figures in the "whole chamber" cells include all legislators, regardless of whether they participated in the final vote on NDEA. In nine cases in the House and two in the Senate, scores were taken from 1959 because the eleven legislators did not have 1957 scores. In the case of one senator, only the 1958 score is available, and it was used for these calculations. The House had five vacancies when the NDEA vote took place.

SOURCES: Congressional Quarterly Inc. 1959, 414–15 and 461 for the votes on the NDEA and Americans for Democratic Action website for 1957 ADA scores. (1957 scores downloaded October 21, 2005, from http://www.adaction.org/1957.pdf.) 1958 and 1959 ADA scores from Sharp 1988.

Description of National Defense Education Act Votes in Congress

Throughout this chapter, I have included the 1957 ADA scores of individual legislators as a provisional indicator of their conservative or liberal leanings, but I do not draw conclusions about the ideological orientation of these legislators solely on the basis of their ADA scores. Indeed, I believe that the content and context of their comments is a better source of information about their values and beliefs concerning the specific topic of federal aid to schools. In this section, I take a brief detour away from congressional argumentation to examine the final votes on the National Defense Education Act. The votes also enable me to analyze aggregate ADA scores within the House and Senate. Please note, however, that this is a supplemental technique that is simply meant to confirm the existence of the ideological factions identified in my analysis of the NDEA debate in Congress. Neither individual nor mean ADA scores, by themselves, drive this chapter's conclusions. (The votes and ADA scores are deployed in the same way—and with the same limitations—in this book's other episodes.)

Both parties supported the NDEA conference report (that is, the final bill) in the House of Representatives and the Senate. Even though Congress was not divided by party on the National Defense Education Act, there were ideological divisions suggested in the debate and the votes. Both the debate and the votes indicated a separation between liberals and conservatives on this legislation. Table 2 displays the NDEA votes and the 1957 ADA statistics. The table is organized by chamber, party, and NDEA voting position. The ADA data confirm that federal aid to education, as proposed in the National Defense Education Act, drew more support from liberals than from conservatives in Congress. The NDEA "yes" voters in both the House and Senate have substantially higher "liberal quotients" than the "no" voters. Note that these differences are not accounted for by party affiliation—that is, the distinct ideological divide between "yes" voters and "no" voters persists regardless of party membership. It is interesting that the Democrat "no" voters in the House are more conservative than Republican "no" voters, as measured by ADA scores. This phenomenon reflects the conservatism of Southern Democrats in the 1950s (Carmines and Stimson 1989, 163). For the record, Republican President Dwight Eisenhower supported the NDEA bills; the Democrats controlled both houses of Congress.

The Ideological Significance of the
National Defense Education Act for Later Policies

The National Defense Education Act of 1958 is the starting point for my analysis of the expansion of federal aid to education in the last five decades. As such, it might be viewed as an arbitrary choice, because it built on robust precedents and sustains the momentum already established for expanding federal involvement in education. Yet it also broke new ground by delivering large amounts of categorical aid to elementary schools for the first time. It also anticipated the strategies necessary for enacting the larger Elementary and Secondary Education Act in 1965. The National Defense Education Act is important because it marked the beginning of a long and continuing interval when the arguments and political maneuvers against the federal role in education no longer blocked its expansion.

The winning argument in 1958 took the following form: Soviet educational and technical gains threaten U.S. security and economic interests. Meeting this national threat demands federal support for the Cold War's education front. Restrictions can be placed on federal aid that do not compromise state and local-control traditions. Therefore categorical aid for math, science, and foreign-language instruction is a legitimate federal expenditure.

The losing argument was that federal control inevitably results from any kind of federal involvement in schools. Federal control of schools is un-American, so the bill should be defeated. Both pro and con camps tended to underestimate the extent to which federal aid was already being dispensed in 1958. The existence of long-standing, popular federal programs before the NDEA, such as vocational education and the G.I. Bill, challenged the notion that federal control would inevitably result from the new programs. On the other hand, these earlier activities led to expanded federal involvement, the gradual erosion of state and local autonomy, and the increased threat of federal control.

The NDEA debate also placed the education system at the center of federal efforts to solve noneducation problems. This strategy may have helped eclipse long-standing bipartisan suspicion of federal involvement, because schools were portrayed as one front in a broader, ideological struggle against communism. The frequent success of ideological arguments against federal action in schools may have led federal-aid backers to substitute rhetoric based on anticommunist ideology for their painstaking but unsuccessful arguments based on domestic needs.

The passage of the National Defense Education Act did not completely disenfranchise opponents of federal aid. They were outvoted and lost much of the influence they had enjoyed in earlier decades. They were also outfoxed by federal-aid advocates who strategically appropriated conservative rhetoric (anticommunism) to advance a liberal idea (government spending for education). Nevertheless, the influence of federal-aid opponents was displayed in several areas of the new law. For example, the original plan for outright grants to undergraduates was jettisoned because of fears that they would be perceived as a reckless federal handout. A winning bill was crafted by the federal-aid proponents, who respected some of the limits set by the opposition and by everyone's fear of federal control. Opponents also produced a public record of detailed opposition to particular aspects of the law, as well as registering their usual ideological objections.

The events and political maneuvers surrounding the National Defense Education Act suggest an important distinction between arguments and politics. For example, there was significant political momentum during the 1950s toward increased federal action in education. Most legislators also recognized existing federal programs for schools and colleges (for example, vocational education and the G.I. Bill) as bona fide precursors to the N D E A. This momentum was independent of the Cold War and Sputnik and led to numerous provisions of the law that were unrelated to national security. Yet the imperative to stay technically competitive with the Soviet Union was the main argument in the debate. Federal-aid advocates used anticommunist rhetoric to successfully counter conservative objections to federal spending for schools.

By citing international competitiveness, the National Defense Education Act resembles the later Goals 2000. Both laws authorized new federal activities to improve the position of the United States in the global community. Supporters of both acts also anticipated and tried to dodge conservative arguments about federal control. The requirements of both acts were kept intentionally vague because of these concerns. Federal-control objections were addressed in the two episodes but not neutralized. This was also true during other policy debates. The federal-control objection returned with particular ideological and rhetorical strength during the Goals 2000 debate.

Because it paved the way for the first Elementary and Secondary Education Act in 1965, the National Defense Education Act is also a key precedent for the No Child Left Behind Act. It began the steady, incremental expansion of the federal role, an expansion that No Child Left Behind has greatly accelerated. To conservative (and liberal) legislators in the 1950s, No Child Left Behind would have looked like a dangerous form of federal interference. Indeed, provisions of the later law border on the worst federal-control fears of the opponents of federal aid in the 1950s, 1960s, and 1970s. Yet, the expansion of federal involvement occurred so gradually that many of those who opposed the principle on conservative grounds in earlier debates came to endorse it by 2001.

3

lyndon johnson's "billion-dollar baby"

The Elementary and Secondary Education Act of 1965

Federal dollars have a strange and captivating lure. They sing a siren song
which to many is irresistible, and lure off course many an otherwise right-
thinking citizen.

—U.S. Representative Paul Findley (R-IL) (1965)

Seven years after passage of the National Defense Education Act of 1958,
Congress enacted an even larger school-aid package. The Elementary and
Secondary Education Act of 1965 (esea) was a key episode in the long
decline of opposition to federal involvement in education. The legislation
authorized a large increase in the federal contribution to elementary and
secondary schooling. The political compromises that led to its passage
helped align various factions behind the bill and thereby override the
diminished cadre of unconverted conservative opponents to expanded
federal assistance to schools. The Elementary and Secondary Education
Act is important to this study because it shows how backers of school aid
within the federal government were able to manipulate the factions of
"potential opponents" into supporting their bill. These factions were
frequently exploited by the opponents of federal aid in earlier episodes.

Even though the Elementary and Secondary Education Act has been
well studied, some of the conventional wisdom about its original passage
needs updating. For example, the legislation was not unprecedented, contrary
to what many commentators and congressional orators contend. It had
novel aspects, including politically sophisticated authors and managers,
but virtually everything in the bill had been seen before in other federal
education programs. The architects of the bill in Congress and the Johnson
administration rediscovered and redeployed the categorical-aid design used
in earlier programs to deflect controversy about "general aid." The Elementary and Secondary Education Act entailed a huge fiscal outlay ($1 billion

in its first year), but an earlier federal education program did too; the G.I. Bill cost $13 billion between 1944 and 1956 (Jennings 1967, 77).

In addition, existing accounts of the Elementary and Secondary Education Act do not concentrate on the ideological points of view of federal-aid opponents, nor do they spell out the content and meaning of the rhetoric and arguments wielded by different sides of the debate. Given the importance of congressional rhetoric in this book, it is crucial that we understand what this legislation meant for proponents and opponents at the time and how it both divided and united them. The Elementary and Secondary Education Act is the ideological touchstone for federal support and regulation of elementary and high schools to this day, so it needs to be studied carefully.

The Elementary and Secondary Education Act is significant because it accelerated the expansion of federal assistance to elementary and secondary education, much like the No Child Left Behind Act of 2001 greatly increased the federal role in school accountability. The 1965 deliberations show that Congress was still divided about the appropriateness of federal involvement generally and the strategy embodied in the Elementary and Secondary Education Act. Liberal and conservative positions were easy to identify and describe, a task that became more difficult in later episodes, such as the Education for All Handicapped Children Act of 1975 (P.L.94-142) and No Child Left Behind. Supporters of the Elementary and Secondary Education Act engineered a liberal victory by aligning various factions of "potential opponents" behind the legislation. Conservatives were outvoted, but they were active participants in the debate. They helped define the political and ideological parameters of the ESEA by clearly registering their objections to the bill.

The rhetoric of the different factions for and against the Elementary and Secondary Education Act revealed ideologies about the appropriate role of the federal government in education. These ideologies are important because they help explain the motivations for political action and behavior. Much of the ESEA story is about the needs and interests of different groups inside and outside Congress. In most cases, these needs can be understood in terms of deeper ideological commitments regarding government, education, religion, and race.

The Legislative and Historical Context of the Elementary and Secondary Education Act

The Elementary and Secondary Education Act is a turning point in the evolution of federal involvement in education. The political and ideological landscape had been changing since at least the 1958 congressional elections (Carmines and Stimson 1989, 70–71), and conservative opponents of federal aid to schools were losing their power to "veto" these proposals. Federal-aid advocates engineered this switch by placating the same groups of potential opponents (or swing voters) that the hard-line opponents had manipulated during past episodes. The liberal position was also strengthened by gains in the 1964 election, which added more legislators to Congress who favored federal involvement in education.

Both the Elementary and Secondary Education Act and its predecessor, the National Defense Education Act, overcame opponents of federal assistance to schools by employing a categorical-aid design for their programs. The Morrill Act of 1862 and the Smith-Hughes Act of 1917 were also categorical-aid programs for higher education and vocational education, respectively. The backers of the National Defense Education Act and the Elementary and Secondary Education Act successfully outvoted federal-aid opponents by exploiting events of the day that were independent of the educational system. These laws were aimed at narrower targets than were other, more controversial and unsuccessful proposals for general aid. The federal-aid success stories since the late 1950s stemmed in part from proponents' ability to persuade and maneuver Congress into approving educational solutions to international and domestic problems.

The winning strategies of the National Defense Education Act and the Elementary and Secondary Education Act did not lessen the controversy over the expanding federal role, however. The Elementary and Secondary Education Act was more controversial than the National Defense Education Act and passed with slightly smaller, although ample, margins (Congressional Quarterly Inc. 1959, 414 and 461; Congressional Quarterly Inc. 1966, 946 and 1035). The National Defense Education Act was opposed by a variety of interests and individuals questioning the need for federal involvement in math, science, and foreign-language instruction and loans to college students. It was also opposed on broader, ideological grounds as an unwelcome government intrusion into state and local school systems.

Several important controversies lingered during the period between the National Defense Education Act and the Elementary and Secondary Education Act. These controversies strongly suggest that the main danger faced by proposals to expand the federal role in elementary and secondary education was not hard-core ideological opposition. It was the political influence of *possible* opponents: those factions that believed that their needs were not addressed by a given proposal. In 1961, for example, President John F. Kennedy proposed a major aid package for teacher salaries and school construction. The proposal failed because it incited opposition by parochial-school advocates who found their interests largely excluded from the bill's provisions. The National Defense Education Act reinforced the precedent for federal assistance to elementary and secondary education and appeared to portend a loosening of federal resistance to unrestricted education aid. Nevertheless, Kennedy's education bills failed because he did not broker solutions to issues that remained contentious, such as substantial aid to private schools (Price 1962, 20–30; Graham 1984, 18–25). These issues blocked the expansion of what, as of the 1950s and early 1960s, was a long-standing but tightly circumscribed federal role in education.

The situation changed after President Lyndon B. Johnson's landslide win in 1964, for along with it came a large liberal majority in each chamber of Congress. Johnson also had a deeper commitment to education and better skills at "playing" Congress than Kennedy. Moreover, he was not politically encumbered by his religion. Kennedy's Catholicism was seen as a liability during the 1960 campaign and therefore precluded his open support for public aid to parochial and other private schools (Graham 1984, 21).

The Elementary and Secondary Education Act was packaged as an educational contribution to the federal civil rights movement and the War on Poverty. Poverty became a prominent public policy issue in the early 1960s (Majone 1989, 145). The Johnson administration and school-aid activists in Congress also wanted to parlay their gains in the 1964 election into a large new federal program for the nation's schools, and the ESEA was the vehicle for accomplishing both these goals. Advocates had long argued that there was a legitimate role for the federal government in supporting elementary and secondary education. Now they had the legislative formula and votes to deliver a new program linking education to a pressing domestic problem. (Much of the rhetoric associated with the National Defense Education Act, by contrast, cited competition with the Soviets.) The legislative window of opportunity for a new program might slam shut at any time, so school-aid advocates had to move quickly.

Again, foes and potential foes of federal assistance were a major consideration as the legislation was drafted. The administration was acutely aware of the bitter school-aid defeats that had occurred regularly into the early 1960s. There were three potential deal-breakers facing federal education proposals in the decade between the *Brown* decision on school segregation and the mid-1960s. Authors of the Elementary and Secondary Education bill attempted to minimize the volatility of two of these issues—race and aid to parochial schools—and thereby weaken the third threat, fears about federal control. Collectively, these controversies were known as "the 3Rs—Race, Religion, and Reds."

Organization and Development of the Elementary and Secondary Education Act

The Elementary and Secondary Education Act is best remembered for Title I, "Financial Assistance to Local Educational Agencies for the Education of Children from Low Income Families." Title I was the act's most expensive program and has led many observers to use the terms "ESEA" and "Title I" interchangeably. From the time the Elementary and Secondary Education Act was enacted, Title I has been the most reliable source of "compensatory" education funds in the United States—money to supplement state and local revenues for schools serving students from poor families. The other programs of the 1965 act included supplementary support for school libraries and instructional materials (Title II), supplementary educational centers and services (Title III), educational research and training (Title IV), grants to strengthen state departments of education (Title V), and general provisions (Title VI). A separate House bill included a title to establish a cabinet-level Department of Education. This version was not considered seriously. With the exception of final appropriations, the legislation that was enacted was essentially the same as what the administration proposed. The administration's bill was conceived largely by President Johnson's 1964 Task Force on Education, chaired by John W. Gardner. Gardner was head of the Carnegie Corporation at the time and was later named Johnson's Secretary of the Department of Health, Education, and Welfare (Bailey and Mosher 1968, chap. 2; Meranto 1967; Eidenberg and Morey 1969. See also *Report of the President's Task Force on Education* 1964).

Title I was worth almost $1 billion—80 percent of the funds appropriated by the act. It stipulated that federal funds go to schools with large numbers and/or high concentrations of children from low-income families. Congress recognized "the impact that concentrations of low-income families have on the ability of local educational agencies to support adequate educational programs" (P.L.89–10, Title I, sec. 201). The distribution formula for Title I funds used the comparatively rough indicator of poverty to identify needy schools, and the finer indicator of low achievement to identify students within high-poverty schools who deserved additional attention. Once eligible schools and students were targeted, local educators were directed to design supplemental educational programs for the low-achieving students in these schools.

An additional goal of Congress was to get supplementary funds into poor schools to help equalize per pupil expenditures within states. Proponents of the Elementary and Secondary Education Act conceded at the time that federal aid could not effectively address resource inequalities between states or regions, even though high-poverty school systems in the South were supposedly favored by the Title I formula (Wirt and Kirst 1975, 156). ESEA critics thought proponents were ignoring real needs, disregarding their own antipoverty rhetoric, and reinforcing existing inequalities in the distribution formula for Title I funds.

Despite these criticisms, a liberal Congress under the spell of a new crisis—domestic poverty—passed the Elementary and Secondary Education Act. Legislators endorsed crucial compromises on parochial schools, desegregation, and Title I funding formulas that ensured wide distribution of funds. These factors helped overcome the "race, religion, and reds" objections to federal aid. Poverty was operationalized as an extremely broad category, thereby distributing Title I funds to every state and congressional district, virtually every county, and the vast majority of the nation's school districts. An unanswered and perhaps unanswerable question is how much of the "yes" vote on the ESEA endorsed the Title I funding formula as a covert general-aid vehicle versus an educational attack on poverty. Clearly, the political advantages of spreading the benefits of each program as widely as possible were known to the bill's authors in the administration. At the same time, the rhetorical appeal of education as a "temporary" antipoverty strategy was also clear. It is likely that many "yes" voters in Congress simultaneously believed in both purposes. Conservative foes of federal involvement tried to exploit what they saw as an inconsistency between the two objectives.

When the administration bill arrived in Congress, the House General Subcommittee on Education of the Committee on Education and Labor, and the Senate Subcommittee on Education of the Committee on Labor and Public Welfare, quickly scheduled hearings. The whole legislative process took only three months from receipt of the bill to passage and presidential signature. In addition to debate about federal control and public funds going to parochial schools, several other issues came up during the committee hearings and floor debates.

It is interesting that the issue of race was not an overt part of the public congressional debate. This absence is difficult to explain, given the intense controversy engendered by the federal stake in desegregation since the

Supreme Court's *Brown* decision. Amendments to deny federal assistance to racially discriminatory school systems killed a major school construction bill in 1956. The 1964 passage of the Civil Rights Act was tainted by massive dissent from the southern delegation in Congress, including a three-month Senate filibuster (Meranto 1967, 32). This dissent was not a surprise, given the sweeping ideological declaration made in Title VI of the Civil Rights Act of 1964: "No person in the United States shall, on the ground of race, color, or national origin, be excluded from participation in, be denied the benefits of, or be subjected to discrimination under any program or activity receiving Federal financial assistance" (P.L.88-352, Title VI, sec. 601). Applicable programs and activities in educational institutions were included in these protections. The Department of Justice was charged with enforcing the Civil Rights Act.

Why was race practically absent from education deliberations less than a year after passage of the divisive Civil Rights Act? Backers of the Elementary and Secondary Education Act worked hard to anticipate and dispel controversies due to race in the congressional debate. Opposition to racial integration and civil rights legislation united the South and made it a powerful bloc of potential opposition to federal education policies that required desegregation. At the same time, schools in the South desperately needed outside dollars because of their persistently small, rural southern tax base. One of the strategies in the ESEA was to allocate disproportionate shares of Title I funds to southern states with the hope that the carrot of federal assistance would look better than the stick of compliance with desegregation orders (Wirt and Kirst 1975, 156).

How did the Title I formula benefit the South? Thirteen states are defined by Congressional Quarterly Inc. as "southern": Alabama, Arkansas, Florida, Georgia, Kentucky, Louisiana, Mississippi, North Carolina, Oklahoma, South Carolina, Tennessee, Texas, and Virginia (Sharp 1988, x). At the time, with 28 percent of the nation's population of five- to seventeen-year-olds, these states received almost 42 percent of the funds authorized in Title I. However, the region had almost 55 percent of the nation's school-age children from families earning less than $2,000 a year (part of the Title I definition of "poverty"). Because existing per pupil expenditure rates were also part of the Title I funding formula, the southern share of Title I was pushed down by southern states' low education spending. (These calculations are based on figures provided in U.S. House of Representatives 1965a, 110.) Hence, the South got more than its share of Title I funds, according to the general-aid theory of the Elementary and Secondary Education Act and less than its share according to the antipoverty theory.

It is not clear whether the southern strategy won or lost votes in Congress. The South did not vote as a bloc. The Elementary and Secondary Education Act won among every subset of voter in the Senate (Republicans, Democrats, and southerners). The bill lost the southern vote in the House by a vote of 42–70 (calculations based on data in Congressional Quarterly Inc. 1966, 946–47 and 1035). However, the southern vote was not necessary for passage.

The apparent silence on race during public congressional consideration of the Elementary and Secondary Education Act may have been an artifact of the administration's attempt to defuse one of several potentially explosive factions—southerners—by "exporting" the race issue to separate legislation administered by the Justice Department (Stoner 1976, 49). Past experience demonstrated that race could become highly politicized by different groups in Congress, so downplaying race in the fine print of the Elementary and Secondary Education Act was an important strategy. According to the ESEA votes in Congress, this approach was only marginally successful in placating the South and, by itself, probably unnecessary. However, combined with other tactics on parochial schools and the Title I spending formula, the race gamble paid off. Southern interests did not block the legislation procedurally, nor was it indirectly sabotaged by explicit antisegregation amendments. It also seems to have helped that the race controversy was diluted by spreading it across two years, two statutes, and two agencies (the Department of Health, Education, and Welfare and the Department of Justice). The sequence of the two laws was probably important, too; the Elementary and Secondary Education Act raised the stakes of the Civil Rights Act by dramatically increasing the federal contribution to education.

Yet the race issue was not dispelled indefinitely. Busing, for example, was a controversial issue in future debates over the Elementary and Secondary Education Act and during the Reagan administration two decades later. The near absence of race from the formal debate is puzzling, and it reminds us that pivotal ideological issues may be hidden without being completely absent. (Racial categories were built into the subgroup accountability reporting rules for No Child Left Behind, an interesting twist on racial politics for the new millennium.)

Controversies from Congressional Consideration of the Elementary and Secondary Education Act

The issues that engendered the most controversy during consideration of the Elementary and Secondary Education Act were the funding formula for Title I, the procedural tactics used to speed the bill through Congress, federal aid for private schools, and the threat of federal control perceived by conservatives in the bill's various provisions. These controversies relate to other topics that were germane to development and passage of the bill.

The proposed funding formula for Title I generated intense debate and disagreement. Despite explicit congressional intent to use these funds to help solve the problems of poverty and educational deprivation, many federal-aid critics believed that the formula did not adequately target federal funds to high-poverty areas. Several facts bolstered the position of these critics. Title I grants went to every congressional district and to 95 percent of the nation's counties (Meranto 1967, 5). Moreover, state grants were calculated with a multiplier that included that state's average per pupil expenditure. According to critics, this calculation favored states that were already outspending others on education and where poverty was likely to be a smaller problem. (Another element of the formula, the number of children from poor families, tried to account for the effect of poverty and shift more funds to southern states.)

Senator Peter H. Dominick (R-CO; 1966 ADA score: 10) rose in opposition to the Title I funding formula during floor debate in the Senate. (Like many ESEA opponents who criticized the Title I formula, he also had other objections to the bill.) He was puzzled that one of the main arguments in favor of the federal compensatory education program—Title I—was the unequal ability of state and local school systems to support their schools. Yet the distribution formula for Title I appeared to do nothing to equalize school expenditures. Dominick wondered why Title I did not do more to help equalize expenditures across the nation. It seemed wrong to him to base the calculation of state Title I grants on the same unequal per pupil expenditure rates that were cited as problems to begin with (*Congressional Record* 1965, 7331).

An indirect answer to this concern is suggested by the commentators and congressional insiders who called the Elementary and Secondary Education Act a general-aid bill with a categorical label (Stoner 1976, 11–13). An anonymous Democrat on the House Committee on Education and Labor described the issue as follows: "The bill itself was really categorical aids with categories broad enough to resemble general aid. We made the categories so broad that the aid splattered over the face of the entire school system and could be called general aid in principle while politically remaining categorical aids" (quoted by Eidenberg and Morey 1969, 90–91). The category of educational disadvantage was broad, but it clearly differentiated the ESEA from earlier, ill-fated proposals to fund teacher salaries and school construction.

The House Committee on Education and Labor voted to recommend passage, but the vote was not unanimous. In the "Minority Views" section of the committee report, Representatives William H. Ayres (R-OH; 1966 ADA score: 12), Robert P. Griffin (R-MI; 1964 ADA score: 8), Albert H. Quie (R-MN; 1966 ADA score: 12), Charles Goodell (R-NY; 1966 ADA score: 6), John M. Ashbrook (R-OH; 1966 ADA score: 0), Dave Martin (R-NE; 1966 ADA score: 0), Paul Findley (R-IL; 1966 ADA score: 12), and [Arthur] Glenn Andrews (R-AL; 1966 ADA score: 0) collectively criticized the logic of the formula, their main objection to the bill. "These weird consequences" (where school districts in wealthy counties receive Title I grants), they wrote, "stem from the political decision to spread the funds as thinly as possible by establishing entitlements county by county. Were the funds allotted to the States (the normal procedure in Federal grant programs), it is inconceivable that any State would pour the funds into its wealthiest areas" (U.S. House of Representatives 1965b, 70).

The signers of the minority report also criticized the bill for ignoring early childhood education, and the administration for requesting only $150 million for Head Start that year (ibid., 67 and 71). Representative Charles Goodell believed that educational and social intervention in early childhood should be part of any antipoverty program and saw the Elementary and Secondary Education Act as flawed because it targeted only school-age children (ages five to seventeen) (U.S. House of Representatives 1965a, 164).

The committee minority continued the fight during floor debate on the bill in the House of Representatives. Representative Goodell was the most vocal critic in the House and made numerous charges against the bill and its sponsors, including the following: "This bill is a thinly veiled attempt to launch a general Federal aid to education program by means of a spurious appeal to purposes which it would not adequately serve [that is, ameliorating poverty]. It manages to incorporate the worst features of general aid with the worst features of specialized aid, while disbursing limited funds to 90 percent of our school districts without regard to need" (*Congressional Record* 1965, 5768).

Later, during the same lengthy speech, Goodell elaborated further: "The reason for these inadequacies is probably a political one involving the administration's determination to get an initial amount into as many school districts as possible, which will not limit funds in areas of greatest need. This can be done only by a juggling of outdated and inadequate data to achieve a predetermined initial outlay of $1 billion" (ibid., 5771).

These criticisms were answered in several ways. Representative Carlton R. Sickles (D-MD; 1966 ADA score: 100) justified the disbursement of funds to wealthy counties by pointing out that poverty occurs in both wealthy and poor counties and that the bill is designed to help educationally disadvantaged children wherever they are found (ibid., 5977). Oregon Democrat Wayne L. Morse (1966 ADA score: 85) responded to similar concerns in the Senate by noting that grants to states also reflected their federal tax contribution (ibid., 7340). This feature was built into the bill to protect it from anticipated charges of excessive interstate redistribution of federal tax revenue. (Scattered criticisms to this effect were actually made by some of the same legislators who faulted the bill for *not* helping to equalize education spending.) Rather than strenuously defend the formula as proposed, however, federal assistance advocates were more likely to concede its imperfections and to assure critics that the formula could be revised during later appropriation and reauthorization hearings.

Certain federal-aid advocates were more likely than their opponents to question the utility of the focus on poverty. Some witnesses who favored unrestricted general aid acknowledged the strategic value of the antipoverty connection. George J. Hecht, publisher of *Parents* magazine, testified along these lines: "But if proposing the provisions in this title on an antipoverty basis will get the bill through more rapidly, I am for it, nevertheless" (U.S. Senate 1965a, 2393). Senator Jacob K. Javits (R-NY; 1966 ADA score: 90), responding to Hecht, declared his own support for general aid but viewed Title I as a legitimate antipoverty measure. "I am not for doing one under the guise of the other" (ibid., 2398). The president's education task force favored general aid but cited political and ethical reasons for directing funds to high-poverty areas (*Report of the President's Task Force on Education* 1964, 77 and 82).

Federal-aid opponents attacked the proposed formula because they believed it did not legitimately address the problems of poverty. It is possible, however, that a bill with a "valid" formula (for example, one that better equalized overall spending or encompassed early childhood education) would have lost. The Elementary and Secondary Education Act won, at least in part, because the funds in each of its titles were distributed widely and encompassed every congressional district. It irritated the foes of federal aid that a viable bill was also deceptive. Technical criticisms of the formula made by conservatives in 1965 anticipated similar attacks on Title I/ Chapter 1 targeting by numerous experts almost three decades later (Commission on Chapter 1 1992; National Assessment of Chapter 1 Independent Review Panel 1993. [Note that "Title I" was renamed "Chapter 1" from 1981 until 1995]). The formula for Title I/Chapter 1 was one of the most prominent issues in the 1994 ESEA reauthorization debate. During the

2001 No Child Left Behind debate, the Title I funding formula was not criticized, but the adequacy of the administration's funding request was.

Another major confrontation in the debate was related only indirectly to the contents of the bill. The administration did not want two versions of the bill to pass in the House and Senate and then risk losing everything in a bicameral conference committee. (An ad hoc conference committee representing both houses of Congress is convened to iron out differences whenever the two chambers pass two versions of the same legislation.) Education legislation often had died in previous conference committees and in the House Rules Committee (Price 1962). If the two houses passed identical bills, a conference committee would not be necessary and the legislation could be sent directly to President Johnson for his signature. The House considered the Elementary and Secondary Education Act first and made slight amendments to the bill. That version then went to the Senate, where the Democratic Party leadership was under strong pressure from the administration to pass it unamended.

Reaction by opponents to this tactic was strong, especially in the Senate, where the no-amendment discipline was vigorously and successfully enforced. Senators Jacob K. Javits (R-NY), Winston L. Prouty (R-VT; 1966 ADA score: 25), Peter H. Dominick (R-CO), George L. Murphy (R-CA; 1966 ADA score: 0), and Paul J. Fannin (R-AZ; 1966 ADA score: 0) filed a "Minority Views" section to the Senate report that recommended passage of the bill. These Republicans were not opposed to reporting the bill; indeed, the committee unanimously voted to report the bill to the full Senate (Bailey and Mosher 1968, 63). They were opposed to the strong-armed intimidation against Senate amendments and asked: "Will legislation henceforth originate in the House, to be accepted supinely by the Senate without a murmur? Are conference committees a thing of the past?" (U.S. Senate 1965b, 81). They then went on to criticize their compliant committee colleagues. "It is ironic, indeed, that while this committee speaks out on behalf of this billion dollar plus measure to liberate children from the shackles of ignorance, at the same time it draws close about it—and about the Senate which has entrusted to it this important responsibility— the strong but subtle silken threads of legislative impotence" (ibid., 82).

The House also had been pressured to reject certain types of amendments lest they alter the bill's base of support. As House members rejected numerous amendments with limited or no debate, Representative Goodell exclaimed: "The Great Society has turned today into a great steamroller. I think every liberal who calls himself a liberal sitting on the other side of the aisle who believes that these things should be debated and exposed to the light of day to arrive at a proper decision and a proper policy for our country should be ashamed" (*Congressional Record* 1965, 6020).

Making laws in Congress can appear chaotic because of the mix of democratic and autocratic principles and traditions that govern the institution. The adoption of complex, seemingly arbitrary procedures is legendary in Congress. These procedures are often used to kill bills as well as save them. Formal and informal rules that restrict debate and amendments are subject to intense criticism, even though these maneuvers have long histories. For the sponsors and architects of the Elementary and Secondary Education Act, the draconian procedures were a calculated risk. Despite pointed outcries, the strategy worked. The unamended House version passed the Senate and eliminated the need for a conference committee.

A related issue and, at times, a response to criticisms of the speedy consideration of Elementary and Secondary Education Act was the admission by many of its supporters that the bill was "imperfect." "It has imperfections" was also an answer to attacks on the Title I funding formula. Again, the administration's strategy was to get a law on the books as quickly as possible by almost any means necessary. The go-for-broke strategy was risky not only because it alienated and infuriated conservative opponents of federal aid but also because it also tested the patience of potential allies who favored a freer legislative hand. One of these legislators was Representative Edith Green (D-OR; 1966 ADA score: 82), who ended up voting for the final bill. Senator Prouty was an alienated ally in the Senate. Before voting in favor of the bill, he attacked it, saying: "The advocates of this legislation do not claim its present form is perfect. Instead, they argue that it should be passed and that the necessary revisions can be added later in this Congress. This is like an auto dealer delivering three-quarters of a new car, with a note saying that the wheels and transmission will be sent later if the company feels like it. Yet in both cases the customer will pay the full price" (*Congressional Record* 1965, 7319).

As political considerations, the funding formulas and formal procedures were not explicitly ideological. However, I believe that these political calculations were undertaken in the name of deeper values and ideological beliefs, such as the desirability of federal action on behalf of schools and equality of educational opportunity. Ideological disputes are usually mediated through political proxies, enabling both sides to negotiate political compromises without appearing to abandon their deeper principles. This was true even with the more obviously ideological disputes, such as aid to parochial schools and federal control. These issues were operationalized as political problems.

We now move on to the divisive question of giving public aid to religious and other nonpublic schools. Most participants in the ESEA debate were wary of the private-school issue. The American tradition of separation of church and state is taken quite seriously by many secular and sectarian interests. Yet by 1965, the issue could no longer be ignored. Leaders of the Catholic church, for example, gradually realized that federal education aid could, should, and, finally, must benefit children attending parochial schools. Because children who attend private schools would eventually enter the workforce or otherwise generate benefits for the whole society as citizens, the quality of their education was of public concern and a legitimate object of public funds. Moreover, as numerous private-school educators have repeatedly contended, parents of children attending private schools must still pay public-school taxes. Thus, they believed that private schools were entitled to at least some public tax revenue. This burden is often called "double taxation." (The double-taxation argument is not especially convincing: citizens without children in school and corporations also pay school taxes in the name of general community welfare [Powell 1960, 21].)

The increasing demands for aid to private schools ended the political practice in earlier episodes of silently evading and downplaying the issue. The National Defense Education Act, for example, provided limited financial assistance to private institutions. These were mostly institutions of higher education, a category of school that, until 1956, received tuition payments from discharged military personnel under the G.I. Bill. President Kennedy's 1961 proposal for federal aid for elementary and secondary teacher salaries and school construction excluded private schools, thereby mobilizing the opposition of Catholic education leadership and some influential Catholic legislators (Price 1962, 64). Kennedy, who was not passionate about education and therefore was reluctant to spend much political capital on his bill, was also unwilling to risk the political firestorm that might occur if he, as the nation's first Catholic president, openly advocated federal aid for parochial schools. Kennedy declared flatly that such aid was unconstitutional. Throughout his presidency, he was unwilling to negotiate a compromise on the issue.

The lessons of the 1961 defeat were not lost on the authors of the Elementary and Secondary Education Act. The bill had to include a plausible vehicle for aiding nonprofit, private schools. Titles I, II, and III were all intended to assist children enrolled in private schools, justifying their inclusion on the basis of "child-benefit theory." The principle of child benefit originated in the 1930 U.S. Supreme Court decision *Cochran v. Louisiana State Board of Education*. According to the court majority in that case, the principle of separation of church and state is preserved if the children attending private schools—rather than the institutions—are the ultimate beneficiaries of public funds. The assumption underlying child-benefit theory is that the public interest is served by high-quality schooling for all children, including those attending religious and other private schools. For example, providing nonsectarian textbooks (in the case of *Cochran*) and transportation (as in a later case, *Everson v. Board of Education of Township of Ewing* [1947]) with public funds benefits the children attending these institutions and advances the interests of society as a whole. The *Everson* decision further refined the principle by declaring that such subsidies neither favor nor harm private schools, thereby preserving state neutrality toward church-related institutions, including those receiving public aid (Doak 1968, 247–48). (Case summaries adapted from Zirkel and Richardson 1988, 17–19.)

Other Supreme Court judgments during the 1930s upheld the constitutionality of federal assistance to education per se. These rulings help explain the decline of claims in subsequent decades that federal aid to education was unconstitutional. Senator Strom Thurmond (R-SC; 1966 ADA score: 0) was the only identifiable holdout as of 1965 (*Congressional Record* 1965, 7633; see also Goldwater 1960, 77). Legal precedents allowing public funds to benefit children attending private schools were not as convincing. President Kennedy, for example, cited *Everson* as a judgment *against* providing federal aid to nonpublic schools (Graham 1984, 19–20). Four years later, numerous critics testified before congressional subcommittees about their unqualified opposition to aid for private schools, including representatives from many non-Catholic religious groups. This testimony was made even though their schools—if they had them—would be eligible for several ESEA programs. For its part, the Catholic church had an extensive infrastructure of parochial schools far larger than the combined educational efforts of other faiths. The political push for aid to parochial schools came from the Catholic church and from legislators who were eager to forge a compromise on the issue that had "torpedoed" the 1961 Kennedy bill. Opposition came from almost everyone else.

The main opposing argument was that such aid was unconstitutional at the federal level and, redundantly, in the majority of states. (Information about state constitutional prohibitions was presented to the House subcommittee by Edgar Fuller, executive director of the Council of Chief State School Officers. See U.S. House of Representatives 1965a, 1151–60.) Many subscribers to this view warned the respective subcommittees that the private-school provisions would not survive a court test. Another frequently raised argument was the slippery definition of "child benefit." For example, Rabbi Richard G. Hirsh, director of the Religious Action Center, Union of American Hebrew Congregations, asked rhetorically: "If the 'child-benefit' theory is to be used as the basis for providing private-school children with textbooks, instructional materials, and mobile services, then what cannot be given? Would not the individual child also benefit from better teachers, better teaching equipment, better science laboratories, and better buildings to house them?" (ibid., 1502).

The private-school provisions left much to be determined by public-school authorities. Title I funds were to be made available to educationally disadvantaged children attending private schools with comparatively high concentrations of poor children relative to the school district average. Services "such as dual enrollment [in private and public schools], educational radio and television, and mobile educational services and equipment" were permitted (P.L.89-10, Title I, sec. 205[a][2]). Funds were not intended to cover the salaries of private-school teachers or equipment purchases for ownership by the private school. Title II funds for library, textbook, and other instructional materials purchases were also intended to benefit private-school students, although all purchases would remain the property of public-school agencies.

On the private-school issue, Title II was more controversial than Title I. Several witnesses and legislators were skeptical about how these materials would be selected and controlled by public-school personnel. The anti-poverty focus of Title I was absent here, as were practical guidelines for ensuring that materials purchases would add educational value to the school experience of children rather than simply supplant private-school resources. Edgar Fuller, of the Council of Chief State School Officers, enthusiastically favored Title I but strongly opposed Title II, again on the grounds of state unconstitutionality (U.S. House of Representatives 1965a, 1119–20). The child-benefit theory was a better argument for Title I than for Title II.

There were numerous exchanges about the implementation of the private-school services. (Several implementation issues were still being resolved twenty years later. In *Aguilar v. Felton* [1985], the Supreme Court ruled that public-school teachers could not provide remedial services on private-school grounds, because such services required unconstitutional monitoring by public-school administrators [Zirkel and Richardson 1988, 36].) During House subcommittee interrogation of a panel of big-city superintendents, James Tobin, assistant superintendent of Boston Public Schools, philosophized about what kind of aid to parochial schools would survive a constitutional test. He guessed that there might be a constitutional distinction between remedial and nonremedial teachers, thereby enabling remedial teachers from public-school payrolls to teach in private schools (U.S. House of Representatives 1965a, 594). Representative Goodell reacted with exasperation:

> It seems to me on this whole question you people walked right off the cliff. Blindly pursuing this billion dollars up in the sky which is about to come to you, you walk right along with your hands outstretched and go right off this constitutional cliff. It is one thing to talk about the fine distinctions of shared time, with students going to public-school facilities and utilizing them. After all, their parents are taxpayers in the public-school system. It is another thing to talk about sending public school teachers into the private schools to teach and then saying it is all right if it is remedial. (Ibid., 595)

Goodell also warned a panel of Catholic educators who favored the bill that parochial-school aid carried with it the constant threat of federal control. "I do not believe that there is a disposition on this subcommittee to [impose] that kind of requirement but it could well be imposed in future years" (ibid., 823).

Catholic educators seemed to reconcile their simultaneous desires for public funds and freedom from state control by acknowledging their desire to comply with state accreditation standards. In addition, Monsignor William McManus, superintendent of the Department of Catholic Schools of Chicago, averred that all parochial-school educators were acutely aware of parent demands for coverage of secular topics comparable in scope and quality to those of the public schools (ibid., 821).

Like many other calculated risks of the Elementary and Secondary Education bill, its private-school provisions were necessary political gambles. Opponents of parochial-school aid were vocal, but they failed to force changes in the bill. The constitutionality gamble ultimately paid off; later court rulings on Title I services for private schools upheld its underlying purpose, stipulating only minor changes regarding how services were delivered to private-school children.

The passage of the Elementary and Secondary Education Act suggests that the calculated risks undertaken to sidestep traditional obstacles to federal-aid legislation were successful. Not every potential opponent was swayed by assurances that the bill was not general aid, that the bill could be repaired in later sessions, or that giving substantial public aid to private schools was not a mistake. Enough opponents were swayed, however, and none of the factions that might have sidelined ESEA was able to do so. The remaining hard-core, ideological opponents (numerous conservative Republicans and Southern Democrats) tried to exploit these issues. By the time the Elementary and Secondary Education Act was enacted, these opponents of federal aid were less influential than they had been in most previous episodes. The preferred theme for their attack on the bill remained the specter of federal control. This was the ideological core of conservative opposition to most areas of government action, especially areas, such as education, that have strong if largely rhetorical traditions of state and local autonomy.

Warnings about federal control took many forms during the debate over the proposed Elementary and Secondary Education Act. A common form was to outline the future risk posed by the legislation. This is an important theme, because claims made about the future in 1965 can be revisited in retrospect with the benefit of an intervening generation of policy developments and rhetoric. Indeed, there has been a continual extension of the federal reach into schools and expansion of the scope of federal action. The Education for All Handicapped Children Act of 1975 (P.L.94-142), the elevation of Education to cabinet-level status in 1979, and the No Child Left Behind Act of 2001 all attest to the growth of federal involvement. Moreover, they all build on the ESEA precedent to varying degrees.

Several legislators warned that federal control was likely to result from ESEA programs once they were implemented and modified by future federal action. The threat versus the actual manifestation of federal control was an important distinction in several of the comments by these concerned legislators. The distinction has two possible explanations: the dangerous novelty of the Elementary and Secondary Education Act in the eyes of its opponents and their desire to add their warnings of federal control to the legislative history. (Personnel in administering agencies rely on committee hearings, reports, and floor debates to establish congressional intent when they write rules and regulations for new programs. Courts do the same thing if legislation is challenged there.) Emphasizing this threat is a good strategy, because each faction in the federal-involvement debate declares its opposition to federal control.

Most of the charges of federal control leveled at the Elementary and Secondary Education Act consisted of warnings about the likely or inevitable implications of provisions that initially appeared to be innocuous. (Recall that the same types of warnings were sounded during consideration of the National Defense Education Act. The Elementary and Secondary

Education Act itself can be viewed as a vehicle for escalating the federal interference threat of the Civil Rights Act; ESEA funds were subject to the nondiscrimination litmus test of the earlier law.) In many remarks, there were intimations of something vaguely sinister or deceptive in these "first steps." Representative Ayres (R-OH) "deplore[d] the use of such a worthy objective ["helping the educationally deprived child"] as a cloak for their attempt to create the first step for bureaucratic Federal control of the education of our children" (*Congressional Record* 1965, 5748).

If the Elementary and Secondary Education Act was a "first step," then what did previous federal education programs count as? Both proponents and foes of increased federal involvement in education tended to overlook the existence and significance of federal education precedents. For starters, there was little agreement about what counted as a precedent. Considering the National Defense Education Act in retrospect, the Secretary of Health, Education, and Welfare, Anthony J. Celebrezze, called it a defense act, not an education act (U.S. House of Representatives 1965a, 67). He may have done this to portray the Elementary and Secondary Education Act as a really new idea with wider appeal than a national-security measure. On the other hand, downplaying precedents can also benefit foes of federal aid: an action that is without precedent may also be unjustified, according to conservative ideology.

It is worth noting that the actual track record of earlier federal programs was almost totally ignored during congressional consideration of the Elementary and Secondary Education Act; proponents did not extol positive performance, nor did foes emphasize shortcomings. Actual performance data were rare, a fact that explains why Senator Robert F. Kennedy (D-NY; 1966 ADA score: 100) was so interested in strengthening the evaluation provisions of the Elementary and Secondary Education Act (U.S. Senate 1965a, 903 and 3084–87; Graham 1984, 78–79). One legislator, Senator Fannin (R-AZ), cited incompetent federal administration of education programs for Native American students as one reason for his opposition to the ESEA (*Congressional Record* 1965, 7556).

Representative Goodell was convinced that increased federal control would come at the hands of Congress itself. His warning to a panel of Catholic educators about this threat was quoted above. Goodell said that his eyes were open to the threat of federal control embedded in federal-aid proposals and that he wanted to make sure that local educators also foresaw this scenario. "When you get this money in successive years and you come down and ask for more, we are going to put strings on it, more and more. We are going to tell you what we think you should do as educators.

You are not only going to deal with your State people, you are going to deal with the Federal people. I think you should understand this and have your eyes wide open, too" (U.S. House of Representatives 1965a, 596).

Opponents of federal aid saw numerous federal-control threats in the legislation. In Title I, the main controversy was the authority given to the U.S. Commissioner of Education to determine the criteria by which state education agencies could approve district-level Title I plans (P.L.89-10, Title I, sec. 205[a]). The legislation was intentionally vague about the intended design of local programs. The alternative, greater specificity, would have made the bill vulnerable to further charges of federal control. Nor did it spell out possible approval criteria. This final accountability checkpoint was too open-ended and gave too much authority to the commissioner, according to many critics.

Title II, the program that subsidized school library, textbook, and instructional materials purchases, was seen by some critics as a dangerous intrusion into the jurisdiction of local educators. (It also drew fire for not having an antipoverty focus. States simply received grants based on the number of children enrolled in public and private elementary and secondary schools [P.L.89-10, Title II, sec. 202(a)].) Representative Quie believed that textbook support under this title "puts the Federal Government awfully close to influencing and determining what is in the curriculum" (*Congressional Record* 1965, 5752). Quie's colleague, Representative John J. Rhodes (R-AZ; 1966 ADA score: 0), shared his concern that Title II opened the way for further government domination in the future: "Although the choice of textbooks is left to the localities where it belongs, no language can guard against subsequent federal controls. By creating dependence upon the Federal Government, no matter how minor it might be initially, for the purchase of textbooks and school library materials, the possibility of Federal control over the choice of these textbooks and materials becomes a clear danger" (ibid., 5767).

The most odious manifestation of federal control is a centralized national curriculum. At the time, virtually no one supported extensive national involvement in curriculum policy. Earlier federal support for curriculum reform in science through the National Science Foundation's Physical Science Study Committee (PSSC) and later projects was highly specialized, voluntary, and, like the National Defense Education Act, partly explained by the context of the Cold War (Marsh and Gortner 1963). Nevertheless, Representative Ashbrook saw these kinds of programs (Title II and PSSC) as an ominous trend against local control: "We appear to be headed for a degree of centralization of curriculum, text development, teacher preparation, and so forth." Representative John Brademas (D-IN; 1966 ADA score: 82) replied that "[t]here is no excuse for defending outmoded mathematics and sloppy physics in the name of local control" (U.S. House of Representatives 1965a, 431). In this remark, he edged closer than most legislators to defending national curriculum initiatives, but he did so only in the name of pedagogical rigor. Three decades later, voluntary national curriculum standards were hotly debated in connection with Goals 2000.

Several legislators expressed misgivings about fostering state and local dependence on federal resources. State education agencies, in particular, might become too fond of funds from Title IV (educational research and training) and Title V (grants for state capacity-building), according to this view. Arguments about state dependence on federal resources echoed the case made against the ill-fated Blair bills eighty years earlier.

Title III authorized funds for supplementary education centers to be run as cooperative ventures between public-school systems and other partners (state education agencies, universities, nonprofit private schools, and other public and private "cultural and educational resources" such as museums). These partnerships would be formed to design and deliver model school programs (P.L.89-10, Title III, secs. 301 and 304). The eight Republicans who signed the "Minority Views" section of the House committee report worried that these centers would become separate school systems run by the U.S. Office of Education. The existence of such centers would represent a blatant attack on state educational autonomy, especially in conjunction with the research and training provisions in Title IV and state subsidies in Title V (U.S. House of Representatives 1965b, 76–77). Edgar Fuller, of the Council of Chief State School Officers, the main national lobbying organization for state education agencies, believed that states should be parties in the operation and supervision of projects established under Titles III and IV (U.S. House of Representatives 1965a, 1121).

Commissioner of Education Francis Keppel denied that state and local educational autonomy would be compromised by Title III. He cited the requirement that local public-school systems be partners in centers established under Title III (ibid., 1717).

The points raised separately by Keppel and Fuller expose a collision of intergovernmental interests that occurs frequently in many federal-aid debates. There are distinct layers of educational governance and finance through which all federal policies are interpreted (Elmore and McLaughlin 1988, chap. 3). The powerful ideology of local school control is tempered by the reality of state control. States and school districts try to preserve their own autonomy while demanding unrestricted funds from the U.S.

Treasury. Local educators were accustomed to working in state bureaucracies in the mid-1960s and may have been better able to assimilate the
trade-off between more money and less autonomy than were state
bureaucrats. Congress envisioned several provisions of the Elementary
and Secondary Education Act as vehicles for bypassing recalcitrant states
as it worked to reform local education practice. For his part, Senator
Robert F. Kennedy viewed school districts as part of the problem (U.S.
Senate 1965a, 513–15). As a former cabinet officer, Senator Kennedy of
New York may have had a more national frame of reference for defining
the national priorities of the Elementary and Secondary Education Act;
virtually all his fellow advocates for federal aid—and most opponents—
seemed to trust local educators. Title V capacity-building grants to states
were the strongest formal indication that Congress and the administration wanted to reform state practice. This is why the Gardner task force
recommended grants to state education agencies (*Report of the President's
Task Force on Education* 1964, 68).

As the House floor debate progressed toward passage of the bill, the
warnings about federal domination intensified. The desperation of the
ideological rear guard was clear. Representative Donald D. Clancy (R-OH;
1966 ADA score: 0) claimed that the bill was an actual incarnation of
federal control. "Under this legislation, decision-making with respect to
course content, curricula, instructional materials and professional standards
for teachers would be centralized in the U.S. Office of Education" (*Congressional Record* 1965, 5980). The ramifications of the bill were probably
exaggerated in Clancy's remarks, but they were mild compared with
Representative Edward J. Derwinski's (R-IL; 1966 ADA score: 0) charges.
Derwinski captured most of the main criticisms of the bill quite succinctly:
"Mr. Chairman, this bill, H.R.2362, is a massive fraud being perpetrated
against the American public and, more specifically, the teachers, students,
and taxpayers of the country. It is of dubious constitutionality and creates
contradictory administrative situations. It is built entirely on false promises
and, as we plainly see, is being stampeded through the House by brute force
and demagoguery. This bill, in its formation, presentation, and legislative
processing, exposes the complete hypocrisy and dictatorial philosophy of
the Democrat administration" (ibid., 6117–18).

The vitriolic spirit of these remarks continued several months after
passage of the Elementary and Secondary Education Act. In a September
1965 House debate on the request by the Department of Health, Education,
and Welfare for supplemental ESEA appropriations, Representative Robert

H. Michel (R-IL; 1966 ADA score: 6) exposed the ESEA as a secret plan for federal takeover of education:

> Mr. Speaker, this is a veiled attempt to strike at the heartbeat of the local-State control of our education system by putting a tourniquet of Federal direction on our educators. Direction of education, including the making of curricula and curriculum materials will be in the hands of "regional education laboratories" and "model demonstration centers." They will be liberally funded. Government funds will be—and are being—supplemented with funds from foundations staffed with centralist-minded officers.
>
> The "model" for American education will be spun, not out of the minds of men, but out of computers in Washington, D.C. Computers will design what kind of education is needed for the kind of society which the computers say we will have by 1984. (Ibid., 23220)

These conspiracy theories were expressed with entertaining rhetoric. More interesting from a philosophical standpoint were the widespread claims that federal control would necessarily result from any attempt at federal regulation. We have already seen this paradox at work in earlier episodes. The paradox is that federal regulation is necessary to responsible government while federal control, a logical consequence for conservatives, is abhorred by all. The situation is simultaneously contradictory and inevitable. Senator Absalom W. Robertson (D-VA; 1966 ADA score: 5) expressed the structural inevitability and paradox of federal control during Senate floor debate: "not only does Federal control follow Federal funds, but it is the constitutional duty of a Congress which appropriates Federal money to supervise its expenditure" (ibid., 7523).

The same thing came up during House subcommittee hearings. Representative Goodell conceded the necessity for some degree of federal control:

> It seems to me what we get into every time in this discussion is that the Federal Government moves into this field because we want to accomplish certain things. Then you say there will be no control. Then we say if there is no control, you cannot be sure you are going to accomplish your objective, so we have to put some control in to be sure that it goes to the areas and the places that we are concerned about. It is just a question of how you

define control. Obviously there has to be some control. (U.S. House of Representatives 1965a, 146–47)

A little later in the same hearing, Goodell pressed HEW Secretary Celebrezze to make the same concession and identify federal control by name. Celebrezze did not budge and suggested that the dispute between Goodell and himself was a semantic one.

> Goodell: I support [the principle of federal school aid] with my eyes wide open that certain controls are there and are necessary if we are to spend our Federal money effectively. What always makes me tear my hair in frustration is when people like you come and say there are no controls. . . .
> Celebrezze: You call it control. I refer to it as [accountability to the] objectives of the legislation. (Ibid., 148)

The same dispute over semantics continued during Representative Alphonzo Bell's (R-CA; 1966 ADA score: 41) interrogation of Secretary Celebrezze.

> Bell: Sometimes there is inadvertent domination that creeps up; for instance, in matters of financing. When you grant money and place restrictions on its use there is domination to a certain extent. For example, would you be willing to give money to all States in the same proportion for educational purposes without any restrictions?
> Celebrezze: The fact that you say it is for educational purposes means you have a restriction. (Ibid., 160)

A second issue is raised in Representative Bell's question: giving money "without any restrictions." This is the root of all questions of federal control: to what degree should the federal government offer assistance to education, specify the uses of resources that are offered, and ensure that these funds are supporting education in the ways intended by Congress? For conservatives, the threat of federal control begins the minute funds are appropriated. The responsibility to safeguard federal expenditures means that the federal government is exerting some level of control over the institutions that receive federal funds. As programs grow and multiply, federal domination inevitably increases. The only safeguard against federal control is to withhold all assistance.

If governmental audit authority entails the beginning of federal control, then congressional specification of funding categories extends the risk even further. Charges of federal control, as defined by conservatives, are automatically invited by categorical aid because the Congress and the administration get to define the categories.

Liberals have a different interpretation of the intent of the authors of the Constitution with respect to a limited national government. When a national interest is widely accepted and other levels of government or the community cannot meet it, then a liberal sees a legitimate call for federal action. Education is one of these national interests. To advocates of increased federal involvement in education, government actions taken to address a national interest are not equivalent to federal domination. The responsible management (or "control") of federal resources is not the same thing as, nor will it lead to, the dictatorial control of state and local school systems.

To conservatives, once the camel's nose gets inside the tent, as the famous federal-control metaphor goes, the fine distinctions and assurances made by liberals mean nothing. The "first step" warnings are important for conservatives because they see federal control as inevitable once illegitimate federal action begins. To use another metaphor, categorical aid or any other promise of federal restraint is a Trojan horse for outright federal control and domination. (No Child Left Behind makes these warnings seem remarkably prescient, especially because conservatives appear to have forgotten making them.)

Description of Elementary and Secondary Education Act Votes in Congress

Data from the 1965 Elementary and Secondary Education Act votes analyzed with 1966 ADA scores confirm the existence of the liberal and conservative blocs suggested in the congressional debate. This consistency reinforces my assumption that the factions for and against expanded federal involvement in schools tend to vote according to their values and beliefs. Liberal legislators were disposed to support the Elementary and Secondary Education Act, whereas conservatives tended to oppose it.

Table 3 shows that liberal and conservative voters, as defined by 1966 ADA scores, were sharply divided on the Elementary and Secondary Education Act in both the House and the Senate. ADA "liberal quotients" appear to be less ambiguous than party label in differentiating the different factions. Notice that "yes" voters, both Democrats and Republicans, have higher average ADA scores than the groupings that opposed the ESEA. As points on a continuum, the scores also appear to make finer distinctions

Table 3   1965 ESEA Votes with 1966 ADA Statistics

ESEA 1965 votes with 1966 ADA scores	House March 26, 1965	Senate April 9, 1965
Final vote on H.R. 2362 final (i.e., ESEA bill)	263–153 (63.2% "yes")	73–18 (80.2% "yes")
Democrats	228–57 (80% "yes")	55–4 (93.2% "yes")
Republicans	35–96 (26.7% "yes")	18–14 (56.2% "yes")
ADA Score Analyses		
Mean ADA score of "yes" voters	60.6 (n=263)	52.9 (n=73)
Mean ADA score of "no" voters	5.1 (n=153)	1.9 (n=18)
Mean ADA score of Democrat "yes" voters	65.9 (n=228)	60.1 (n=55)
Mean ADA score of Republican "yes" voters	26.4 (n=35)	31.1 (n=18)
Mean ADA score of Democrat "no" voters	8.0 (n=57)	2.5 (n=4)
Mean ADA score of Republican "no" voters	3.3 (n=96)	1.8 (n=14)
Mean Democrat ADA score (whole chamber)	53.4 (n=293)	52.7 (n=68)
Mean Republican ADA score (whole chamber)	10.0 (n=140)	18.3 (n=32)
Mean ADA score of whole chamber (1966)	39.4 (n=433)	41.7 (n=100)

NOTE: ESEA = Elementary and Secondary Education Act; ADA = Americans for Democratic Action; n = the number of legislators in each cell with 1966 ADA scores. ADA figures in the "whole chamber" cells include all legislators, regardless of whether they participated in the final vote on ESEA. In eight cases in the House and two in the Senate, scores were taken from 1964 because the ten legislators did not have 1966 scores. The House had one vacancy when the ESEA vote took place.
SOURCES: Congressional Quarterly Inc., 1966, 946–47 and 1035 for the votes on ESEA; Sharp 1988 for ADA scores.

than party labels. Part of the ambiguity of "Democrat" and "Republican" in the mid-1960s is regional; Southern Democrats tended to resemble conservative Republicans on education votes because of racial politics.

The Politics and Ideology of the Elementary and Secondary Education Act

The Elementary and Secondary Education Act significantly expanded federal support for K-12 schooling and stands as a major tribute to Great Society optimism of the 1960s. Conservatives were outvoted in 1965 by a liberal majority. Pro-federal-aid operatives in the Johnson administration and in Congress devised a winning legislative formula that delivered substantial new federal resources to the nation's schools. Reauthorizations of the same program continue to receive strong support in Congress, including increased levels of support from conservatives.

The Elementary and Secondary Education Act extended the precedents for categorical aid to elementary and secondary schools that had been reaffirmed with the National Defense Education Act of 1958. More important, the 1965 statute spread federal funds more widely than before by employing a broad definition of poverty. At the same time, the National Defense Education Act and the Elementary and Secondary Education Act set national goals—ameliorating poverty and competing with the Soviets, respectively—that schools were expected to accomplish. Earlier federal programs had gradually defined federal responsibilities for supporting education without explicitly altering state and local priorities. Federal-aid advocates believed that the new goals set by the ESEA were consistent with the status quo of limited federal involvement. Federal-aid foes saw the same goals as "first steps" toward unwanted federal control of education.

The deliberations on and passage of the Elementary and Secondary Education Act show that it is important to be aware of the multiple and shifting factions on federal-aid questions. In this case, the dominance of the core liberal bloc was enhanced by its ability to deliver benefits to potential opponents. These groups—parochial-school interests and southerners—could have sided with liberals or conservatives, depending on the content of the legislation. Before the ESEA, conservatives had usually blocked new education proposals by manipulating their content and dictating unworkable procedures for considering the bills. In 1965, it was the liberals' turn to do similar things in the name of increasing federal aid to schools.

The political maneuvers necessary to align various factions behind the Elementary and Secondary Education Act were complex. The maneuvers had more influence over the final action of Congress than any one argument or ideological rationale. This is probably true in many other cases as well. Nevertheless, to the extent that the supporters of the ESEA had values and beliefs about the appropriate role of the federal government in schools, the rhetoric and arguments expressed during the deliberations reveal important ideological information. The ESEA debate shows that ideological concerns were at the root of political maneuvers by liberals to convert potential opponents. Liberals believed that there was a legitimate role for federal action in schools in order to reduce poverty, protect civil rights, and help equalize educational resources. The ideological dispositions of conservatives were also revealed in their rhetoric, namely, their deep fear of federal control of schools and their strong belief in state and local control. (Southerners called this ideology "states' rights.") Even if the victories won by ideologically motivated blocs are due to their political tactics rather than the persuasiveness of their arguments, the underlying rhetoric is still an important indicator of the beliefs, values, and larger ideologies of legislators in Congress.

Once the Elementary and Secondary Education Act passed, it became the centerpiece of federal assistance to elementary and secondary education. It garnered strong, fairly consistent support from most liberals and from many conservatives in Congress. Opponents of federal aid lost their ability to block education legislation. Occasionally, the opposition was virtually nonexistent, as during the passage of P.L.94-142 in 1975 and the 1988 reauthorization of the ESEA (Congressional Quarterly Inc. 1989, 330 and 24-H). Other debates, however, such as the decisions to establish the U.S. Department of Education and to enact Goals 2000, are clear reminders that opposition to the expansion of federal assistance to schools has almost always been present and has usually been influential in shaping the final form of federal education laws.

The Elementary and Secondary Education Act also represents another change. As federal assistance to schools expanded, new constituencies found a stake in it. They exerted grassroots pressures on Congress to maintain and increase education spending and federal action on behalf of children in poverty. An early evaluation of the ESEA's Title I program conducted by the Washington Research Project and the NAACP Legal Defense and Education Fund (Martin and McClure 1969) profoundly influenced the accountability and assessment requirements for this program for the next twenty-five years (Jeffrey 1978, 132). Outside interest groups were not the only forces at work in shaping and sustaining federal education programs, but their importance was increasing. As we will learn in the next chapter, the political strength of the special-education lobby helps explain strong congressional support for the Education for All Handicapped Children Act in 1975.

Finally, supporters of federal assistance to schools may have succeeded too well in outvoting and then converting their conservative opponents. The fact that federal dollars were flowing to schools in virtually every congressional district was not lost on legislators, including those who had previously opposed federal education programs. With the passage of No Child Left Behind thirty-seven years later, the magnitude of federal involvement in schools was close to what foes of federal control had warned about in earlier episodes. Even more surprising, this expansion came about at the behest of a conservative president with the strong support of conservative legislators. Of course, there was a respectably conservative argument for the dramatic increase of federal authority under NCLB:

mandatory testing is the only way to make sure the government does not continue wasting money on low-performing public schools. Conservatives disparaged the track record of federal spending on education as a basis for imposing new controls on schools.

4

civil rights and unfunded mandates

The Education for All Handicapped Children Act of 1975

[The Education for All Handicapped Children Act of 1975] contains a vast array of detailed, complex, and costly administrative requirements which would unnecessarily assert Federal control over traditional State and local government functions. It establishes complex requirements under which tax dollars would be used to support administrative paperwork and not educational programs. Unfortunately, these requirements will remain in effect even though the Congress appropriates far less than the amounts contemplated in [the conference report].

—U.S. President Gerald R. Ford (1975)

The Education for All Handicapped Children Act of 1975 (P.L.94-142) was a milestone for disabled children, civil rights, and federal involvement in education. The legislation spelled out detailed due process and administrative requirements for educating children with disabilities. The protections provided by the law were overdue, given the number of handicapped children who were being excluded from school in the early 1970s. At the same time, the federal government took bold new steps into the nation's schools and classrooms. The tension between the principle of educational opportunity for disabled students, the definition and enforcement of these rights by the federal government, and the cost of providing them has been continuous during the three decades of this law's existence.

The significance of the Education for All Handicapped Children Act is widely acknowledged, but the statute also has a mysterious side. Why were the law's momentous implications for federal interference with state and local school systems virtually ignored in the original debate? The only exception to this silence was President Ford's signing message. The ideological vacuum around P.L.94-142 is quite puzzling; congressional debates on education usually expose different values and beliefs about the federal role. It is clear that political pressures were at work during consideration of the bills that became P.L.94-142, pressures that make the law resemble the political origins of the No Child Left Behind Act of 2001.

The P.L.94-142 episode teaches the following lessons. First, politics and ideology are distinct and sometimes completely separate. Second, the absence of public and fundamentally ideological criticisms of the Education for All Handicapped Children Act was due to the political pressure to pass it, not to the lack of ideological objections. It was not practical to ask even the mildest questions about the appropriateness of the federal role in setting the special-education regulations contemplated for P.L.94-142. Third, the federal share of the cost of this mandate was reduced to ensure passage. It was not until later that the "unfunded mandate" charge was made against P.L.94-142.

The Deliberations and Passage of the Education for All Handicapped Children Act, P.L.94-142

By the time the Education for All Handicapped Children Act of 1975 became law, P.L.94-142, there was already significant and increasing government action on behalf of the approximately eight million disabled children between the ages of three and twenty-one. The courts and many state governments had decided that more should be done to ensure equal educational opportunity for these children (Atkin 1980, 91; Guthrie 1982, 517–18). Pennsylvania and Maryland were examples of states under court order to guarantee disabled students access to special education (U.S. Senate 1975, 41 and 139). Still, it was estimated at the time that half of all children with disabilities were not pursuing educational activities at home, in schools, or in other institutions.

To Senator Jennings Randolph (D-WV; 1976 ADA score: 45), chair of the Senate Subcommittee on the Handicapped, the need for federal action was obvious. During the Senate debate on the S.6 conference report, the bill that became P.L.94-142 when it was passed and signed, he said: "Mr. President, with almost 4 million handicapped children needing the help that this legislation offers, it is imperative that positive action be taken. Delay in action to meet the needs of handicapped children has far-reaching implications for the futures of these children and their families. We must act now to give these children the educational services they need to compete in today's changing world" (*Congressional Record* 1975, 37410–11).

By adding the congressional mandate to existing state requirements and court orders, legislators intended "to assure that all handicapped children have available to them . . . a free appropriate public education which emphasizes special-education and related services designed to meet their unique needs, to assure that the rights of handicapped children and their parents or guardians are protected, to assist States and localities to provide for the education of all handicapped children, and to assess and assure the effectiveness of efforts to educate handicapped children" (P.L. 94-142, sec. 3[c]).

Support for this act was almost unanimous in Congress, despite its cost and prescriptiveness. The S.6 conference report passed by a vote of 404–7 in the House of Representatives and 87–7 in the Senate in November 1975 (Congressional Quarterly Inc. 1976, 162-H and 77-S). To some observers, this level of assent suggested that federal aid had grown so noncontroversial by the mid-1970s that strong support for education bills was a foregone conclusion (for example, Halperin 1978, 65–66). There was some truth to this claim at the time; federal support for civil rights did grow stronger during the 1960s and 1970s, along with public support for the federal role in these areas (Guthrie 1982, 520; Elam 1978, 318 and 330–31). However, there was stronger evidence that the consensus on P.L.94-142 was an artifact of political pressures rather than of ideological agreement. Moreover, congressional efforts to reduce the federal share of the costs incurred by the legislation seemed to explain some of its popularity. Some members of the House and Senate appear to have supported the legislation because its costs were passed downward. Of course, this possibility raises the crucial question of why no legislators commented about the "unfunded mandate" they were passing, or about the new level of federal interference it entailed with or without the money.

What little dissent was publicly aired during the formulation of the bill concerned its cost. According to their public comments, the fourteen conservative legislators in both chambers of Congress who voted "no" on the conference report did so because they were concerned that the formula for the federal share of special-education costs would result in prohibitive costs. (Many "yes" voters had the same misgivings.) Several formulas were considered; an early House version would have cost almost $4 billion a year by the time the law was fully implemented (U.S. House of Representatives 1975, 59–61). Authorizations (that is, broad spending goals) in the final statute were much lower than this figure and actual appropriations (that is, the funds budgeted), and final expenditures were lower still, leaving states and school districts to fund almost all of the law's mandated costs. This has been true ever since P.L.94-142 was passed.

Federal underfunding was anticipated by state leaders and local educators who testified on behalf of P.L.94-142. State and local interests wanted federal assistance for meeting the needs of disabled students, because state and local education agencies were already incurring substantial costs in this area. Massachusetts Lieutenant Governor Thomas O'Neill III (son of then–House majority leader Representative "Tip" O'Neill, D-MA; 1976 ADA score: 60) warned the Senate subcommittee that the legislation could become "impotent" if inadequately funded (U.S. Senate 1975, 44–45). Larry Harris, special assistant to the superintendent of the Minneapolis Public Schools, spelled out the same concern in his written testimony to the subcommittee. "[I]t would be another cruel hoax if the Congress passed a piece of legislation which was based on supporting 75 percent of the excess costs of providing appropriate educational opportunity to the handicapped, but was actually funded at a much lower level." Harris said that few urban districts would support S.6 if they knew the federal government was going to renege. "State education agencies, local education agencies, state legislators, and, most of all, our parents and our handicapped children must not be led to expect great support for their efforts from the Congress only to find out that there are in actuality few resources provided to carry out the intent of the law" (ibid., 126).

The same warnings about cost were voiced by the Ford administration and by several members of Congress (ibid., 159 and 166; U.S. House of Representatives 1975, 59–61). The gist of these warnings was that it would be fiscally irresponsible for the federal government to take on a large percentage of the cost of special education, and deceptive to pass legislation stating that Congress intended to do so. As ideological objections, these warnings were fairly mild. In addition, only a small minority of legislators expressed their concerns publicly. Denials of these points were also rare. Obligatory remarks about moral duty and humanity were more common. Representative Herbert Harris II (D-VA; 1976 ADA score: 80) made these appeals but also denied that the legislation was an "overcommitment." He made the following remarks during the House floor debate on H.R.7217 (the original House version of the Education for All Handicapped Children Act). "While there are some who will argue that this bill is an 'over-commitment,' I believe it offers a proper and appropriate incentive to States and localities to provide adequate educational programs for the Nation's 7.8 million handicapped children. Indeed, it is difficult for me to imagine that the Federal Government could ever 'over-commit' to this special segment of our school population" (*Congressional Record* 1975, 25538).

Some legislators took pride in simultaneously supporting the legislation and working actively to curtail authorized spending levels. Reporting back from the conference committee that was convened to iron out differences between the House and Senate bills, Representative Albert H. Quie (R-MN; 1976 ADA score: 10) bragged about bringing back a reduced funding authorization ($100 million for fiscal year 1976 instead of the $680 million originally passed by the House) (ibid., 37026). Representatives John Ashbrook (R-OH; 1976 ADA score: 5) and Robert H. Michel (R-IL; 1976 ADA score: 5) cited this reduction as their reason for supporting the conference report after opposing H.R.7217 (ibid., 37028–29 and 25543). In the Senate, Senator Robert T. Stafford (R-VT; 1976 ADA score: 60), a key architect of the legislation, seemed to suggest that the symbolism of even a modest federal commitment to the disabled was more important than the size of the federal contribution to actually meeting their needs. "The conferees agreed to limit the amount to be appropriated in order to meet the administration's objections to the enormous cost of the bill. We feel that this is too important a statement for the handicapped children of the nation to risk a veto on the level of authorization" (ibid., 37412).

The cost-containment effort is one of the mysteries of the P.L.94-142 debate. On the one hand, it is a responsible government that monitors and attempts to minimize the cost of its programs. On the other hand, if the reduced federal share passes additional costs to states and school districts, then that government looks a little less responsible. Moreover, Congress was caught between moral, legal, and political pressures to do something for disabled children and counterpressures to cut government spending and avoid President Ford's threatened veto. Because special education in most settings is more labor-intensive than mainstream schooling, civil rights in this form are very expensive.

Why did the total cost of this legislation to all levels of government receive so little scrutiny in Congress when it was first enacted? Fiscal conservatism was the one safe way to criticize this legislation without directly opposing the principle of federal enforcement of special-education rights. Even so, few lawmakers chose to do this. Legislators who were worried about the law's impact on the federal budget may have known that appropriations would always lag behind the statutory targets, a common situation in federal budgeting. The symbolism of any amount of federal funds was important to both Congress and the special-education lobby, so the ultimate allocation of costs across the system was conveniently forgotten.

Many consequences of disability are heartbreaking and expensive, especially forgone educational opportunities. Policy analysts David Neal and David Kirp recognized the intertwined political and moral pressures exerted by children with disabilities and their families. "The issue of educating handicapped children had undoubted appeal. Once one could argue that such children were educable it became well-nigh impossible to mount a politically palatable argument denying handicapped children's claims to education; while educating handicapped youngsters might be expensive, how could costs be weighed against reclaimed lives?" (Neal and Kirp 1986, 346–47).

Representative Michel, a vocal conservative from Illinois—the Land of Lincoln—defended the S.6 conference report on quasi-conservative grounds, the only such rationale in the entire debate record. "Abraham Lincoln gave us the concept that the Government ought to do for its citizens only those things which they were unable to do for themselves. Well, there are many things that the handicapped are unable to do for themselves, and, frankly, I can think of no areas which more legitimately come under Lincoln's definition than services to the handicapped" (*Congressional Record* 1975, 37029).

The humane impulses that impelled community aid for disabled children were reinforced by political and legal imperatives engineered by special-education interest groups. Advocates for the disabled sought to exploit natural altruism and the legal system to overturn the persistent institutional neglect of the real needs of exceptional children. The political sophistication of such groups as the Council for Exceptional Children was considerable and, as the votes on P.L.94-142 suggest, almost irresistible. The disabled joined the civil rights movement a little late, but they quickly became the most powerful interest within it. The Council for Exceptional Children, the Children's Defense Fund, and other groups were helping draft special-education bills and testifying in favor of them (Guthrie 1982, 519).

During hearings conducted by the Senate Subcommittee on the Handicapped special-education legislation in 1973, a disabled high school student named Peter Hickey proved a captivating witness and a partisan fighter. "Mr. Nixon and his various Republican cohorts who are all-fired concerned about saving our budget and cutting down our cost, they say this isn't a good program, they say we shouldn't finance special education. Well, I challenge that person, I challenge him to spend 1 day in a wheelchair and then see if he is so all-fired up against having special education and I'd like to see if he'd actually be opposed to this bill" (U.S. Senate 1973, 384–85).

It continues to be politically unwise to question the rights of disabled Americans or to suggest competing demands on public resources. This tendency was cited by Raymond Waier, superintendent of the North Kansas City School District, during field hearings on P.L.94-142 in 1980. He also mentioned the law's effect on local decision-making, an issue ignored by everyone except President Ford in 1975:

> Section 504 [of the Rehabilitation Act of 1973] and Public Law 94-142 have brought needed aid to the handicapped but they have, at the same time, virtually neglected local decision-making at the public school level. Even the most outspoken educators willing to be critical of some aspects of this legislation are fearful that advocate groups, the media, and Federal bureaucrats will focus upon them as insensitive, inhumane and unsympathetic to the needs of all children. Wishing to avoid such wrath, their voices are too often stilled. (U.S. House of Representatives 1981, 317)

Waier later referred to the power of the special-education lobby: "In my opinion, Federal bureaucrats are easily manipulated by the complainant, media pressure and vested interest group influence" (ibid., 320). James W. Guthrie and Julia Koppich explain the same phenomenon more colorfully: "handicapped children constitute a politically sanctified classification which is subject to attack only by electoral campaign kamikazes and those who would denigrate motherhood and apple pie" (Guthrie and Koppich 1987, 35).

Of course, sympathy for the disabled is not simply a political calculation. Legislators are just as likely as the rest of the population to be touched by disabilities of their own or in their families. Several legislators referred to disabled family members in their comments supporting the legislation, including Representative Thomas R. Harkin (D-IA; 1976 ADA score: 85) and Senator Hubert H. Humphrey (D-MN; 1976 ADA score: 90) (Congressional Record 1975, 25541 and 37411). The lingering question is whether the actual or perceived power of the disability lobby was strong enough to force political consensus on a federal law with major ideological ramifications.

Answered and Unanswered Ideological Questions

Fiscal conservatism is an ideological position that is typically, although not always, associated with other conservative beliefs about limited government. (The principle of limited government, in turn, is inherited from classical Liberalism.) However, the budgetary criticism of P.L.94-142 was fairly tame, given the massive regulatory presence that went along with modest amounts of federal assistance. It is difficult to believe that conservative and liberal objections to such a major federal-control threat were silenced by the fact that most of the costs were passed elsewhere or because it was not "politically palatable" to speak out or vote against the rights of disabled children. Yet this is a possible explanation; no ideological objections were made to the bill except for mild dissent about the budget. Let us imagine a vocal conservative taking a longer view in 1975. She might have wondered how "one of the sharpest intrusions of the federal government into the details of teaching practice" (Atkin 1980, 92) could be contemplated in a nation with such a rich tradition of state and local educational autonomy. She would have had more fundamental misgivings about the costs of the legislation at all levels of government, not just in Washington, D.C.

We can assume either that such opinions existed in silence or that they did not exist at all. The fact that fundamental criticisms from liberals or conservatives could not be found in the debate record does not mean nobody made them. Warnings about federal control may have been sounded privately or in closed committee sessions to "mark up" the bill. Later criticisms of federal interference under P.L.94-142 and other programs suggest that conservative views were not absent in 1975 but that their dormancy had something to do with the continuing symbolic value and political necessity of congressional support for civil rights legislation.

It is also possible that there was genuine ideological consensus about the need for civil rights and due-process protections for the disabled. Moreover, it was necessary and acceptable for the federal government to enforce these rights. Attitudes about race, desegregation, poverty, and the rights of neglected populations evolved rapidly during the twenty-one years between the *Brown* decision and the passage of P.L.94-142. Federal activism reflected these attitudes, and the Education for All Handicapped Children Act solidified the federal commitment.

I am less persuaded by the second explanation, because of the return of plentiful arguments against the expansion of the federal role in later episodes. However, special education may have been such a special case that ideological objections (other than fiscal conservatism) simply did not exist. The first explanation is more plausible to me because it supports the distinction between political consensus (which P.L.94-142 did seem to have at the time) and ideological consensus (which it probably did not have). Indeed, what I think this episode best illustrates is the sharp difference between politics and ideology on sensitive questions of civil rights for the disabled in the 1970s.

Special education is an interesting mandate because it casts a larger shadow than the resources that go with it. From the federal perspective, it is a cost-effective way to enforce a moral vision. Today, this is called an "unfunded mandate," and it is a frequently deployed—if unpopular—strategy for influencing local practice. In 1975, however, federal underfunding was one of the reasons P.L.94-142 enjoyed such wide support in Congress.

Unanimity by the Numbers

In Chapters 2 and 3, congressional voting data were analyzed to confirm the existence of liberal and conservative voting blocs on education and to demonstrate that these blocs mostly voted according to the arguments and beliefs expressed in the congressional debates. The votes on P.L.94-142 were a different story. They did not reflect a split between liberals and conservatives. Rather, the votes appeared to represent the large extent to which legislators felt political pressure to support the legislation. A divide between liberals and conservatives still existed at that time; it simply was not reflected in the votes or the debate on P.L.94-142. As we know from the arguments, scattered opponents voted "no" on fiscal grounds. Fiscal conservatism is ideological, to be sure, and the legislators who publicly opposed the legislation took a courageous and unpopular stand in the name of that principle. The distinctive fact about P.L.94-142 is that so few members of Congress felt moved to oppose it publicly and that no member publicly opposed it as an overextension of federal authority.

The statistics in Table 4 show that legislators in each chamber strongly supported the measure. The S.6 conference report received strong and at times unanimous assent from Republicans, Democrats, conservatives, and liberals. "No" voters were likely to be more conservative according to their ADA scores, but legislators with low ADA scores were not especially likely to oppose the bill. The division between liberals and conservatives, as measured by their liberal quotients, was quite weak on these votes.

The Relationship Between P.L.94-142,
No Child Left Behind, and Other Laws

The passage of the No Child Left Behind Act of 2001 makes the Education for All Handicapped Children Act of 1975 (P.L.94-142) less anomalous than

Table 4   1975 P.L. 94-142 Votes with 1976 ADA Statistics

1975 P.L.94-142 votes with 1976 ADA scores	House November 18, 1975	Senate November 19, 1975
Final vote on S.6 (i.e., conference report)	404−7	87−7
	(98.3% "yes")	(92.6% "yes")
Democrats	271−3	58−0
	(98.9% "yes")	(100% "yes")
Republicans	133−4	29−7
	(97.1% "yes")	(80.6% "yes")
ADA Score Analyses		
Mean ADA score of "yes" voters	42.8 (n=404)	46.9 (n=87)
Mean ADA score of "no" voters	13.6 (n=7)	4.3 (n=7)
Mean ADA score of Democrat "yes" voters	56.1 (n=271)	54.2 (n=58)
Mean ADA score of Republican "yes" voters	15.8 (n=133)	32.2 (n=29)
Mean ADA score of Democrat "no" voters	23.3 (n=3)	— (n=0)
Mean ADA score of Republican "no" voters	6.2 (n=4)	4.3 (n=7)
Mean Democrat ADA score (whole chamber)	55.2 (n=288)	54.3 (n=62)
Mean Republican ADA score (whole chamber)	15.4 (n=145)	25.7 (n=38)
Mean ADA score of whole chamber (1976)	41.9 (n=433)	43.4 (n=100)

NOTE: P.L.94-142 = Education for All Handicapped Children Act; ADA = Americans for Democratic Action; n = the number of legislators in each cell with 1976 ADA scores. ADA figures in the "whole chamber" cells include all legislators, regardless of whether they participated in the final vote on P.L.94-142. 1974 ADA scores were used for three representatives who did not have 1976 scores. The House had one vacancy in the house when the P.L.94-142 vote took place. In the Senate, Senator James L. Buckley (Conservative-NY) was counted with the Republicans and Senator Harry F. Byrd Jr. (Independent-VA) was counted with the Democrats. SOURCES: Congressional Quarterly Inc. 1976, 77-S and 162-H–163-H for the votes on P.L.94-142 and Americans for Democratic Action website for 1976 ADA scores. (1976 scores downloaded October 26, 2005, from http://www.adaction.org/1976.pdf.) 1974 scores from Sharp 1988.

it was in 1975. Like P.L.94-142, No Child Left Behind imposes unfunded mandates on state and local educational agencies. Both laws increased the federal regulatory presence in schools and were overwhelmingly supported in Congress when first enacted. Both episodes teach us that long-standing ideological values in Congress can be either temporarily or permanently transformed.

P.L.94-142 and the Elementary and Secondary Education Act set the federal civil rights enforcement precedents for No Child Left Behind. For example, children with disabilities make up one of the subgroups for which adequate yearly progress must be reported under NCLB. Supporters of the new law have portrayed its subgroup accountability requirements as a continuation of the federal role in protecting the civil rights of children with disabilities, English-language learners, and disadvantaged students. Legislators of all ideological stripes have become extremely reluctant to challenge the federal expansion and protection of civil rights in schools. Today, conservatives willingly link civil rights rhetoric to fiscal conservatism and school choice, even if it means rethinking their traditional commitment to limited government.

There are some other lessons about federal education policy that enable us to compare the deliberations on P.L.94-142 with those of other laws. The first lesson is that presidential backing can help get a federal education proposal to and through Congress, but such support is neither necessary nor sufficient to pass the laws. This is an obvious lesson from the history of federal education policy-making (and federal policy-making generally). Indeed, other observers have touched on this theme (for example, Cross 2004, 148–49). Active presidential involvement can motivate Congress to pass important education laws. President Lyndon B. Johnson campaigned on his commitment to increasing federal aid to schools, and his administration devised a winning formula for delivering federal dollars to virtually every school district in the country. Almost four decades later, George W. Bush campaigned on his commitment to education generally and on the purported gains students had made while he was governor of Texas. Two Texans, one liberal and one conservative, made—and delivered on—education-related campaign promises. The Elementary and Secondary Education Act and No Child Left Behind were touted for their potential to remake the landscape of public education. Again, both laws were shaped and aided by their White House backing.

Of course, presidential support is not necessary for key education laws to be passed. President Gerald R. Ford opposed the Education for All Handicapped Children Act and would have vetoed it in 1975 if it had not had almost unanimous support in Congress. Nor does presidential support guarantee success, as was the case with President Ronald Reagan's desire to enact a constitutional amendment permitting school prayer in 1984. Both President Jimmy Carter and President Bill Clinton won education victories in Congress (establishing a cabinet-level Department of Education and passing Goals 2000, respectively), but the resulting laws came under fierce ideological attack despite (or perhaps because of) their presidential support.

The second lesson is to remember the origins of the unfunded mandate charge in federal education policy. Both P.L.94-142 and No Child Left Behind are widely viewed as unfunded mandates because of the mismatch between funding levels and the costs incurred by their requirements. P.L.94-142 passed along most of its costs to states and school districts, a fact that received little attention when the law was enacted. Since passage, however, the law has become the poster child for unfunded mandates. The federal government has been repeatedly criticized for being unwilling to meet the funding levels originally envisioned in P.L.94-142. The issue of funding for the earlier law was debated at length during consideration of No Child Left Behind in 2001. (It is interesting that when Senator James Jeffords left the Republican Party in May 2001 to become an Independent, one reason he cited was the failure of President George W. Bush and congressional Republicans to use some of the nation's budget surplus to increase funding for special education [Manna 2006, 3].)

Like P.L.94-142, critics accused No Child Left Behind of spawning many unfunded mandates, especially with regard to the cost of fulfilling the law's testing requirements. (Several states have objected to the costs of NCLB's testing requirements, and at least one—Connecticut—has filed suit against the federal government.) More significant is that concerns about inadequate funding for Title I of No Child Left Behind almost derailed the Senate bill, although it later passed that chamber by a huge margin. Hence, the unfunded mandate charge was leveled at No Child Left Behind more vocally than at P.L.94-142 during the original debate. In neither case, however, has inadequate federal financing for the ambitious purposes of the original laws led to reductions in their reach. Over the past thirty years, it has become more acceptable for the implementation costs of federal education policies to be passed down to states and school districts.

5

the house that jimmy built

The U.S. Department of Education

[The Department of Education] is a barnacle that has grown on the ship of state, and the quicker we scrape it off the better for the Government and the people.
—ATTRIBUTED TO U.S. REPRESENTATIVE THEODORE M. POMEROY (R-NY) (1868)

In the ten years between the passage of the Elementary and Secondary Education Act of 1965 and the Education for All Handicapped Children Act of 1975 (P.L.94-142), federal involvement in the nation's schools had become more extensive and, apparently, less controversial. Many ideological impulses and divisions were hidden during debate over P.L.94-142. The divisions were exposed again within a few years, even as federal education activities continued to grow. When presidential candidate Jimmy Carter promised to establish a cabinet-level Department of Education, politicians of various ideological persuasions worried that the federal role would become more centralized. What started as a proposal to reconfigure the federal education bureaucracy became an ideological reexamination of federal involvement in schools.

The decision to create a U.S. Department of Education is important for understanding the No Child Left Behind Act because both laws increased the visibility of the federal role in schools. Both episodes also demonstrated that traditional differences between liberals and conservatives were less pronounced than they had been in the debates of the 1950s and 1960s. Numerous liberals, for example, opposed the Department of Education measure and No Child Left Behind because they feared federal control. More puzzling, however, was the scattered support the Department of Education received among conservatives in the 1970s. Most paradoxical of all was the strong support conservatives gave No Child Left Behind in 2001. The softening of ideological differences between liberals and conservatives partly explains why federal authority for schools has steadily increased since the 1950s.

Department of Education Proposals Before 1977

Proposals for a cabinet-level education department date to the mid-nineteenth century. One such department was established in 1867 with the limited mission of compiling statistics and disseminating information about the nation's schools. Many professional educators favored a national bureau for educational affairs, and support for it in Congress suggested that education was a growing national concern. There was also a hostile reaction to the idea by those who feared federal encroachment on state and local school systems, especially in regions where schools were already well supported (for example, New England). President Andrew Johnson signed the bill "only after he had received definite assurances that no centralization of educational activity was envisioned." Advocates of the department claimed that it did not entail federal control. Controversy persisted, however, and the department was downgraded in 1868 to a bureau in the Department of the Interior; it retained the same functions but lost much of its budget and prestige. This episode and the earlier Morrill Act (1862) solidified the factions for and against federal involvement in schools as early as the nineteenth century (Lee 1949, 21–28, quotation on 26; see also Peskin 1973).

In 1919, efforts to establish a cabinet-level education department were renewed, but they met with even less success than in the 1860s. The latter proposal did not survive Congress. Yet it is important to recognize that this ill-fated idea reflected a widespread impulse to centralize, standardize, and professionalize public education during the Progressive era. In addition to many professional educators sympathetic to Progressivism, an education department was favored by "Nativist" groups who were anti-Catholic and alarmed about the large influx of immigrants during the preceding decades. The Masons and the Ku Klux Klan favored the bill, viewing a national education department as a means for assimilating (and brainwashing) newcomers and as a weapon against parochial schools (Dumenil 1990, 499–518 and 523).

Opponents of the department of education proposal, which was debated in the early 1920s, included the Catholic church and many other groups fearing the increased reach of the federal government. Many members of the business community opposed the bill because they wanted to reduce federal expenditures. These concerns apparently struck a deeper chord than did arguments supporting the bill. Lynn Dumenil calls this feeling "antistatism." The Great War had led to additional powers for the national government. These along with other actions, such as prohibition, were sobering reminders of increased federal interference with private life and individual freedoms (ibid., 510–12).

Finally, in the 1960s an early House version of legislation leading to the Elementary and Secondary Education Act included a title that would have established a Department of Education. This proposal was not seriously considered at the time, in part because Congress and the president wanted to give money to schools rather than establish a national education department.

These earlier episodes anticipated some of the issues that would be controversial during consideration of President Carter's proposal for a federal Department of Education. Praise for and warnings of centralization, for example, and the debate over what a national education department might mean for private schools, recurred in the later debate. The 1970s debate also exposed ideological divisions that had been largely hidden since the Great Society era. Indeed, whereas the passage of the Education for All Handicapped Children Act was distinguished by its near unanimity and apparent absence of public controversy, the decision to establish the Department of Education was hotly debated. Opposition took two broad forms: (1) ideological objections to the growing federal role in schools and (2) counterarguments to the organizational rationale for creating a new department. Conservatives were most likely to oppose creating the department on these grounds, but they were joined by large numbers of liberals who were also critical of the reorganization and the motives of their president.

The 1970s Department of Education Debate

Establishing a cabinet-level Department of Education was the campaign promise of a moderate Democrat—Jimmy Carter—to a liberal constituency: members of the National Education Association (NEA). It also gained initial support in the Senate from Senator Abraham Ribicoff (D-CT; 1980 ADA score: 56), having been endorsed on previous occasions by him and other liberals in Congress. Its liberal origins did not mean that it had universal support among liberals in Congress, however, nor did the proposal repel all conservatives. In fact, the weakening of previous ideological divisions between liberal support for and conservative opposition to federal involvement in education is the distinguishing feature of the 1970s debate over the Department of Education.

Ironically, advocates of the Department of Education in the administration and in Congress tried to keep the proposal ideologically neutral. They claimed, for example, that the proposal was not designed to expand the federal role in education but would simply consolidate diffuse federal educational functions—which themselves had been growing rapidly—into a well-organized department with greater prestige and visibility than the mere Office of Education in the Department of Health, Education, and Welfare. This claim, if believed, set the proposal apart from earlier, usually liberal schemes to expand federal spending in schools. A department was to be established in the name of efficiency and coherence. In this way, advocates of the Department of Education attempted to sidestep the traditional liberal case for federal activism.

Opponents of the Department of Education objected to the proposal on a number of grounds. Many of their arguments against the new bureaucracy invoked dire warnings of federal control. Virtually all opponents (and supporters, for that matter) implicitly recognized that federal involvement in education had grown quickly, was firmly established, and required some type of reorganization either within existing agencies or in new ones. Hard-core opponents sometimes ignored the complexity of existing arrangements or the fact that federal programs had grown rapidly, but they did not automatically oppose federal involvement per se. In this regard, many conservative opponents of the Department of Education had changed their attitudes about federal involvement during the years since the National Defense Education Act of 1958 and the Elementary and Secondary Education Act. This transformation was almost complete by the time No Child Left Behind was considered in 2001.

Even though the concept of an education department was contested both before and after one was created, the legislation may have passed despite that because enough legislators actually believed the organizational efficiency arguments in its favor. Indeed, reorganization may have been less controversial to some policy-makers than voting to establish new federal programs. (This seems to have been the belief of many within the Carter administration.) President Carter was willing to expend precious political capital and win one of his rare victories in Congress. The arguments for and against creating the Department of Education may not have altered individual opinions and votes in Congress, but they did represent the values and allegiances of legislators. In other words, although the arguments did not necessarily affect the outcome, they do help explain why the proposal won.

Public opinion did not help explain the proposal's success, either. The 1977 Gallup Poll of Public Attitudes Toward Education indicated divided sentiments on the question, "with slightly more respondents voting to keep it in the present department [Health, Education, and Welfare] rather than make it a separate department" (40 percent in favor; 45 percent opposed) (Elam 1978, 320–22).

The rhetoric also shows that the opposition to forming the Department of Education was not strictly Republican or conservative. Opposition and support came from unexpected quarters, as the following examples show. Liberal Congresswoman Patricia Schroeder (D-CO; 1980 ADA score: 94) opposed the bill and cited a bruising episode regarding loss of Title I funds in Denver in her remarks. Schroeder, representing a western congressional district during the "sagebrush rebellion"—a movement of western states against federal land-use regulations of the 1970s—opposed the department because she believed it would entail federal control of schools: "No matter what anyone says, the Department of Education will not just write checks to local school boards. They will meddle in everything. I do not want that" (*Congressional Record* 1979, 1820–21). Exceptions like this and those cited below might have been unexpected at the time, but in general they are not uncommon in a pluralist democracy with a relatively weak party system. More significant from an ideological standpoint were the defections of several previous supporters of federal education programs who worried deeply about the ramifications of reorganizing the federal role in education. Senator Daniel Patrick Moynihan (D-NY; 1980 ADA score: 72) was one of these "defectors," as was Representative Leo J. Ryan (D-CA; 1978 ADA score: 55). Alongside the arguments in favor of the department, these exceptions show that the reorganization proposal was simultaneously more and less controversial than a new federal program. The reorganization was a lightning rod for many hopes, dreams, and fears about national education policy.

A defection to the pro–Department of Education ranks was made by the notoriously conservative Senator Strom Thurmond (R-SC; 1978 ADA score: 17). Thurmond strongly favored the bill on pragmatic grounds, perhaps because he represented—for forty-eight years—a southern state that had grown dependent on federal education dollars:

> Mr. President, with the creation of this new Department, we will have a responsible, high-level Federal official whose only concern will be education. This person will be held accountable not only when there are advances in education, but also when there are failures. Education will have an advocate in Washington for its needs and to work hard toward solving its problems. When the Congress or the public desires to inquire into the status of education in this country, there will be one central office, a Cabinet-level Department from which the information can be obtained.

Finally, Mr. President, I want to emphasize my understanding that this bill, with all of its benefits through centralization and effective management, will not mean more control. I am bitterly opposed to Federal control of education. By this, I mean that the policy decisions and curriculum to be taught in local schools will remain at the State and local levels where it belongs. A new Department of Education can do an important job by assisting the States and localities without infringing on their rights to establish their individual educational needs. (*Congressional Record* 1978, 374)

It is astonishing that Senator Thurmond would hold or express these views, even late in his career. His opinions on civil rights and desegregation were softening during this period (Cohodas 1993, chap. 14), but nothing in any part of Thurmond's political biography suggested that he would favor consolidating federal education activities. Yet his sentiments that day reflected the will of Congress with respect to establishing the Department of Education.

The Case for the Department of Education

There were two major impetuses for creating a cabinet-level education department. The first was as a political payoff to the National Education Association for endorsing Jimmy Carter for president in 1976 (and 1980). The second was President Carter's desire to make existing federal education functions more efficient and coherent through some type of reorganization. The proposal needed bipartisan support, so the administration emphasized the organizational rationale. No one in Congress or the NEA forgot the proposal's political origins, however. A few legislators cited the NEA payoff as part of the reason for voting against the department, including Representative Shirley Chisholm (D-NY; 1980 ADA score: 78): "While others may choose to debate this issue in terms of the lofty and admirable ideals supposedly associated with creation of the Education Department, I find it extremely difficult to disassociate formation of this department from its onerous political origins" (U.S. House of Representatives 1978b, 379).

The organizational case took the following generic form. Myriad education functions—from Head Start to overseas dependent schools to college loans—were spread throughout the executive branch. This dispersion resulted in costly duplication of effort and lessened the prestige of federal education programs. The prestige part of this argument could also be read as the need to build a better constituency for federal education programs.

The organizational case was made to deflect ideological criticism that the new department would threaten federal control of schools (Radin and Hawley 1988, 9).

During the many hearings conducted on the proposals in Congress, numerous witnesses advanced supposedly apolitical arguments in favor of the reorganization of federal education functions. A panel from the Citizens Committee for a Cabinet Department of Education (CCCDE) testified before the Senate Committee on Governmental Affairs during consideration of an early proposal to establish the Department of Education. A front for the National Education Association, the Citizens Committee for a Cabinet Department of Education was represented by a panel consisting of Stephen Bailey and Samuel Halperin, both well-known commentators on the federal role in education, and Rufus E. Miles Jr., a former assistant secretary of Health, Education, and Welfare. Panel members summarized a CCCDE study on forming a department of education and argued that the visible presidential appointment of an education secretary would ensure accountability for the complex education functions of the national government (U.S. Senate 1977, 34).

A succinct rationale for the Department of Education proposal is given in the 1978 report of the House Committee on Government Operations:

> H.R.13778 will create a Department of Education to be headed by a Secretary of Education who will be a member of the President's Cabinet. The department will help insure that education issues receive proper attention at the Federal level and will enable the Federal Government to coordinate its education related activities more effectively. Federal support for education has grown significantly during the past decade and the activities now being carried out on the Federal level are of such magnitude that they merit consolidation in a separate executive department. (U.S. House of Representatives 1978a, 1006)

Thus, the case in favor of establishing a department of education relied on many of the same pragmatic and organizational-efficiency arguments that were advanced in support of earlier consolidation proposals. A new department would facilitate the efficient administration of existing federal education functions by reorganizing them in a single and prestigious cabinet-level department. Proponents attempted to keep the 1970s Department of Education debate free of ideology and party politics by emphasizing the reorganization rationale.

Of course, the consolidation rationale did not dispel fears about increased federal control, as the ideological arguments against the bill repeatedly demonstrate. Both advocates and foes of creating the Department of Education eschewed federal control, but certain opponents were convinced that federal control would result from the actions that proponents wanted to undertake in the name of visibility and efficiency. The federal-control charge was at the core of the ideological response by many opponents of the department.

The Case Against the Department of Education

Less than five years after the nearly unanimous passage of the Education for All Handicapped Children Act, an extremely prescriptive yet progressive civil rights measure, many legislators worried that reorganizing federal education activities was a covert attempt to capture control of the nation's schools. As indicated above, many of the arguments made against the Department of Education proposal took the form of warnings about federal control.

Ever since the first Department of Education in the 1860s and the ill-fated Hoar bill of 1870, federal education overtures have been attacked as schemes to take over the nation's schools (Peskin 1973, 573; Lee 1949, 23–25 and 55). Proponents of the National Defense Education Act of 1958 attempted to defuse this charge by permitting a broad range of spending within specified areas (strengthening math, science, and foreign-language instruction in schools and offering loans and fellowships to college students). By designing a categorical delivery system for the Elementary and Secondary Education Act programs, the Johnson administration prevented its "billion-dollar baby" from being derailed by charges of federal control. Federal control was still a damning accusation during the debate about the Department of Education, even though it was curiously absent from the deliberations on P.L.94-142, the Education for All Handicapped Children Act.

A popular strategy for raising the federal-control issue was to expose the unintended but inevitable consequences of a proposed education program or strategy. Several legislators warned about the "first steps" toward federal control embodied in the Elementary and Secondary Education Act. Even though warnings of federal control were not made in connection with P.L.94-142 in Congress, legislators were still implored to consider the future effect of mandated increases to the federal share of special-education costs. During the debate about the Department of Education, the fear of federal control returned and was invoked by name under the same "delayed reaction" syndrome. From the vantage point of No Child Left Behind, these warnings turned out to be quite prescient.

In his dissent to the House Committee on Government Operations report recommending passage of H.R.2444, the 1979 House bill to establish the Department of Education, Representative William S. Moorhead (D-PA; 1980 ADA score: 56) wrote the following:

> Proponents of the Department maintain that local control of education is assured by statutory language in the bill. Yet, it is my experience that too often the intent of Congress is passed over by the natural inclination of dedicated bureaucrats to regulate—even to legislate. To me, the creation of this Department provides a potential for a centralization of the control of ideas, a potential which may or may not be realized but one which will be latent for as long as the Department exists. And, as we all know, where there is potential for a thing to be done, there are eventually people who attempt to realize that potential for whatever purposes— good or evil. (U.S. House of Representatives 1979b, 1161–62)

Several legislators agreed with the threat, including onetime federal education booster Senator Moynihan, who despaired of witnessing what conservatives warned against and liberals promised would not happen in earlier episodes. Moynihan bemoaned what he saw as the excessive politicization of education at the national level, a veiled reference to Carter's campaign promise to the National Education Association: "Mr. President, I have to say that it comes as something of a disappointment to me, although perhaps it should not come as a surprise, that everything we said would not happen to Federal aid to education when we were battling for it in the later days of the Eisenhower administration and throughout the Kennedy administration, everything we said would not happen is happening here today" (*Congressional Record* 1979, 780–81).

Representative Clarence E. Miller (R-OH; 1980 ADA score: 11) extended this warning by spelling out the dynamic of increasing federal control over time. He also opposed the bill, as is clear from the following remarks he made during floor debate in the House:

> It has been said that this bill is not a prescription for a Federal takeover of education or a national policy on education. However, the entire thrust of the legislation leads toward increasing Federal involvement in education. . . . A separate Department of Education,

employing more than 24,000 bureaucrats and having a budget of $14.5 billion annually would soon seek to enlarge its role in an effort to justify its existence. And like all bureaucracies, it would fix itself firmly on the political landscape by issuing more regulations and expanding paperwork requirements. (Ibid., 1538)

The warning was spun out even further by Senator Harrison H. Schmitt (R-NM; 1980 ADA score: 17), a former NASA astronaut with a Ph.D. in geology. He described an alarming sequence of events leading from the Great Society to the creation of the Department of Education and to federal control through fiscal dependence:

> The proposed department is expressly designed to provide more money and more Federal control of education. No one, I think, will deny that. It is not difficult to imagine this department establishing national "advisory" standards at some point in the future. Later, the department could require adherence to the compulsory standards, if Federal aid is to be continued. Next, standard tests, developed by the Federal Government, could be mandated to check whether the compulsory standards are being met. Last, State and local authorities will be coerced into acceptance of a standardized curriculum as the "only possible" guarantee of meeting compulsory standards. (*Congressional Record* 1978, 299)

Certain provisions of Goals 2000 (passed in 1994) and much of No Child Left Behind (passed in 2001) came close to Senator Schmitt's warnings about standards and assessments. Like his colleague Senator Moynihan, Schmitt referred with alarm to the gradual transformation of the federal role. The relatively innocuous provision of funds during the 1960s had become something more threatening by the next decade. "During the last decade, the Federal Government has become more and more involved in education. What started out as assistance, primarily financial assistance, to State and local authorities, has emerged as de facto control through the threat of withholding funds upon which local systems had become dependent. The creation of a department of education obviously will strengthen this trend toward centralized decision-making in the field of education" (ibid., 298–99).

Senator Schmitt supplemented these warnings with a concise description of how fiscal dependence becomes the "mechanism of Federal control":

[R]egulations are being imposed through financial coercion. The proposed department of education would accelerate the process of bureaucratic takeover of our educational system. The Federal Government provides about 10 percent of the finances spent on elementary and secondary education in this country. However, as education is marginally financed—Mr. President, I emphasize that phrase, "marginally financed." As it is, it permits almost 100 percent control in many school districts, if not most, in the country. No educational system can afford to lose 10 percent of its funds off the top once [it has] become dependent on them. Thus comes the mechanism of Federal control. (Ibid., 298)

Schmitt made these remarks as a conservative Republican senator. Similar warnings of federal control were also made by members of President Carter's party (for example, Representative Patricia Schroeder). Another Democrat, Representative Leo Ryan, declared that the proposed Department of Education "is more than a benign 'reorganization' of the Office of Education. It is a massive shift in the emphasis by the Federal Government from supporting the local efforts of school districts and State departments of education to establishing and implementing a national policy in the education of our children" (U.S. House of Representatives 1978a, 1044).

In another dissent, Republican Representatives John N. Erlenborn (IL; 1980 ADA score: 11), John W. Wydler (NY; 1980 ADA score: 28), Clarence J. Brown (OH; 1980 ADA score: 11), Paul N. McCloskey Jr. (CA; 1980 ADA score: 78), Dan Quayle (IN; 1980 ADA score: 0), Robert S. Walker (PA), Arlan Stangeland (MN; 1980 ADA score: 0), and John E. (Jack) Cunningham III (WA; 1978 ADA score: 5) asserted that the decision to create a department of education would have one of two undesirable consequences: "Since education in this Nation is a function reserved to the states under the Constitution, this reorganization will either be a colossal bureaucratic blunder wasting tens of millions of dollars, or if successful it will result in the domination of education by the Federal Government" (ibid., 1048).

Another traditionally conservative objection to most government programs is the cost to taxpayers. As quoted above, Senator Schmitt claimed that "no one . . . will deny that" a federal department of education means more money for education. He may have been referring only to opponents of the department, because no advocates made the connection publicly. (It was wise for proponents to keep silent, even if they did have this objective.) It was true, in general, that most liberals favored increased funding for education. The National Education Association was on record as favoring a federal share of one-third of all public education expenditures (U.S. House of Representatives 1978b, 64). In these deliberations, however, commentators and legislators who were in favor of a federal education department were more likely to argue that the department would cost less because consolidation of existing functions would be more efficient. The savings would not be dramatic, but they were tangible. One analysis by the President's Reorganization Project in the Office of Management and Budget attributed cost savings of $100 million (less than one percent of all education expenditures at the time) to the new department (Radin and Hawley 1988, 122).

Rather than attack the weak economic-efficiency rationale for a federal education department, legislators opposed to its creation accused advocates of using the department to deliver more money to schools. Representative Erlenborn explained the endorsement of the Department of Education by the National School Boards Association as follows. "I have come to believe that their endorsement was based—and this is based on conversations with some of the members—on the concept that, with a Cabinet-level Department, more Federal funds would flow into various school districts" (U.S. House of Representatives 1978b, 568). Similar charges were made against the National Education Association and other groups by opponents, including Representative Leo Ryan: "I think that the public system is already so stuffed with money, and so inefficient in its operation because it is stuffed with money, that more stuffing will only do more harm. The liberal idea and the idea of the Democratic Party—that somehow more money means better education for kids, is in my experience a false assumption. It was when I was in Sacramento. It is here now" (ibid., 578). Ryan also estimated that more than half the employees of the California Department of Education were paid with federal funds (ibid.).

If the objective in establishing the Department of Education was simply to increase education appropriations, President Carter could do so without a new department, according to Representatives Ryan and John Conyers Jr. (D-MI; 1980 ADA score: 78) (ibid., 598). If their assertions were true, they actually reinforced the veracity of claims by proponents that the creation of the department was unrelated to obtaining additional funds but rather designed to make existing programs more cost-effective.

Senator Moynihan made a subtler point against the consolidation argument. He believed that concentrating funds in a single agency threatened to politicize education and quoted sociologist David Riesman, a commentator who shared Moynihan's opposition to forming a federal education department: "I would not want something so comprehensive that anybody could get his hands on it. Education is safe in Washington as long as it is hidden, distributed, inaccessible, and nobody controls more than 5 percent of it" (U.S. House of Representatives 1979a, 201–2).

Warnings of federal control and excessive spending are traditional weapons in the conservative arsenal. What is noteworthy about their appearance in this debate is the extent to which legislators other than hard-core conservatives made these charges. Senator Moynihan, an early neoconservative at times, had close connections with the Kennedy, Johnson, and Nixon administrations and a record of scholarship addressing welfare and education policy. Moynihan was skeptical about certain educational strategies for African Americans, but he always advocated federal action on their behalf. Moynihan wrote the 1964 Democratic Party platform plank that, he claims, "led some eight months later to the Elementary and Secondary Education Act of 1965" (Moynihan 1988, 48).

Speaking of scholarly inquiry, an educational researcher tested one of the claims made in Congress after the Department of Education legislation was enacted. Dennis J. Encarnation examined the one fiscal rationale advanced by the National Education Association and others in favor of an education department. The department will help education, according to this argument, because the "uncontrollable" entitlement programs in the Department of Health, Education, and Welfare (for example, Social Security) put education programs at a disadvantage during annual appropriations. Encarnation tested this claim statistically and found that education expenditures would fare no better under the Department of Education than they did in the Department of Health, Education, and Welfare. Instead, he found that variation in the overall domestic budget accounted for increased education appropriations (Encarnation 1982, 8 and 21).

By exploiting the risks of federal control and increased funds to schools, opponents of the Department of Education attributed motives that were simply denied by the advocates. Supporters of the proposed department surely would have lost if they had openly favored more money or more control. Opponents also tried to counter the overt arguments in favor of the Department of Education. In these cases, they did not have to rely on conspiracy theories to make their cases against the proposed department. For example, in response to proponents' claims that the prominence and prestige of federal education activities would be enhanced by concentrating most of them in the Department of Education, the following dissent was filed in the 1978 House report on H.R.13778. In it, five Democrats— Benjamin S. Rosenthal (NY; 1980 ADA score: 78), John Conyers Jr. (MI), Henry A. Waxman (CA; 1980 ADA score: 83), Peter H. Kostmayer (PA;

1980 ADA score: 89), and Ted Weiss (NY; 1980 ADA score: 100)—opposed establishing the Department of Education and disputed the prestige rationale. "It is argued that a Cabinet-level Department of Education is needed to increase the visibility and status of Federal education programs and to improve their coordination. 'Visibility' and 'status' are undefined catch phrases which hardly justify creation of a Cabinet-level Department of Education. These goals can be achieved with the present structure of HEW [the Department of Health, Education, and Welfare]" (U.S. House of Representatives 1978a, 1042).

If increased visibility was the main reason for establishing the Department of Education, that goal could be accomplished by other means, according to these Democrats. This dynamic was apparent in the comments above on increased funding. At times, different opponents attempted to identify different key motives of proponents of the Department of Education and attack them in isolation from the others. The proponents, however, had several reasons for political action that operated simultaneously: prestige, efficient and coherent organization of existing education functions, and so on. The case in favor of the Department of Education was politically strong because it rested on more than one argument.

Albert Shanker, president of the American Federation of Teachers, also countered the prestige argument in favor of a Department of Education by declaring in his written statement to the Senate Committee that "[a]n expansion of prestige will come with programmatic success. A separate department certainly will not do it." He further warned that the creation of [the Department of Education] could backfire by "spotlight[ing] education in a negative way." He urged frank discussion of the potential for federal control in the 1978 Senate Department of Education bill, S.991 (U.S. Senate 1978a, 160 and 162). Of course, these comments come from the head of the large national teachers' union that was *not* wooed by Carter during the 1976 campaign, so some political resentment may underlie Shanker's opinions. Although they represented similar constituencies, the National Education Association and the American Federation of Teachers were often on opposite sides of national education policy questions at the time (Radin and Hawley 1988, 97).

Another argument in favor of the Department of Education was the contention that consolidation would lead to greater administrative efficiency, coherence, and cost-effectiveness. This argument was the key administrative strategy for keeping the proposal above politics. It is interesting that many of the proposed organizational transfers became the most politicized elements of the debate. Several programs originally slated for transfer never made the move to the Department of Education, a circumstance that can be seen as nullifying the original efficiency rationale. Implicit counter-arguments were made everytime legislators contested the transfer of a program to the new agency. Nevertheless, consolidation may be the main reason most legislators supported the Department of Education in 1979.

Contested program transfers made up the bulk of the debate at the subcommittee, committee, and full chamber levels in the House and Senate. This situation led Senator Robert Morgan (D-NC; 1980 ADA score: 22), an opponent of the Department of Education, to muse: "We had no comparable difficulties in deciding what to put in the Department of Energy, which to me implies there was a much better rationale for creating it" (*Congressional Record* 1979, 766).

The debates over program-by-program transfers frequently revealed different attitudes about national government generally, as well as about its role in education. An amendment by Senator Ted Stevens (R-AK; 1980 ADA score: 39) to delete the transfer of Native American schools from the Bureau of Indian Affairs to the new department and the ensuing debate illustrate some of these attitudes. Here, as in the case of several other contested transfers (science education programs from the National Science Foundation, Head Start, and Department of Defense schools for dependents of American personnel stationed overseas), there were arguments for and against the transfer. Senator Barry Goldwater (R-AZ; 1980 ADA score: 0), an opponent of the Department of Education, wanted to retain administration of these schools in the Bureau of Indian Affairs because he believed that Native American culture would be preserved (*Congressional Record* 1978, 237). Senator James G. Abourezk (D-SD; 1978 ADA score: 60) disagreed, calling the Bureau of Indian Affairs politicized and negligent. In his words, "the best thing that can happen for the country and for the Indian people is to transfer education out of the Bureau of Indian Affairs and the hopeless state in which it is found in that agency. I do not know how well the Department of Education will do it, but they cannot possibly do any worse than the Bureau of Indian Affairs has done, and for God's sake I hope they can do it better" (ibid., 243).

The reorganization debate included people of all political and ideological stripes with wide-ranging views on the federal bureaucracy. In the case of the Bureau of Indian Affairs, the cultural preservation of a relatively powerless Arizona constituency was invoked by an ideological opponent of an education department (Senator Goldwater) to justify continued activity by another part of the government. This is an indication of the drift in attitude that occurred for some conservatives during the twenty-one years between passage of the National Defense Education Act and the decision to establish the Department of Education. Conservative opponents of the proposed department attached disturbing ideological motives to the administration's desire to reorganize existing federal education programs, but they did not always criticize the programs themselves. In several cases, they defended them in their current configurations.

American Federation of Teachers President Albert Shanker wondered about the efficiency rationale when he posed the following rhetorical question to the members of the Subcommittee on Legislation and National Security of the House Committee on Government Operations:

> If this Department is going to be such a great thing for education of this country, why does everybody that is supposed to be moved over there come before you and demand to be taken out? Demands [are] voiced . . . with such strength and such vociferousness that the committee takes them out without a fight. First, the Indians and then the Head Start program. What do the Indians know that we do not know? Why is it that they do not want to be in such a department? We ought to think about why it is.
>
> If a department is good for education then those who want out are wrong, and their programs should be included. If they have some good reasons for staying out, maybe there are others who have some good reasons for staying out as well. (U.S. House of Representatives 1979a, 227)

Vocal lobbies spoke on behalf of other specific programs. Like Shanker, William E. Murray, rural area development specialist for the National Rural Electric Cooperative Association, cited the Head Start omission in his argument against the transfer of child nutrition programs from the Department of Agriculture: "I might just add in my covering the hearings on the Senate side, Senator Ribicoff, in asking that the Head Start program be exempted from transfer—and this was during the markup—mentioned the reason he was making that request was that Head Start was working very well where it was and it would not make good sense to disturb it. We think the same logic applies to the child nutrition program. It doesn't seem logical to us to transfer it" (U.S. House of Representatives 1978b, 337).

Senators Charles H. Percy (R-IL; 1980 ADA score: 39), Muriel Humphrey (D-MN; 1978 ADA score: 68), and John C. Danforth (R-MO; 1980 ADA score: 50) betrayed hard feelings toward schools rather than federal agencies in their written opposition to transferring child nutrition programs into the new Department of Education. In their "Additional Views" attachment to the Senate Committee report on S.991, they cited their belief that "[e]ducators have had a history of obstructing the placement of these programs within the schools," preferring instead to raise money by promoting junk food (U.S. Senate 1978b, 220 and 222).

During the two decades before consideration of the Department of Education, enforcement of civil rights was a major federal activity through the courts and, increasingly, in Congress. The transfer of the Office for Civil Rights from the Department of Health, Education, and Welfare to the new Department of Education elicited much criticism from those who felt that civil rights enforcement would be compromised (Radin and Hawley 1988, 124). Many civil rights advocates believed that the new department would cater to the needs of the educational establishment and state education agencies and thereby neglect concerns about equality of educational opportunity. This view was expressed by Phyllis McClure, director of the NAACP Legal Defense and Education Fund, in a written statement to the House subcommittee that considered H.R.13778 (U.S. House of Representatives 1978b, 268–69). Representative Shirley Chisholm also had concerns about the Department of Education's "obvious inability to insure equal educational opportunity for all Americans through effective and efficient enforcement of the civil rights laws passed by Congress" (ibid., 378).

Vernon E. Jordan Jr., president of National Urban League, doubted the civil rights commitments of some of those who supported the Department of Education. In his remarks before the House subcommittee considering H.R.2444, he couched his civil rights comments in this context: "There are those who share our enthusiasm for a separate department but do not share equally our enthusiasm for the enforcement of civil rights. Because of that and so as to insure the enforcement of civil rights receives the same equity and the same weighting as does the Department of Education, we are insisting on this. We have reasons grounded in history and experience to suggest that after this the Office of Civil Rights in fact may be compromised, and we would not like to see that happen" (U.S. House of Representatives 1979a, 192).

Civil rights attorney Joseph Rauh believed it unwise to strengthen the hand of the education establishment against desegregation by giving the Department of Education control of the Office of Civil Rights. The effectiveness of the Office of Civil Rights under the Department of Health, Education, and Welfare, he said, was due to its independence from professional educators with vested interests in the status quo (ibid., 327).

Representative John Erlenborn, a leading critic of creating the Department of Education, declared his commitment to civil rights in the following exchange with the Children's Defense Fund director, Marian Wright Edelman.

> Mr. Erlenborn: My principal concern is the threat to local and State control of education that would come from a strengthened Cabinet-level Department of Education. Do you personally see any threat in this regard?
>
> Mrs. Edelman: Mr. Chairman, I think that you obviously have a right to ask and to express that concern and to get a thoughtful answer to it, again, before you exercise your vote, if that is your priority concern.
>
> I guess I have always seen the role of the Federal Government in education as one of dealing with those problems of equity which State and local districts have not responded to adequately.
>
> Second, I guess I have seen the Federal role as one of leadership and innovation and of being able to do the kind of policy planning and thoughtful thinking about education in the future that people who are delivering direct services on a day-to-day basis are not able to do or don't do for whatever reason.
>
> So I guess that my principal concern, without being able to answer your question, has been continuing to insure equal educational opportunity.
>
> I think some people call that enforcement and others call it intrusion. I think that depends on what your ends are and how you do that.
>
> But I think that, clearly, I am concerned that the strong Federal enforcement efforts continue to insure that those kids most in need who are not adequately protected by local and State policies are protected.
>
> Now I don't know whether you would view this as intrusion. I don't necessarily view that as intrusion, but clearly it seems to me that we must reach those children and strengthen the abilities of States and localities to reach those children more effectively in ways in which they have not in the past.
>
> Mr. Erlenborn: I would not call that intrusion. I think that is a proper role for the Federal Government to play. (Ibid., 247–48)

Had Edelman or someone with her beliefs testified during the decade after the *Brown* decision, conservative legislators would have interrogated her about the "intrusiveness" of federal civil rights enforcement. Decades later, conservative Erlenborn agreed that enforcing civil rights "is a proper role for the Federal Government to play." By the time No Child Left Behind was debated, the protection of educational civil rights was one of the principal arguments for increased federal regulation of schools.

The Rev. Jesse Jackson favored the proposed department on civil rights grounds, despite the skepticism of many of his colleagues. To the Senate Committee, he said, "we are not appealing for more Federal control. We are appealing for Federal responsibility so that we can be equally protected under the law. That will not happen at the local level" (U.S. Senate 1979, 23).

Along with varied opinions on the appropriateness of program transfers, different organizational schemes elicited debate. One amendment that did not pass sought to establish an assistant secretary of private education in the new department. The amendment was proposed by Representative Tom Tauke (R-IA; 1980 ADA score: 33), who argued: "[w]e need to have someone in the Department who looks after private education, to prevent excessive control. On the other hand, if we do have federal involvement in private education, we need a spokesman to make certain that that involvement serves the best interests of the private sector" (*Congressional Record* 1979, 1380). Representative Millicent Fenwick (R-NJ; 1980 ADA score: 67) was uneasy about the amendment. "I am troubled always by the idea that the Federal Government is going to control private education," she said. "And when one sees a special arrangement allowing for Federal influence which I fear controls private education, I think it is dangerous" (ibid., 1380). Representative Dan Glickman (D-KS; 1980 ADA score: 56) shared this view:

> Private schools would have everything to lose and nothing to gain by this kind of hierarchy. They would be competing with and subject to higher institutionalized level requirements, regulations, and burdens that our public schools inevitably have to deal with and fight against every single day.
>
> In my judgment, Mr. Chairman, H.R.2444 is bad, because it presumes ultimate Federal control over the policy of education, and for that reason, I oppose it; but an assistant secretary for private education throws the towel in for private schools, too, and assumes that ultimate Federal control over private education as well as public education. (Ibid., 1383–84)

In general, private-school interests were opposed to creating the Department of Education. The basic rationale was expressed by Monsignor Wilfrid H. Paradis, secretary for education of the U.S. Catholic Conference, in his 1978 testimony before the Senate Committee. He worried that the Department of Education could "become dominated by public school interest groups almost exclusively committed to public school education and perhaps with very little understanding for and appreciation of the values and the rights of nonpublic education" (U.S. Senate 1978a, 170–71). Monsignor Paradis applauded the Elementary and Secondary Education Act of 1965 in his written statement because it made large sums of federal money available to parochial schools. On the other hand, he felt that an education department was unnecessary and would threaten parental rights and educational pluralism (ibid., 174).

The debates over program transfers and other organizational issues were infused with ideological considerations. Systems of belief about civil rights and private schools, for example, were discernible in the arguments for and against certain configurations. The federal-control concerns about an education department were patently ideological as well, even though they often strayed from the traditional conservative and liberal divisions that had identified these concerns in the past. Several other issues came up in the debate that exposed raw ideological nerves: the belief that federal-aid causes or is correlated with declining school quality, federal incompetence, and categorical aid as an insidious form of federal control.

Senators Goldwater and Schmitt equated federal aid with federal control and blamed federal control for what they perceived as the declining quality of education (*Congressional Record* 1978, 240). During a 1978 Senate floor debate, Schmitt made the following remark: "Ironically, however, as we have been spending more money on education, as we have seen more and more Federal control and manipulation of education, the general quality of education has been declining. Obviously, more money and more bureaucratic control has not improved education overall" (ibid., 299).

The same theme was taken up the following year by Senator Robert Morgan. For him, the Elementary and Secondary Education Act marked the beginning of achievement declines and increases in violence, vandalism, and drug use in schools. "For lack of better evidence, I am hesitant about asserting the existence of a cause and effect relationship between the increasing Federal role and decline in our schools" (*Congressional Record* 1979, 756). Nevertheless, Morgan was more impressed with this possible correlation than with the evidence that federal involvement improves schools.

The same argument was made by Senator Malcolm Wallop (R-WY; 1980 ADA score: 22) against S.210, the 1979 Senate bill to establish the Department of Education. What is noteworthy about Wallop's opposition to S.210 is that he was a sponsor of the 1978 Department of Education bill, S.991 (ibid., 854–55). (There were several bills under consideration in both chambers in the 95th and 96th Congresses.) "It is only in the last twenty years that the Federal Government has taken an extremely active role in placing conditions on the money it grants to school systems and requiring their compliance. No one can deny that some of these 'conditions' have created a more equitable educational system in America. Yet many are as quick to point out a demise in the quality of learning over the last ten years for our children in public schools, in no small part, due to over-regulation and Federal intervention" (ibid., 865–66). Wallop's message is clear: equal educational opportunity has led to a deterioration of the nation's schools, and federal intervention is responsible for both.

Longtime critic of federal involvement Representative Robert H. Michel (R-IL; 1980 ADA score: 6) sustained this line of reasoning in the House. This is the same legislator who believed that the Elementary and Secondary Education Act was part of a secret, computer-based federal takeover of education. Of the Department of Education, Michel said: "We are going to be handing over a brand new department to those whose educational philosophy either contributed to or was unable to stop this decline [of test scores and other educational indicators]. This new Department will not start anything new. It will simply solidify, institutionalize, and perpetuate the old, tired, discredited, weary, stale, flat, and unprofitable array of education innovation and social experiment we have been conned into believing helps kids" (ibid., 1211–12).

Federal involvement might be responsible for a variety of ills, according to Representative L. C. Fountain (D-NC; 1980 ADA score: 17), but only a social scientist would know how to tell for sure:

> teacher strikes, . . . violence in the schools, . . . functional illiteracy, . . . declining test scores. . . . No one can point to one factor and say it alone is the reason for all the troubles afflicting public education.
>
> However, it appears that as Federal involvement in all areas of education has increased dramatically over the past several years, the overall quality of public education has decreased concurrently. If it were possible to quantify and plot out all the many complicated variables in the equation, we just might find a verifiable

relationship there. That is something we should all think about as we continue to consider this legislation. (Ibid., 1809)

Paul Copperman, a reading specialist and conservative author, did weigh in on these questions. As president of the Institute of Reading Development in San Francisco, he too spoke of the relationship between academic achievement and the federal role in education. His complex reasons for opposing the Department of Education are worth quoting in detail from his 1979 testimony before the House Subcommittee. "I suggest that the twin historical anomalies of extensive Federal involvement in public education and declining academic achievement are not coincidental. In fact, four years of research into the decline in academic achievement in our public schools have convinced me that the Federal Government bears significant culpability for that decline" (U.S. House of Representatives 1979a, 285).

Copperman traced the history of federal participation in education during the twentieth century: "During the first sixty-three years of this century, when academic achievement was on a steady upswing, Federal involvement in American public education was quite restricted. The Federal Government contributed to Department of Defense schools, to schools on Indian reservations, to land-grant colleges, and during the last part of that period, to programs designed to improve the science and math education of our brightest students. During this period, our public schools received little financial support from the Federal Government and were subjected to few Federal regulations" (ibid.).

Copperman contrasted the focus of the National Defense Education Act on "our brightest students" with the misplaced emphasis on low-achieving "disadvantaged minority children" under the Elementary and Secondary Education Act. This shift exacerbated the achievement losses due to federal aid. Copperman continued:

The astonishing gains in academic achievement recorded during the post-sputnik era were largely due to the focus on the education of above-average-ability students, with the consequent hike in performance standards for all students.

The achievement decline of the past fifteen years can be partially attributed to the Federal policy and program focus on below-average-ability students and the consequent reduction in performance standards for all students. It is important to note that high-ability students have recorded a much more striking drop in academic achievement during the past fifteen years than low-ability students. (Ibid., 287)

Some of the purported instructional travesties Copperman blamed on the federal government were career education and heterogeneous grouping. He deplored work-study components of vocational education programs because they reduced time spent on academic subjects: "My experience with students in these programs is that middle-class kids use them to earn money to support their cars, stereos, and clothes." Regarding what he perceived as a centralized attack on ability grouping in schools, he declared: "This is an example of misguided educational policy adopted by the Federal educational bureaucracy which is being forced on local schools" (ibid.).

According to Copperman, not only was the federal government culpable for teaching the wrong students the wrong things, its educational enterprises have been run as a special interest and a "jobs program" since the passage of the Elementary and Secondary Education Act. "The mass of Federal regulations which public schools must obey when spending this money [under Title I] virtually insures that the money will not be used to serve the needs of children; but, in fact, will only serve the needs of politicians who pass the legislation, the bureaucrats who administer it, the professors of education and commercial interests it employs, and the community residents who use it as a jobs program" (ibid., 286).

Copperman accused the House Subcommittee of aiding and abetting these special interests by hearing testimony from national education lobbies and "self-serving" education professors rather than local teachers and administrators. "I have a very strong feeling that you people are not talking to people at the local level. You are talking only with very high ranking people and the big educational lobbying organizations. You are talking with people who only talk to each other. You do not talk with local schoolteachers. You do not talk with principals and superintendents. You do not talk with people who have to deal with the day-to-day operation of schools" (ibid., 291).

In sum, Copperman condemned the federal government for creating "a self-serving parasitic superstructure on local education," for "[acting] to stab the classroom teachers in the back on a wholesale level," and for "sucking the blood out of the American public education" (ibid., 288, 291, and 293).

Part of the superstructure of "parasites" decried by Copperman was also assailed by Representatives John Erlenborn (R-IL), Benjamin Rosenthal (D-NY), Peter Kostmayer (D-PA), John Wydler (R-NY), Clarence Brown

(R-OH), Paul N. McCloskey Jr. (R-CA), Thomas N. Kindness (R-OH; 1980 ADA score: 6), Robert Walker (R-PA), Arlan Stangeland (R-MN), M. Caldwell Butler (R-VA; 1980 ADA score: 17), Jim Jeffries (R-KS; 1980 ADA score: 6), Olympia J. Snowe (R-ME; 1980 ADA score: 28), and Wayne Grisham (R-CA; 1980 ADA score: 6) in their dissent to the 1979 House report. Representing one-third of the full Committee on Government Operations, they were concerned that the Department of Education formed under H.R.2444 would codify a categorical-aid strategy as the main delivery system for federal funds. These dissenters preferred less-restricted block grants or education revenue sharing. "The countless legions of regulation writers employed by the Department to dictate precisely how localities and States must use the Federal education largesse would no longer be needed under these latter approaches" (U.S. House of Representatives 1979b, 1170).

Recall that the Johnson administration's rediscovery of the categorical program design was widely credited with making the Elementary and Secondary Education Act politically acceptable. The categorical-aid strategy supposedly anticipated and neutralized suggestions that the ESEA was general aid. The act's programs of targeted assistance were also intended to minimize accusations that they would lead to federal control of schools. Of course, numerous foes of the Elementary and Secondary Education Act were not convinced that specific categories of assistance reduced the risk of federal control, but categorical aid seemed to be a winning formula for the ESEA (and earlier programs like the National Defense Education Act).

After the 1965 passage of the Elementary and Secondary Education Act, the views of many federal-aid critics evolved from opposing federal aid outright to tacitly accepting restricted aid to endorsing much less restricted funding vehicles. President Richard Nixon advocated sharing federal tax revenue with states for educational purposes (Jeffrey 1978, 208–9), and President Reagan engineered the first educational block grant in 1981 (Congressional Quarterly Inc. 1982, 465). (Block grants resulted from collapsing several categorical programs into one, more flexible grant.) Both conservatives and liberals expressed skepticism about the categorical-aid strategy as time passed. It was condemned during the debate on Goals 2000 and charged with becoming a mechanism for federal control during consideration of No Child Left Behind.

The gradual accumulation of categorical programs over the two decades preceding the proposal to establish the Department of Education confirmed that these—and not unrestricted grants—would be the primary delivery system for federal aid. The idea of a department of education seemed to

Table 5   1979 Department of Education Votes with 1980 ADA Statistics

1979 ED votes with 1980 ADA scores	House September 27, 1979	Senate September 24, 1979
Final vote on S.210 (i.e., ED conference report)	215–201 (51.7% "yes")	69–22 (75.8% "yes")
Democrats	185–77 (70.6% "yes")	51–5 (91.1% "yes")
Republicans	30–124 (19.5% "yes")	18–17 (51.4% "yes")
ADA Score Analyses		
Mean ADA score of "yes" voters	57.1 (n=215)	54.4 (n=69)
Mean ADA score of "no" voters	29.4 (n=201)	25.5 (n=22)
Mean ADA score of Democrat "yes" voters	59.6 (n=185)	59.4 (n=51)
Mean ADA score of Republican "yes" voters	41.5 (n=30)	40.2 (n=18)
Mean ADA score of Democrat "no" voters	51.7 (n=77)	49.0 (n=5)
Mean ADA score of Republican "no" voters	15.6 (n=124)	18.6 (n=17)
Mean Democrat ADA score (whole chamber)	57.0 (n=274)	58.2 (n=59)
Mean Republican ADA score (whole chamber)	21.1 (n=159)	29.3 (n=41)
Mean ADA of whole chamber (1980)	43.8 (n=433)	46.4 (n=100)

NOTE: ED = U.S. Department of Education; ADA = Americans for Democratic Action; n = the number of legislators in each cell with 1980 ADA scores. ADA figures in the "whole chamber" cells include all legislators, regardless of whether they participated in the final vote on ED. In three cases in the House and one in the Senate, scores were taken from 1978 because the four legislators did not have 1980 scores. The House had one vacancy when the ED vote took place. A few legislators quoted or mentioned in this chapter (for example, Representative Leo J. Ryan [D-CA]) participated in the ED debate but were not seated when the final vote occurred in 1979. Their individual 1978 scores are included in the text of the chapter, but they are not part of the analyses in Table 5.
SOURCES: Congressional Quarterly Inc. 1980, 136-H–137-H and 51-S for the votes on ED and Americans for Democratic Action website for ADA scores. (1980 scores downloaded October 20, 2005, from http://www.adaction.org/1980VotingRecord.pdf. 1978 scores downloaded May 23, 2006, from http://www.adaction.org/1978.pdf.)

conflict with the bipartisan commitment to limited federal involvement. Was the coordination and consolidation of existing policies to be the first step toward federal control of education?

Description of the Department of Education Votes

The votes on the Education for All Handicapped Children Act (P.L.94-142) indicated what turned out to be a temporary, politically motivated consensus on federal education policy in 1975. Pre-1975 divisions reappeared in the debate over the Department of Education. The 1979 votes in the House and Senate to establish the Department of Education confirm the discernible but weak divisions by ideology and party indicated in the congressional rhetoric. Table 5 shows that the vote was quite close in the House of Representatives, reflecting the intensity of controversy about the Department of Education in that chamber. House Democrats tended to support the new department, while House Republicans were likely to oppose it. As measured by ADA scores, Republicans were more conservative than Democrats, especially those Republicans who voted "no." In the Senate, the Department of Education won with the support of both parties. Except for the majority vote in each party, the same broad differences between Democrats, Republicans, liberals, and conservatives in the House also applied to the Senate on this vote.

The Politics and Ideology of the Department of Education

The proposal that created the Department of Education was a reorganization measure born of partisan politics. The debate over the proposal incited a bruising reexamination of the federal role in education. A number of critical issues surfaced during these deliberations: whether federal control of schools was a growing threat, the politics of bureaucratic reorganization, and the proliferation of lobbies for different federal programs. Despite the growing federal role and stable support for that role, the Department of Education debate showed that federal involvement remained politically and ideologically controversial.

Traditional divisions between liberals and conservatives were weaker during the Department of Education debate than they had been in the 1950s and 1960s. Many liberal Democrats openly opposed President Carter's reorganization plan as a threat to state and local control of schools. Some liberal legislators also had serious concerns that the federal government was altering its commitment to civil rights enforcement. Numerous conservatives supported the reorganization scheme. When certain conservatives opposed the transfer of particular programs to the Department of Education, they argued in favor of existing arrangements and either tacitly or explicitly endorsed federal involvement as it had evolved to that point. The Department of Education was not a liberal victory, like the Elementary and Secondary Education Act and the National Defense Education Act were, because the measure depended on conservative and Republican support to offset dissenting liberals and Democrats. The Department of Education episode shows that it is not always sufficient to explain the growing federal role in education after the mid-1950s by citing only the power of liberals and Democrats in Congress. Neither their president nor the Department of Education proposal unified them in 1979.

Nevertheless, the proposal won with discernible liberal and Democratic support. Despite its "onerous political origins," the initial proposal was shaped by President Carter's penchant for organizational efficiency. The reorganization rationale was also a deliberate attempt to keep the legislation above politics and ideology. A majority of legislators, representing liberals and conservatives in both parties, seem to have believed that the Department of Education would improve the coordination of the disparate raft of federal programs in different agencies. Several programs did not make the move to the Department of Education—Head Start and Department of Defense schools, for example—but the consolidation rationale remained viable and convincing in Congress. Moreover, the new department and its programs withstood the ideological attack of President Ronald Reagan.

For twenty years, the department was a bane to many conservatives, Republicans, and others who perceived it as a threat to state and local authority over education. Abolishing the Department of Education was an official Republican commandment until presidential candidate George W. Bush lobbied to remove a plank calling for eliminating the Department of Education from the 2000 Republican platform (Rudalevige 2003, 34). Under the George W. Bush administration and No Child Left Behind, the Department of Education has become an active enforcer of federal testing and accountability regulations.

The most interesting ideological stories from the debate over the Department of Education were the challenges made to the usually reliable assumption of liberal support and conservative opposition to federal action in schools—an assumption that worked well in the 1950s and 1960s. President Carter's inability to lead the Democrats in Congress may explain some of the liberal defections and the close final vote in the House of Representatives. The ideological content of liberal fears about the new department also shows that liberals as well as conservatives could be counted on to oppose excessive federal involvement in schools. Both liberals and conservatives eschewed federal control in earlier debates; several liberals made a special effort to do so as an argument against the new department.

Of course, these liberal dissents were not the whole story of the Department of Education. The formation of the department shows that many conservatives and liberals accepted federal involvement and voted to improve the coordination of the growing number of federal programs. The Department of Education was born of an agreement between liberals and conservatives to support reorganization. At the same time, as many conservatives and some liberals warned in this and earlier episodes, the growing acceptance of federal involvement in schools would make it harder to hold the line against increases in federal authority in the future.

6

standards-based reform meets federal education policy

The Goals 2000: Educate America Act

It is really tragic that we have gotten so emotionalized in America that people actually believe Goals 2000 is part of some plot by the federal government to seize control of education. It's hard to fathom how someone could be that illogical.

—C. Richard Cranwell (D), Virginia House of Delegates (1996)

By the time Ronald Reagan was elected president in 1980, federal support for elementary and secondary education had strong, bipartisan appeal in Congress. Schools were widely viewed as tools for ensuring civil rights and equal opportunity for English-language learners, students of color, and the disabled. Even though it was controversial, the decision to establish the U.S. Department of Education the previous year demonstrated that legislators of various ideological persuasions accepted a permanent, albeit limited federal role in education. President Reagan wanted to scale back this role and change its direction, but he failed to convince legislators in Congress to enact his agenda.

Although the federal role in education was widely accepted by the 1980s, dissatisfaction with the quality of public schools was growing during the same period. This dissatisfaction was expressed most forcefully in the influential and widely praised 1983 report, *A Nation at Risk*. The report was based on the work of the National Commission on Excellence in Education, which was convened by President Reagan's Secretary of Education Terrel H. Bell. Reagan had mixed feelings about the commission's findings because he, unlike others, did not concede that the federal government might be even partly responsible for remedying the deficiencies identified in the report (Bell 1988, chap. 10).

President Reagan was succeeded by his Vice President, George H. W. Bush. The new president was more inclined than the old to take action on behalf of the nation's schools, and in 1989 President George H. W. Bush convened the Education Summit of state governors in Charlottesville, Virginia, where the governors set six national education goals. Later in his term, President George H. W. Bush attempted to pass America 2000, a goals-driven, school-reform package. His efforts were thwarted by congressional opposition to the school-choice provisions in the America 2000 proposals and other election-year maneuvers by both parties (Alexander 1993; Congressional Quarterly Inc. 1993, 455–56). However, the concerns about school quality and international competitiveness that infused *A Nation at Risk* and the Education Summit continued to grow and evolved into the systemic-reform and standards-based reform movements of the 1990s.

President Bill Clinton picked up the education mission of his predecessor in 1993. He installed at the Department of Education some of the key architects of the national standards movement, among them South Carolina governor (and Charlottesville summit participant) Richard W. Riley as Secretary of Education, and Stanford School of Education dean Marshall S. Smith as Education Undersecretary. The president and his education team quickly proposed a systemic-reform strategy for federal education programs and indirectly for public schooling at large. The Goals 2000: Educate America Act of 1994 provided a standards-based framework for the Improving America's Schools Act of 1994, which reauthorized and renamed the multi-billion-dollar Elementary and Secondary Education Act. The Clinton administration was more aligned ideologically with the 103rd Congress than the George H. W. Bush administration had been with the 101st and 102nd Congresses, so Clinton's proposals fared better than America 2000. Nevertheless, Goals 2000 was contentious; indeed, it was the focal point of 1990s disputes about the appropriate federal role in education.

By establishing a means for developing and "certifying" model national standards and state standards, the Goals 2000 legislation signaled a new role for the federal government. The new role was controversial, however, and Congress and the Department of Education quickly retreated from several key provisions of the initiative. Advocates of Goals 2000, victorious at first, had to stand by while many of the program's innovations were diluted or eliminated in the name of state and local autonomy. Liberal legislators and their allies in the administration discovered that it is one thing to endorse a standards-based reform movement and quite another and more controversial thing to put the federal government at the head of it.

Goals 2000 may have been the last concrete instance of widespread conservative opposition—on ideological grounds—to expanded federal

authority for education. The Goals 2000 debate has assumed new significance in light of the ideological shifts underlying the passage of the
No Child Left Behind Act seven years later. Both laws were ideological
departures from the tradition of limited federal involvement in schools.
Conservatives resisted these departures during consideration of Goals
2000 but celebrated them under No Child Left Behind. In fact, No Child
Left Behind represented a larger expansion of federal authority than Goals
2000 did.

Outline of the Goals 2000 Legislation

The Clinton administration's Goals 2000 bill was sent to Congress in
April 1993, and hearings were conducted almost immediately in both the
House and the Senate. Senator Edward M. Kennedy (D-MA; 1993 ADA: 90),
chair of the Committee on Labor and Human Resources, gave a concise
rationale for S.846, the early Senate version of the legislation that would
become Goals 2000: "By codifying the National Education Goals, this legislation will strengthen our commitment to reach them. By providing for
the development and certification of voluntary standards for learning in
seven basic courses—math, science, English, history, foreign languages, art,
and geography—this legislation will help to end the growing confusion about
what students should be learning in their classes" (U.S. Senate 1993a, 1).
    The eight national education goals were codified in Title I of the final
Goals 2000 law, P.L.103-227. (Two more goals had been added to the
original six set by the governors in 1989.) Title II spelled out duties of the
new National Education Standards and Improvement Council (NESIC, as
it came to be known) and the existing National Education Goals Panel. From
the standpoint of states and everyone else, Title III was most prominent
because it authorized funds for state and local systemic improvement
grants. The National Skills Standards Board and other workplace programs
were established by Title V, and the Office of Educational Research and
Improvement was reauthorized in Title IX. The remaining titles were
relatively minor when measured in dollars and controversy. The National
Education Standards and Improvement Council and all of Title III were the
most controversial parts of Goals 2000 before and after passage of the act.
    The provisions for state and local grants in Title III required states to
submit formal plans to the Department of Education. In conjunction with
the goals panel and the National Education Standards and Improvement
Council, the department would approve these plans if they showed

reasonable promise of success and reflected a standards-driven school-improvement strategy for all K-12 students. As a condition of receiving Goals 2000 grants, states were directed to either adopt "voluntary national model" curriculum and performance standards and "opportunity-to-learn standards or strategies" or devise their own. (Opportunity-to-learn standards, or standards for assessing the adequacy of school resources, were another ideological lightning rod during the Goals 2000 debate.) The national standards were to be "certified" by the NESIC and "approved" by the goals panel, perhaps by consulting actual standards from the several federally funded standards development efforts under way at the time. The NESIC was also charged with certifying state content standards and performance assessments, if states chose to submit them. Despite assurances of the voluntary nature of some of these certification procedures (and the option for states to decline moneys under Title III), advocates of Goals 2000 were never able to quell objections to the law's requirements for federal approval of state curriculum, performance, and opportunity-to-learn standards. (By contrast, No Child Left Behind state accountability plans are mandatory. The fact that these state plans are now required by law has not generated the same level of controversy as the voluntary plans under Goals 2000.)

The Case for Goals 2000

Concerns about the international competitiveness of the U.S. education system were invoked during the Goals 2000 debate. This strategy is reminiscent of how federal-aid advocates exploited the Soviet Sputnik launches to help pass the National Defense Education Act. The place of the United States in the world economy of the 1990s, in fact, was the most frequently cited argument for this ambitious federal blueprint. Secretary Riley expressed these concerns in his written statement to the Senate Committee on Labor and Human Resources: "Many other countries against which we compete for jobs expect all of their students to take challenging academic and/or occupational course work" (U.S. Senate 1993a, 6).

Similar sentiments were expressed later that year during House floor debate by Representative Ron Klink (D-PA; 1993 ADA: 65). "This legislation will help make the United States competitive in the global economy of today and into the twenty-first century. Goals 2000 will encourage and support state and local communities to reinvent our education system so that all American students can achieve internationally competitive standards" (*Congressional Record* 1993, 24292).

Students and schools would become internationally competitive if they met internationally competitive standards. The National Education Standards and Improvement Council and the National Education Goals Panel would ensure that certified and approved standards were internationally competitive. The first task of these panels would be to specify what "internationally competitive" meant. According to Secretary Riley, "[t]his information will be made available by the National Education Standards and Improvement Council. Again, how can we compete internationally if we don't know what we are competing against? 'Goals 2000' will give us that voluntary information" (U.S. Senate 1993a, 7).

Representative Major R. Owens (D-NY; 1993 ADA: 95) worried about our global position too and believed that American students do poorly in international comparisons. In blaming this situation on the American tradition of local control, Owens expressed what was then a very unpopular opinion in Congress:

> Every industrialized nation except this one has some central direction for education. Some overdo it. . . .
>
> But we go to the other extreme. We have this romantic notion that having local school boards in control of education is the best way to go. No, it is not. We are rapidly falling behind. Our students are not performing well in international competitions, and they are not meeting the standards of industry in our own Nation.
>
> So we need help from a central source. We need some help from the Federal Government. (*Congressional Record* 1993, 24334–35)

Certain critics of the Goals 2000 proposal disputed the global competition argument or believed that the U.S. education system had already lost. "Simply throwing more money at the problem is not the answer to our education woes," said Representative Cass Ballenger (R-NC; 1993 ADA: 11). "America spends more on education than any other country, yet American students have one of the lowest achievement ratings" (ibid., 24289). Others saw the argument about competing in the world economy as a convenient excuse for a centralized education system. A letter from Paul T. Mero, legislative director of the Virginia-based Christian Action Network, was inserted in the record of the House debate: "Today, we are told, requires a citizenry educated and trained for the marketplace of tomorrow, and that a centralized system of school boards, curricula, and testing, among other things is essential to fine tune our great economic machine. Such a visionary assessment, neatly packaged in H.R.1804 [the House Goals 2000 bill], is nothing more than new world order nonsense" (ibid., 24330).

Even though the ideological controversy that loomed before and after passage may have been unforeseen or miscalculated, the architects of Goals 2000 attempted to anticipate the objections to the bill and work around them. This had been done in the past as well, especially in the case of the Elementary and Secondary Education Act of 1965, where vital compromises were made on parochial-school aid, civil rights, and targeting of students and schools. There was a key difference, however: most of the compromises on the Elementary and Secondary Education Act were made before the bill was passed, whereas compromises on Goals 2000 were about evenly split between the legislative process prior to passage and hasty retreats by the administration afterward.

Goals 2000 supporters had a single generic rebuttal to many of the charges leveled against the proposal: that participation in the program is voluntary. Moreover, certain activities, such as certification of state standards, would be voluntary even for states that were receiving funds. Because this was the only counterargument to the national curriculum charge, Goals 2000 supporters were vulnerable if enough legislators doubted those assurances. Supporters of Goals 2000 managed to outvote the skeptics, but the perception of involuntary federal mandates persisted after passage.

States were free to decline Goals 2000 funds if they chose not to establish school curriculum and performance standards. In shepherding the legislation through his committee and the full Senate, Senator Kennedy repeatedly emphasized the voluntary nature of Goals 2000, and Secretary Riley agreed with Kennedy's statements:

> Secretary Riley: At some point in time, of course, States could come on a voluntary basis and ask us to look at their standards and see if they are consistent with the Federal standards; if so, we would certify them.
> The Chairman [Kennedy]: I think it's important for people to know that the States don't have to take this money, do they?
> Secretary Riley: No. (U.S. Senate 1993a, 9–10)

States would be allowed to participate in the program without submitting their standards to the National Education Standards and Improvement Council, but the plans sent to the Department of Education had to have assurances that "rigorous" standards were being developed (P.L.103-227, Title III, sec. 305[a]). Even this provision was relaxed in the 1996 amendments to the Goals 2000 law.

Of course, for states that needed the money, it was "ironic" and "absurd" to call the program "voluntary," according to Senator Judd Gregg (R-NH; 1993 ADA: 10) (*Congressional Record* 1994a, 860). The other half of the New Hampshire delegation, Republican Senator Bob Smith (1993 ADA: 15), found seventy-five references to Goals 2000 being voluntary in S.1150 (the second of three numbered Senate bills). However, he believed "there is little about this bill that is truly voluntary."

> Goals 2000 would set up new bureaucracies in the form of the national education goals panel and the National Education Standards and Improvement Council (NESIC), which would be charged with developing national content and performance standards. States would have to conform to these standards in order to qualify for a share of the $400 million in grants authorized by Goals 2000.
>
> This is coercion; States looking for additional funding streams for their educational systems will find it next to impossible to resist the political pressure to apply for these funds, and therefore submit themselves to the dictates of the NESIC. It is difficult to fault States for seeking to recover some of the tax dollars they send to Washington.
>
> It is additionally clear that after these standards are in place, further attempts will be made to link all Federal funding to state compliance. . . .
>
> In effect, then, what we are doing in the name of the noble goal of creating better educational opportunities for our children, is laying the groundwork for a national school board that will use the power of the purse to dictate standards to our schools. This is not right, and is exactly what opponents of the creation of the Department of Education were afraid of. (Ibid., 1540)

Senator Smith cited the 1994 reauthorization of the Elementary and Secondary Education Act as an example of "sliding down the slippery slope toward mandatory compliance with Federal standards" because of its connection to the Goals 2000 framework. Goals 2000 was ahead of the ESEA reauthorization on the legislative calendar for the 103rd Congress, but consideration of the two proposals overlapped. Title 1 of the Improving America's Schools Act (the new name for the Elementary and Secondary Education Act) required that states set and report challenging standards for disadvantaged students as a condition of receiving Title I funds. Of course, this provision did not directly require their participation in Goals 2000, but it pushed them in the same direction by tying standards development to a much larger sum of federal dollars. "Mandatory compliance" had become much less controversial by the time No Child Left Behind was enacted, both because there was a larger amount of money at stake and because of the evolution of ideological viewpoints about acceptable and unacceptable types of federal involvement.

Ironically, some conservatives felt that Congress was giving states and districts too much leeway by specifying too little about what they should be doing with their Goals 2000 grants. For example, Representative William F. Goodling (R-PA; 1993 ADA: 10), former educator and future House education committee chair, worried that states would get implementation funds before their plans were completed and approved: "I just want to keep their feet to the fire and I don't want them getting implementation money until you say the plan is good and it is completed and is approved" (U.S. House of Representatives 1993b, 9–10). Goodling apparently was protective of the education programs he nurtured while in Congress; his strong credentials as a conservative and as a Republican might have led him to advocate more flexibility for states during the 1993–94 debate.

Representatives Richard K. Armey (R-TX; 1993 ADA: 0), Cass Ballenger (R-NC), John A. Boehner (R-OH; 1993 ADA: 0), and Peter Hoekstra (R-MI; 1993 ADA: 20) also faulted the version of H.R.1804 approved by the House Committee on Education and Labor. In their "Supplemental Dissenting Views" section of the House Committee on Education and Labor report, they wrote: "H.R.1804 . . . does not ensure that schools actually use the funds in the bill for reform. The use of the funds only has to be 'reasonably related' to school improvement. This ambiguous term would make any lawyer proud. It can mean funding school-based clinics, multicultural programs, outcome-based education, or any of the number of failed 'reforms' attempted by the education establishment in the past twenty years" (U.S. House of Representatives 1993a, 67).

These dissenters objected that the bill was not more specific about allowable expenditures, because there were clearly some activities that, in their opinion, should not be supported. This issue was problematic for conservatives who desired less government regulation but who also wanted to ensure that federal funds are spent according to the intentions of Congress. Senator Strom Thurmond, then a South Carolina Democrat, objected to the National Defense Education Act in the 1950s because— among other things—it did not require defense-related courses of study for college students accepting federal scholarship aid.

A few legislators, especially liberal Democrats in the House, joined Representative Goodling in wanting strong enforcement of some of the act's provisions. In one controversial amendment to the version of the bill (H.R.1804) reported out of the House Committee on Education and Labor, Representative Jack Reed (D-RI; 1993 ADA: 90) wanted to ensure that standards would be met, not just set:

> This provision asks States, if they choose to apply for Federal planning grants under Title III of Goals 2000, to describe in their application what they will do when a school or school system fails to meet the standards. . . .
>
> We should not sit idly by during this reform debate and watch Federal resources go into another paper drill which will enrich educational consultants and only coincidentally help students because we do not face the tough question of what actions must be taken to ensure that standards are met. (*Congressional Record* 1993, 24299)

Even though Reed's amendment did not make it into the final version of the Goals 2000 law, it is worth noting that at least some conservatives and liberals in 1994 were interested in accountability requirements with teeth. Other legislators announced their intentions to strengthen federal mandates in related areas, especially in connection with the controversial opportunity-to-learn standards. Liberal Senators Paul Simon (D-IL; 1993 ADA: 85) and Carol Moseley-Braun (D-IL; 1993 ADA: 85), Paul D. Wellstone (D-MN; 1993 ADA: 100), and Representative Major R. Owens (D-NY), along with Reed, stood out as legislators who openly pressed for more account-ability by states for meeting the standards and equalizing educational opportunity. It is especially interesting to recall this aspect of the Goals 2000 debate in light of No Child Left Behind's subsequent adoption of a high-stakes accountability system for schools, districts, and states. These sentiments did not carry the day in 1994, but they were starting to emerge.

Representative Thomas C. Sawyer (D-OH; 1993 ADA: 85) made a more typical argument in favor of Goals 2000. These moderate impulses and others like them shaped final legislation that was politically viable, although still controversial.

> The most important feature of the bill is its endorsement of voluntary national content standards in the core subjects. You will hear arguments today that this will lead to the adoption of a

de facto national curriculum. This is simply false. These standards
are strictly voluntary and will provide States and local communities models that they can adopt or adapt to meet their own
educational needs as they define them. In other words, these
voluntary national content standards do not in any way thwart
local diversity or decision-making. The adoption of standards will
provide schools with an organizing tool, to target their finances,
enrich their curriculum and improve their teacher training. For
students the standards are a set of clear objectives for what they
need to know, and be able to do. (Ibid., 24288)

Representative Dale E. Kildee (D-MI; 1993 ADA: 90) also had a succinct,
moderate rationale for the legislation, which, incidentally, was also rooted
in a key idea about systemic reform: "Goals 2000 is built on the idea that
limited Federal dollars can be used to leverage change at the State and
local level" (ibid., 24287). Senator Kennedy agreed: "This is a bottoms-up
education reform with support from the top down. But it is basically and
essentially a bottoms-up program of school reform" (*Congressional Record*
1994a, 852).

Charges that Goals 2000 would lead to an increasingly prescriptive
federal role in schools and a national curriculum were difficult to refute
even though they seemed farfetched at the time. Notice that Representative Sawyer responded by reminding his listeners that the standards were
voluntary. The national curriculum charge stemmed from the constella-
tion of standards specified in the Goals 2000 bills and the national bodies
charged with overseeing them. The National Education Standards and
Improvement Council would become a de facto "national school board,"
according to numerous critics, and eventually force state leaders and local
educators to comply with national curriculum standards, performance
standards, and, worst of all, opportunity-to-learn standards.

Opportunity-to-Learn Standards

Foes of Goals 2000 contended that opportunity-to-learn standards (also
known as "school delivery" or "input" standards) were the most pernicious
of the standards outlined in the legislation. According to their arguments,
these standards would enable the federal government to judge the adequacy
of school resources such as class size, teacher preparation, and facilities
as a condition for receiving federal funds. Opportunity-to-learn standards

were at the center of a broader ideological dispute about the federal role
during this episode. Would Goals 2000 lead to unfunded mandates for
school resource "inputs" that ignored student achievement, as critics contended? Or, might opportunity-to-learn standards simply be a voluntary
model for schools wanting to evaluate whether students had what they
needed to reach internationally competitive content and performance
standards, as supporters maintained? A softened approach to opportunity-
to-learn standards was crafted for the final versions of Goals 2000 (and
the Improving America's Schools Act), but this compromise did little to
placate opponents of the legislation.

The George H. W. Bush administration's America 2000 plan was
amended by congressional Democrats to include strong school delivery
provisions, which partly account for why that proposal lost (Pitsch 1995, 18).
Several iterations of requirements for developing and reporting opportunity-
to-learn standards were later debated in connection with Goals 2000 in
1993–94. In general, liberals were reluctant to set curriculum and performance standards without also ensuring that local educators gave students
a reasonable opportunity to achieve them. Many conservatives, on the other
hand, believed that opportunity-to-learn standards would enable educators
to evade their responsibility for poor student performance by blaming the
lack of resources. The result, some predicted, would be increased litigation
over the adequacy of school resources and increased federal control.

Opportunity-to-learn standards were part of the Clinton administration's
April 1993 Goals 2000 proposal to Congress. Secretary Riley gave some
examples of these "resources, practices, and conditions" in his prepared
statement to the Senate Committee on Labor and Human Resources:
"Through the 'Goals 2000 Act,' voluntary exemplary opportunity-to-learn
standards will be identified in essential areas related directly to teaching and
learning, such as the quality and availability of curricula and materials
and professional development of teachers to deliver this higher content"
(U.S. Senate 1993a, 7).

Misgivings about opportunity-to-learn standards surfaced immediately.
Senator Nancy L. Kassebaum (R-KS; 1993 ADA: 35) stated her concerns in
a statement written before the Senate hearing even began:

> Provisions in the bill relating to the development of school
> delivery or opportunity-to-learn standards also open the door to
> future attempts to decide at the federal level educational "inputs"
> ranging from class size to teacher credentials. I do not believe
> that States should be encouraged to develop such standards in

the image of the model national standards which will be developed by one small group, which may or may not come up with the best approach. Even though States are to develop their own opportunity-to-learn standards, the bill's ultimate goal is to have those State standards eventually mirror the national standards. This is a significantly broader, and I would argue intrusive, role for the Federal Government in education. Furthermore, to ask States to develop these [opportunity-to-learn] standards in concert with the as-yet undeveloped national [content and performance] standards is to require a monumental task, given the lack of available research to show direct correlations between inputs and learning. (Ibid., 3–4)

Kassebaum supported S.1150 as reported by the Senate Committee on Labor and Human Resources, with weakened language on opportunity-to-learn standards. According to another member of the committee, Senator James M. Jeffords (then R-VT; 1993 ADA: 60), "The committee substitute requires all States to address the issue in some fashion in their State plan, but leaves the specifics up to each individual State" (*Congressional Record* 1994a, 855). An amendment by Senator Kennedy during Senate floor consideration of the committee report softened the language even further by introducing opportunity-to-learn "strategies" instead of "standards": "Each State improvement plan shall establish strategies for providing all students with an opportunity to learn" (ibid., 877). The final version of Goals 2000 incorporated the "strategies" language, along with the suggestion that one possible approach was for states to develop opportunity-to-learn standards (P.L.103-227, Title III, sec. 306[d][1]).

Some Democrats in the House of Representatives, on the other hand, insisted on using opportunity-to-learn standards as a lever for ensuring equal educational opportunity. At one point, even the opportunity-to-learn-standards-favoring Clinton administration opposed the stronger House language (Elmore and Fuhrman 1995, 432–33; Riley 1995, 385–86). As reported to the full House by the Committee on Education and Labor, H.R.1804 had the following requirements for addressing opportunity-to-learn standards in state plans:

Each State plan shall establish a strategy and timetable for—
(1) adopting or establishing opportunity-to-learn standards prior to or simultaneous with the establishment or adoption of challenging content and student performance standards;

(2) ensuring that every school in the State is making demons-
trable progress toward meeting the State's opportunity-to-learn
standards;

(3) ensuring that the State's opportunity-to-learn standards address
the needs of all students;

(4) providing for periodic independent assessments of the extent
to which opportunity-to-learn standards are being met throughout the State; and

(5) periodically reporting to the public on the extent of the State's
improvement in achieving such standards and providing all students
with a fair opportunity to achieve the knowledge and skill levels
that meet the State's content and student performance standards.
(U.S. House of Representatives 1993a, 16 [H.R.1804, Title III,
sec. 306(d)])

Opportunity-to-learn standards in this rendering were voluntary only
to the extent that states sought to have them certified by the National
Education Standards and Improvement Council (ibid., 10 [H.R.1804, Title
II, Part B, sec. 213(d)]). They had to be addressed in detail in state plans,
along with related strategies for assessing state progress in meeting them.
Again, language much closer to the looser Senate version was ultimately
inserted in the conference report (the final law), but the House language
seems to have permanently tainted all references to "opportunity-to-learn
standards or strategies."

Senator Claiborne Pell (D-RI; 1993 ADA: 85) supported a stronger definition of opportunity-to-learn standards as a means for holding politicians
accountable for educational quality. "Goals 2000 establishes voluntary
opportunity-to-learn standards that define the teaching and learning conditions necessary for all students to have a fair and equitable chance at receiving
a world-class education. Opportunity-to-learn standards will empower the
public to hold not only schools but also policymakers accountable for the
results they produce. They are essential to an education of equity and
excellence" (*Congressional Record* 1994a, 856).

Senator Gregg (R-NH) did not distinguish between the weaker and
stronger definitions because he opposed them both. "'Opportunity-to-learn,'
that is a nice euphemism," he said. "What it really means is Federal
methodology for teaching. That is really the proper definition of it, if you
are going to be accurate. It is the methodology of how people teach and
what they are taught and the atmosphere in which they are taught" (ibid.,
861). Senator Kassebaum, supporting the more flexible wording in S.1150,

tried to get Senator Gregg to acknowledge the same distinction in the dialogue below. Notice that both senators recognize what I have called the "delayed reaction" threat of federal control in earlier chapters.

> Kassebaum: It is not mandatory language, as you know. It is only there as a voluntary guideline. I share the Senator's concern because I think from that it could lead to other consequences if, indeed, it ever became mandatory.
>
> Gregg: [A]s a practical matter, it is mandatory. I believe it is unquestionably going to end up being language which is not only put in place—directives and specific criteria on what type and how people should be taught—but that it is going to become the enforcing mechanism throughout our school systems in a very short time after its adoption. (Ibid., 862)

Senator Kassebaum ultimately voted against the Goals 2000 conference report but was aware of the different versions of the bill, at least one of which she could support. Kassebaum's Senate colleagues John C. Danforth (R-MO; 1993 ADA: 35), Alan K. Simpson (R-WY; 1993 ADA: 20), and William S. Cohen (R-ME; 1993 ADA: 40) also cited opportunity-to-learn provisions that they saw as too strong as their reason for opposing the conference report. Like Kassebaum, these senators supported S.1150 as passed by the Senate on February 8, 1994. Danforth had an additional concern about opportunity-to-learn standards. "The inclusion of such standards increases the likelihood of litigation with regard to school financing and equity issues," he said, referring to what many conservatives believed was at the core of opportunity-to-learn standards. "The distribution of resources with regard to school financing is a matter of local concern and one in which the Federal Government should not be enmeshed" (ibid., 6983).

This debate raised other issues too. Senator Dave Durenberger (R-MN; 1993 ADA: 75) voted with the committee majority to report S.1150 to the full Senate, but he had philosophical misgivings about opportunity-to-learn standards. He contended in his "Additional Views" section of the committee report that to focus on inputs evaded real reform and real accountability. "Put most simply, real reform down-plays inputs and focuses on outcomes. Opportunity to learn standards, on the other hand, could stop real education reform dead in its tracks by shielding schools from any form of outcome-based accountability. Taken to their extreme, opportunity to learn standards will be a fig leaf behind which failing schools can forever stand because I fear we will never be able to guarantee every school in America the tools that input-oriented regulations will deem necessary to achieve an equal opportunity to succeed" (U.S. Senate 1993b, 59).

Representative William F. Goodling (R-PA) also debated how to sequence inputs and outcomes. During hearings before the House Subcommittee on Elementary, Secondary, and Vocational Education on the initial version of H.R.1804, Goodling said: "[T]he bill requires that States and districts ensure that schools provide an opportunity to learn but does not require that States and districts ensure that students actually learn any more. It is this disconnection between results and opportunity that troubles me. How can we know if students have an opportunity to learn unless we first know what it is they should learn and whether or not they have truly learned it?" (U.S. House of Representatives 1993b, 2).

Opportunity-to-learn standards were troubling to opponents of Goals 2000. Indeed, these standards even made foes out of some potential supporters who feared that opportunity-to-learn mandates would lead to increased federal prescriptiveness, interference, and control. (The same thing happened during consideration of the Improving America's Schools Act, by which time opportunity-to-learn standards had become even more contentious.) Federal-control rhetoric has riddled education debates for decades, and Goals 2000 inflamed the concern in several ways.

Federal and Local Control in Goals 2000

The extent to which Goals 2000 represented a threat to state and local educational prerogatives was a major topic of debate and disagreement in Congress. Some conservatives saw any federal action on behalf of schools, no matter how well-intentioned, as serious threats to local autonomy. Supporters of expanded federal involvement denied these threats but agreed with the principle of state and local responsibility for education. Many other legislators explored the middle ground, seeking the appropriate level of federal assistance and a balance between federal and local priorities.

Senator Kassebaum returned to this issue throughout the Senate deliberations. Her stance with respect to the administration's bill was open-minded but skeptical about certain aspects, especially its possible threat to local autonomy: "My single biggest concern with the bill is that its bureaucratic and prescriptive nature and top-down approach may stifle rather than assist reform efforts which are already being undertaken at the State and local levels. All over this country, States and localities are actively engaged in exciting and innovative reform efforts. They have undertaken these efforts without a great deal of Federal prescription, and I do not think that the Federal Government should infringe on those efforts or redefine what States should be doing" (U.S. Senate 1993a, 3).

As noted above, Senator Gregg (R-NH) remained opposed to the measure for a number of reasons. He was joined by Senators Dan Coats (R-IN; 1993 ADA: 20) and Orrin G. Hatch (R-UT; 1993 ADA: 5) in signing the "Minority Views" section of the committee report on S.1150. They expressed their beliefs about the federal interference entailed by the bill. "Goals 2000 is top-down management, which greatly increases the role of the Federal Government in the area of education—an area which has traditionally been the responsibility of States and local school districts. This Federal intrusion is especially objectionable since Federal education investments account for only about 7 percent of total education spending in the United States. The Federal bureaucracy should not be dictating to the States how and where to spend their education dollars" (U.S. Senate 1993b, 62).

Judd Gregg attended the 1989 Charlottesville Education Summit as governor of New Hampshire. Governors Bill Clinton, Richard Riley, and Lamar Alexander were also there. Senator Gregg had no objection to the national education goals per se, but he believed that S.1150 exceeded that mandate: "It is a significant power grab by the Federal Government for the structure to try to obtain control—control may be too strong a word—but to try to obtain a significant and dominant role in the manner and methodology of education of our children in the elementary-secondary school systems" (*Congressional Record* 1994a, 859). Senator Kassebaum expressed concern about the form of federal involvement under the National Education Goals Panel and the National Education Standards and Improvement Council: "I . . . question whether it is the Federal Government's role to tell communities that the school board they elected is not good enough to make their education decisions for them." She was also concerned about testing provisions designed on a national scale that might not be useful to classroom teachers (U.S. Senate 1993a, 3).

Senator Strom Thurmond (R-SC; 1993 ADA: 10) was interested in the parent and community involvement aspects of systemic reform but believed that Goals 2000 was too prescriptive and gave states and school districts little flexibility for aligning federal funds with their own reform priorities:

> [W]hile we work on education reform legislation, we should try to keep the Federal regulatory requirements to a minimum. The Federal Government should become a partner in State and local

reform efforts, and not a barrier. Unfortunately, this legislation places too many barriers upon the States.

For example, I strongly support the State block grant for systemic education improvement because of the support it provides each State to develop its own reform plan with its own priorities. However, the proposals contained in this legislation are so prescriptive that it virtually writes the plans for the States. . . .

I also believe that the delivery of opportunity-to-learn standards should be left to the local communities. I am concerned that this legislation would lead to Federal regulations as to how instruction should be delivered and how local schools should be organized.

Finally, Mr. Chairman, I believe that more of the funding should be given to the local level and less to bureaucracy. I am concerned that the money provided by this legislation does not flow in the most efficient way to the local levels. (Ibid., 23–24)

Liberal Senator James M. Jeffords (R-VT) reported similar concerns in his "Additional Views" section of the committee report. Jeffords was active on the committee, generally supported the Goals 2000 legislation, and ultimately voted for the conference report. However, he was troubled by the requirement for federal approval of state improvement plans under Title III: "In establishing strategies to improve teaching, learning, standards, and assessments, State planning groups are required to include certain pre-determined strategies in their State improvement plans. I fear that this requirement detracts from local ownership of the reform process and continue to believe that the prescriptive nature of this section should be deleted" (U.S. Senate 1993b, 56).

No advocate of Goals 2000 denied the importance of local decision-making; most supporters simply wanted to supplement local initiatives with national resources. All legislators were obligated to favor a limited federal role in the name of state and local educational autonomy. This rhetoric contrasted with widespread mistrust of local educators that seemed to underlie the debate over the Elementary and Secondary Education Act in 1965. During the Goals 2000 debate, for example, Senator Gregg believed that the "dominant factor" of high-quality schools "is a high degree of local participation in designing the way the school is run." There are other factors too, but local control is key. Continuing, Gregg gored a sacred cow, the Education for All Handicapped Children Act (P.L.94-142), by suggesting that Goals 2000 resembled P.L.94-142 because they both undermined local control:

In fact, Federal regulation is anathema to local control. In fact, probably in the most aggressive experiment the Federal Government has taken on in the area of education is the area of P.L.94-142, which is the curriculums area. In insisting and setting up a Federal structure on how children shall be educated who have handicaps and disabilities, the Federal Government's dominance in that area has become so aggressive that it has in many instances undermined what might have been initiatives on the local level which would have created even a better atmosphere for that child. (*Congressional Record* 1994a, 859)

Representative Owens (D-NY) practically ridiculed the alleged threat to local control in Goals 2000 and supplied a mathematical rationale for his dismissal of it, an argument that assumes an exact correspondence between share of funds and degree of control: "As my colleagues know, if we raise the percentage of the Federal involvement of each school district to 25 percent, . . . there is still the other 75 percent of local control. . . . local control is not threatened at all" (*Congressional Record* 1993, 24335).

In most debates about the federal government's role in education, those who favor expanding that role must overcome the standing assumption that education is primarily a function of local communities and state governments. That assumption was manipulated with great success by federal-aid opponents until the 1950s, when federal action started to increase. Since then, supporters of new federal policies for education have had to justify those actions as legitimate supplements to what was already happening or catalysts for desired behavior by educators. That is, there must be good reasons for alterations to the philosophical tradition of limited federal involvement. A riskier approach—one taken by Representative Owens—was simply to deny that the new program compromises state and local autonomy or, in his earlier comments, to challenge the "romantic notion" of local control. Critics of Goals 2000 did not buy his logic.

School Choice and School Prayer Amendments to Goals 2000

Several components of the final version of Goals 2000 were controversial. A few ill-fated amendments also generated a disproportionate share of controversy, given that there was no way they would pass. From the point of view of Goals 2000 supporters, these tangential debates may have drawn unwanted attention to the program that later led to stronger opposition.

The George H. W. Bush administration's America 2000 proposals foundered in the 101st and 102nd Congresses in part because they included voucher provisions. Many conservatives and Republicans in Congress wanted to keep this agenda alive by amending or replacing Goals 2000 with private-school choice programs. To this end, Representative Richard K. Armey (R-TX) attempted to substitute an entirely rewritten Goals 2000 bill that established a large, federally funded choice program. The amendment received fairly serious attention in the House, even though it was decisively defeated.

School-choice rhetoric inside and outside Congress was likely to refer to competition within the education marketplace as the missing ingredient of school reform. Several legislators viewed "competition" as the philosophical opposite of "bureaucracy." Senator Coats (R-IN) believed that the federal government should foster "competition within the system" rather than "layering additional levels of bureaucracy and administration." Private schools should be studied to learn what makes them more cost-effective and competitive than public schools. Coats also said, "I . . . have real questions as to whether or not we can achieve educational reforms within a single system that is competitive with itself and not competing with an alternative. It is like telling GM, 'You aren't going to have any competition from Honda or BMW or any other car maker—just reform yourself—you've got the whole market—just reform yourself.' I really question whether we can do that without competition from outside the system" (U.S. Senate 1993a, 15–17).

Several months later, Senator Coats tried to amend the Senate Goals 2000 bill to "provide a low-income school choice demonstration program." The program would have initiated six school-district pilot projects at a cost of $30 million (*Congressional Record* 1994a, 1201). Senator Christopher J. Dodd (D-CT; 1993 ADA: 75) opposed this amendment, which was defeated, and added some observations about demonstration projects and the scientific method:

> There is a fundamental difference of view as to whether or not we ought to be in the business of funding a dual system of education, whether it is a pilot program in 1 district or in 10 or in 100. My view is this is fundamentally a bad idea, and bad ideas do not need to be demonstrated.
>
> One might suggest that perhaps we ought to increase the speed limit. Why not try out a 100 miles-per-hour speed limit in certain districts to see how it works? Or others might wonder if people who said they were damaged by nuclear testing were really damaged and test again. (Ibid., 1207)

The Armey substitute amendment in the House of Representatives was the focal point for most remarks about school choice in that chamber. Many comments explicitly contrasted the comparatively prescriptive House version of Goals 2000 and the Armey substitute. Representatives Armey, Hoekstra, Ballenger, and Boehner—the latter two were co-sponsors of the substitute amendment—signed the "Supplemental Dissenting Views" section of the House committee report. The committee had rejected the substitute earlier. These dissenters referred to "merit schools, model schools (including charter schools), school choice programs, and site-based management (with an emphasis on alternative certification)" as "promising approaches to reform." Their dissent concluded: "Throughout the Committee consideration of H.R.1804, one thing certainly became clear—we are faced with a choice in America today—a choice between the old, discredited policies of the status quo, liberal education establishment, or something new, something that will empower parents and communities throughout this country with the ability to make their own decisions about who will educate their children" (U.S. House of Representatives 1993a, 68).

Three months later, when the House was poised to reject his substitute, Representative Armey made one last plea on its behalf: "This is a simple matter, very simple matter. Do you care about union monopoly control over the lives and the future of the children of America more than you care about the rights of parents to do what is best for their children and the ability of children to really, in fact, learn their ABC's instead of how to put a condom on a banana? Give me a break" (*Congressional Record* 1993, 24340).

Representative Goodling opposed the Armey amendment, warning that federal control of private schools might result from the provisions of the substitute (ibid., 24333). For their part, private-school advocates and educators have sometimes been wary of regulatory strings that might be attached to federal aid earmarked for them (Anderson 1997, 137–38).

The school-prayer debate was more of a procedural distraction than a dispute about the appropriate role of the federal government in schools. Senator Jesse A. Helms (R-NC; 1993 ADA: 10) had proposed countless school-prayer amendments to education legislation since entering the Senate in 1972. A few comments from the debate are worth including here because they illustrate broader issues about government control and the history of federal involvement in schools. In the Senate, Senator Carl Levin (D-MI) opposed the Helms amendment because of its threat to local control:

> [T]he Helms amendment is an example of the Federal Government's, in effect, imposing on locally elected school boards the

requirement that they allow voluntary prayer in school as long as it would not violate the Constitution. In other words, it could override a locally elected school board's decision not to allow voluntary school prayer if that school board seeks any funding from the Department of Education.

At a time of increasing concern about Federal mandates and the overriding of local decision-making, this amendment is particularly troublesome because it is in the context of our first amendment freedoms. (*Congressional Record* 1994a, 1100)

In the House, Representative James M. Inhofe (R-OK; 1993 ADA: 10) cited research by David Barton (1988) in urging that school prayer language be inserted in the conference report: "[Barton] charted the behavioral patterns of violent crime, of drug addiction, rapes, teenage pregnancies, and for 200 years that line was a parallel line until 1963 when it shoots off the charts. And what happened in 1963? That is when the Supreme Court took God out of the public schools" (*Congressional Record* 1994a, 6080).

The school-prayer debate was replayed during consideration of the Improving America's Schools Act, along with some of the other issues that shaped the final Goals 2000 law (for example, opportunity-to-learn standards). Yet, there were important differences in the debates and the resulting statutes. The primary focus of this chapter is Goals 2000, but the Improving America's Schools Act (IASA) is important too. Like Goals 2000, the IASA was considered and passed during the 103rd Congress. It also reflected the attitudes of national legislators toward federal aid for educationally disadvantaged students, and education reform generally, in the last reauthorization of the Elementary and Secondary Education Act before the No Child Left Behind Act of 2001.

The Improving America's Schools Act

Even though the Improving America's Schools Act of 1994 descended politically from the much older framework of the Elementary and Secondary Education Act of 1965, its ideological meaning flowed from Goals 2000 and the larger standards movement of the 1990s. As interpreted by the Clinton administration and many legislators in Congress, standards-based reform meant high expectations for all students, including educationally disadvantaged students who received Title I services. Assistant Secretary of Elementary and Secondary Education Thomas Payzant described this new idea to the Human Resources and Intergovernmental Relations Sub-committee of the House Committee on Government Operations in October 1993: "The first principle is based on high standards for all students, not a two-tiered system where we treat those who are served by Title I in one way, with a set of lower expectations than those that we have for our most successful students in the past. We must have the same high standards for all" (U.S. House of Representatives 1998, 9). A full year later, Senator Edward Kennedy described this logic in more detail when he summarized the IASA conference report on the Senate floor:

> First, this bill creates a new Title I Program based on high stan-dards for all students. Over 90 percent of the school districts in the country have been receiving these funds for years. But their use has been focused on bringing some low-income children only up to the standard of other low-income children not in the program. This misguided emphasis has had the unintended effect of creating thousands of separate, watered-down programs that have been found ineffective. We set our sights too low.
>
> The core of this bill will scrap that dead-end low-standard approach and establish high academic standards for all students. It will hold disadvantaged students to the same standards that all other students are held. Why should we target disadvantaged students for special aid, and then educate them to a lower standard than other children? (*Congressional Record* 1994a, 27849)

Again, there were ideological disagreements in the consideration of the Improving America's Schools Act, especially around opportunity-to-learn standards, but the IASA debate also marked the beginning of an ideological convergence of ideas around standards-based reform, high expectations for all students, and accountability. The final legislation incor-porated several key compromises, like making many of the law's most novel provisions unenforceable (McGuinn 2006, 179 and 181), but it started a serious discussion about the need to shift the attention of federal education policy-makers from inputs and spending levels to student out-comes and high standards. Congress stopped short of the kinds of require-ments and sanctions it would impose under No Child Left Behind seven years later, but the direction of future federal involvement in schools was coming into view. In the House floor debate of the IASA bill, Repre-sentative Dale Kildee made a prescient comment about the new federal vision of accountability:

As a matter of fact, the whole bill can be summed up in two words: "flexibility" and "accountability." The legislation is replete with provisions giving educators the flexibility to combine Federal aid in whatever fashion is needed to improve education and to seek waivers from rules and regulations whenever it is necessary to improve achievement. But the accountability with that flexibility is equally clear. If educational gains are not achieved, then school districts are expected to help schools improve, and, if there is still no success, then States are expected to intervene to secure the results. (*Congressional Record* 1994b, H803-H804)

The halting ideological shifts that were in evidence in the debate about the Improving America's Schools Act are important from the standpoint of No Child Left Behind, which was the next reauthorization of the Elementary and Secondary Education Act. At the time, however, political factors played a much larger role in the consideration of the IASA than did the ideological discussion. This phenomenon is understandable, given the fact that the ESEA, compared with Goals 2000, was an established program with a substantially larger sum of federal dollars attached to it. Funding for the first year of Goals 2000 (fiscal year 1994) was $105 million (Congressional Quarterly Inc. 1995, 397). Fiscal year 1995 funding for the Improving America's Schools Act was $12.7 billion, of which $7.4 billion went to Title I (ibid., 383). Goals 2000 was a framework for standards-based reform for all students that included relatively modest grants to states. IASA sponsors intended that the billions of dollars in Title I aid for educationally disadvantaged students would be spent according to the new Goals 2000-inspired thinking in states and school districts.

The politicized elements of the debate over the Improving America's Schools Act drew as much from the twenty-eight-year track record of the Elementary and Secondary Education Act as they did from the IASA's arranged marriage to Goals 2000. The most significant issue from the legacy of the ESEA was the formula for allocating Title I funds to states and school districts. Recall from Chapter 3 that the 1965 ESEA formula managed to accomplish two distinct and not wholly compatible goals: provide supplementary education aid to low-achieving students in high poverty areas *and* funnel program dollars to every congressional jurisdiction and the vast majority of school districts in the United States. The political, ideological, and educational arguments for the Elementary and Secondary Education Act in 1965 demanded a funding formula for Title I that satisfied a number of different interests and viewpoints.

The 1988 reauthorization of the Elementary and Secondary Education Act (P.L.100-297) addressed some of the logical inconsistencies and omissions in the original formula. The 1988 law, also called the Augustus F. Hawkins–Robert T. Stafford Elementary and Secondary School Improvement Amendments, introduced "schoolwide projects" to Title I/Chapter 1. (Title I was renamed Chapter 1 in the 1981 reauthorization of the Elementary and Secondary Education Act.) Schoolwide projects were designed to provide Title I/Chapter 1 assistance to all students in schools with levels of poverty that were 75 percent or greater (P.L.100-297, Title I, sec. 1015), thereby targeting "compensatory education" funds at schools where needs were highest. The schoolwide approach was also intended to reduce pressure on schools to "pull out" Title I/Chapter 1 students from their regular classrooms. (These students still needed to be identified for accounting purposes, but the 1988 law allowed compensatory education services to be delivered to non–Title I/Chapter 1 students [ibid.].)

Several commissions, interest groups, and researchers studied the implementation of the 1988 reauthorization and made recommendations for the 1994 reauthorization of the Elementary and Secondary Education Act (that is, the IASA). One of these panels, the Commission on Chapter 1, stands out because of its influence on the Clinton administration's proposals for Title I/Chapter 1 and the subsequent deliberations in Congress. Among the commission's recommendations was that "funding for this program should be concentrated more heavily in schools with concentrations of children in poverty, where the needs are far greater than in low-concentration schools" (Commission on Chapter 1 1992, 8). The commission also admonished Congress to make Title I/Chapter 1 "a vehicle for improving whole schools serving concentrations of poor children" (ibid., 7) and, it is important to note, to hold these schools more accountable for results.

President Clinton's initial reauthorization proposal to Congress incorporated a Title I/Chapter 1 targeting formula inspired by the commission's recommendations. In general, the proposed targeting recommendation favored urban areas with high concentrations and high numbers of children in poverty. At the same time, the proposal reduced the eligibility threshold for schoolwide projects, enabling more schools to implement whole-school Title I/Chapter 1 programs. To soften the blow to states and school districts standing to lose funds, the new formula would be phased in under what the federal education laws usually call "hold harmless" provisions. Nevertheless, the meaning of the administration's proposal was clear to senators and representatives accustomed to wide distribution of federal education funds. There would be "winners" and "losers" under the new formula for

Title I/Chapter 1 funds. Legislators in both chambers of Congress were very candid about declaring their support for the legislation only if their state or congressional district received its share (or more) of Title I/Chapter 1 dollars. The deliberation about the different formulas—and the types of states and communities they would benefit—was the most dominant issue in the Improving America's Schools Act debate.

Senator Kennedy was one legislator who claimed to see both sides of the effort to correct the Title I/Chapter 1 formula. He conceded that some states would win and some would lose (including Massachusetts), "[b]ut the current formula is badly flawed, and it would be irresponsible to continue it. The new formula is a fair compromise that makes better use of scarce Federal dollars by better targeting funds to States with the greatest need, while mitigating the dislocation to States that have benefited for so long from the old, failed, and flawed formula. No States will lose unduly, and the Nation will gain immensely" (*Congressional Record* 1994a, 27849).

On its face, the formula debate looked more political than ideological. At the time, it was: projected winners and losers of federal funds were engaged in a political struggle. Expressed principles, values, and beliefs about how money ought to be allocated were shaped by individual calculations of gains and losses under different formula schemes and the votes that different proposals would garner. Knowing what we do today about the growth of the accountability movement since the mid-1990s enables us to interpret the IASA Title I/Chapter 1 formula debate through an ideological lens.

The promise of widely distributed federal Title I funds after passage of the Elementary and Secondary Education Act in 1965 gave the program the feel of a de facto institutional entitlement—federal monies that all regions, states, and most school districts and schools were entitled to receive. (Compare this kind of funding with grants for which agencies must compete.) Institutions came to expect these funds, even those that served relatively low poverty communities. Of course, educationally disadvantaged students have needs no matter where they live, and politicians and educators understood that there would be restrictions on the allowable uses of Title I funds. Nevertheless, the Title I/Chapter 1 formula before and after 1994 had the paradoxical effect of generating its own political support by blunting the effectiveness of the program's ostensible purpose: helping students from poor families.

There is one more implication of Title I/Chapter 1 targeting over time. If we understand the Clinton administration's demands for more concentrated targeting of Title I/Chapter 1 funds in light of the subsequent growth of the school accountability movement, the Improving America's Schools Act becomes an important step toward putting the federal government at the center of public-school accountability. It turned out to be a relatively short trip from demands for increased effectiveness and accountability from Title I/Chapter 1 schools—demands that were not fully realized in the IASA—to demands for similar results from *all* schools under No Child Left Behind.

Before turning to the analysis of No Child Left Behind in Chapter 7, there is some unfinished business to settle with regard to Goals 2000.

Description of the 1994 Goals 2000 Votes

The votes on the H.R.1804 conference report, the final version of the bill that became the Goals 2000 law, indicate a decisive split between liberals and conservatives, as measured by 1993 ADA scores (Table 6). Democrats and Republicans were also clearly divided in both chambers. Support by Democrats was virtually unanimous; Republicans opposed the measure by margins of 2 to 1. Within each party, the ideological splits were also unambiguous. Democrats and Republicans who voted for the measure were more liberal than their counterparts who opposed it. It is important to notice, however, that within-party splits did not blur the greater degree of liberalness displayed by Democrats compared with Republicans in the 103rd Congress. For example, Democratic "no" votes were more liberal than Republican "yes" votes on Goals 2000.

The Response to Goals 2000 After 1994

Goals 2000 remained a thorn in the side of conservatives after it passed. The Republican-controlled 104th Congress repealed some key provisions of Goals 2000 after initially threatening to dismantle the whole program. As part of the Omnibus Consolidated Rescissions and Appropriations Act, passed on April 26, 1996, Congress repealed the National Education Standards and Improvement Council and all requirements related to state and federal establishment of opportunity-to-learn standards or strategies. Specific membership requirements for state planning panels were also relaxed, as were requirements for submitting state plans to the Department of Education for review and approval. Congress also authorized districts in states that were not participating in the program as of October 20,

Table 6   1994 Goals 2000 Votes with 1993 ADA Statistics

1994 Goals 2000 votes with 1993 ADA scores	House March 23, 1994	Senate March 26, 1994
Final vote on H.R.1804 (i.e., Goals 2000 conference report)	306–121 (71.7% "yes")	63–22 (74.1% "yes")
Democrats	246–6 (97.6% "yes")	53–1 (98.1% "yes")
Republicans	59–115 (33.9% "yes")	10–21 (32.2% "yes")
Independents	1–0	—
ADA Score Analyses		
Mean ADA score of "yes" voters	65.9 (n=306)	72.2 (n=63)
Mean ADA score of "no" voters	9.6 (n=121)	15.6 (n=22)
Mean ADA score of Democrat "yes" voters	75.8 (n=246)	77.3 (n=53)
Mean ADA score of Republican "yes" voters	24.1 (n=59)	45.5 (n=10)
Mean ADA score of Democrat "no" voters	39.2 (n=6)	55 (n=1)
Mean ADA score of Republican "no" voters	8.1 (n=115)	13.7 (n=21)
Mean Democrat ADA score (whole chamber)	74.9 (n=257)	76.2 (n=56)
Mean Republican ADA score (whole chamber)	13.5 (n=176)	21.2 (n=44)
Mean ADA of whole chamber (1993)	50.0 (n=434)	52.0 (n=100)

NOTE: ADA = Americans for Democratic Action; n = the number of legislators in each cell with 1993 ADA scores. ADA figures in the "whole chamber" cells include all legislators, regardless of whether they participated in the final vote on Goals 2000. The 1995 ADA score was used for one House member who did not have a 1993 score. The House had one vacancy when the Goals 2000 vote occurred.
SOURCES: Congressional Quarterly Inc. 1995, 15-S and 26-H–27-H for the votes on Goals 2000 and Americans for Democratic Action website for ADA scores. (Scores downloaded October 20, 2005, from http://www.adaction.org/1993.pdf and http://www.adaction.org/ 1995.pdf.)

1995 to bypass state agencies and, with state approval, apply directly to the Department of Education for local Goals 2000 grants. The amendments clarified that allowable uses of funds included acquisition of technology for student instruction, making Goals 2000 resemble a flexible block grant. Finally, the revisions clarified that nothing in the legislation was to be "construed to require" outcomes-based education, school-based clinics, or social services (U.S. Department of Education 1996, 36–38).

The same 1994 elections in which the House and Senate changed hands also affected state governments. There were a number of partisan squabbles about state participation in Goals 2000, some of which may have influenced the 1996 revisions. The amendments, in turn, also affected state decisions to apply for grants. In all states where political leaders were reluctant to accept Goals 2000 funds, fear of federal interference in state and local education affairs was cited (Anderson 1997, 168–70). Some state educators and policy-makers negotiated individual arrangements with the Department of Education to use grants to address state priorities. To the chagrin of the Department of Education, some states actually accepted congressional and administration assurances that participation in Goals 2000 was voluntary. Given the relatively small amounts of money involved, compared with the funding levels of the Improving America's Schools Act, and the lack of a strong constituency for a federal role in standards-based reform, it may have been relatively easy to decline Goals 2000 grants on principle. Some states actually did so for a time (ibid., 168–70).

Ideology and the Status Quo

The extent to which Goals 2000 represented a genuine departure from the tradition of federal involvement in elementary and secondary education was in the ideology of the beholder. What Representative Dale E. Kildee (D-MI) referred to as "a process for building a national consensus for education improvement" (*Congressional Record* 1993, 24286), Christian home-schooling advocate Cathy Duffy called "the framework for a cradle-to-grave takeover of America's families" (Duffy 1995, 5). Because of the ideological controversies provoked by this vision of school reform, Goals 2000 eventually was reduced to a symbolic victory for the Clinton administration. Congress and the administration misread the ideological mandate for a federal role in standards-based school improvement in 1993 and 1994, thereby authorizing a program that could not be implemented according to its original plan.

Most supporters of Goals 2000 believed that the federal government was indeed assuming a new role: supporting standards-based reform for all students rather than assisting several categories of special populations in uncoordinated fashion. The new role did not mean that state and local autonomy would be compromised or that the existing federal role would cease. It meant only that the federal approach would assimilate the school-reform trends of the 1990s, a phenomenon called "borrowed strength" by Paul Manna (2006, 103). If supporters thought the legislation would mean anything more radical, they mostly kept quiet about it. Yet, it is also clear that Goals 2000 supporters were pleased with the new ground being broken under the legislation. Representative Kildee, chair of the Subcommittee on Elementary, Secondary, and Vocational Education, and Democratic manager of the floor debate in the House, defended Goals 2000 as a needed departure from past federal reform strategies:

Goals 2000 represents a major departure from the way that the Federal Government has assisted education in the past.

It is the first effort that seeks to use limited Federal funds as an incentive for public-school districts to undertake systemic reform.

Historically, most education reform efforts have dealt with a single part of the system, such as improving testing, or have focused on special populations.

In contrast, Goals 2000 emphasizes systemwide reform because sustained improvements will not occur without coordinated changes in all parts of the education system. (*Congressional Record* 1993, 24286)

Representative Karan English (D-AZ; 1993 ADA score: 90) also supported Goals 2000 as an antidote to the damage done, in part, by federal categorical programs. "Through providing States the tools they need to advance their own school reform initiatives, we will bring focus back to the fragmented and categoricalized American public education system" (ibid., 24293). Representative Barbara B. Kennelly (D-CT; 1993 ADA score: 90) was even more specific in contrasting different approaches to federal aid, praising Goals 2000 because it would supposedly help all children. "This new bill represents a departure from traditional Federal assistance to State and local education reform. This bill will serve as a catalyst to systemic reform. Rather than targeting specific programs, this bill allows for coordinated reform in all parts of the education system. Rather than targeting special groups of children, this bill seeks broad based improvement for all children" (ibid., 24300).

Opponents of Goals 2000 agreed that the legislation entailed a new federal role that would have dire consequences for state and local control of schools. These foes saw an unprecedented and dangerous opportunity for the federal government to establish a national curriculum through content and performance standards. Less than a decade would pass before the traditional opponents of this kind of federal action in schools would change their minds. By the time No Child Left Behind was signed into law in early 2002, the federal government had positioned itself to exert even more authority for education than it had under Goals 2000.

7
the no child left behind act and the federal-control threat

It is not difficult to imagine [the Department of Education] establishing national "advisory" standards at some point in the future. Later, the department could require adherence to the compulsory standards, if Federal aid is to be continued. Next, standard tests, developed by the Federal Government, could be mandated to check whether the compulsory standards are being met. Last, State and local authorities will be coerced into acceptance of a standardized curriculum as the "only possible" guarantee of meeting compulsory standards.

—U.S. SENATOR HARRISON H. SCHMITT (R-NM) (1978)

George W. Bush, like his predecessor Bill Clinton, lived in a governor's mansion before moving to the White House. Both presidents compiled records as education activists when they were governors, and they launched their national education agendas early in their first terms. Indeed, President Bush's proposal for the No Child Left Behind Act of 2001 was sent to Congress almost immediately after he took office. The Senate began its hearings on the measure during the early weeks of the 107th Congress. Just eleven months later, the president signed No Child Left Behind into law. Congressional action might have been even faster without the terrorist attacks of September 11, 2001.

No Child Left Behind is both a continuation of and a departure from previous federal education laws. As we have seen in the preceding chapters, many of the provisions of No Child Left Behind build on earlier policies. For example, the Elementary and Secondary Education Act of 1965 and the Goals 2000: Educate America Act of 1994 included elements that later appeared in No Child Left Behind (funds for educationally disadvantaged students and state planning requirements, respectively). At the same time, the assessment, accountability, and teacher-qualification requirements in

Title I of No Child Left Behind are significant new developments in federal policy for schools. The new law also departs from the concept and practice of limited federal involvement that was the hallmark of most earlier education policies. By strongly supporting No Child Left Behind, most conservatives in Congress abandoned their traditional opposition to increased federal involvement in schools. No Child Left Behind represents a major expansion of the federal role and a dramatic shift in the attitude of conservatives toward this expansion. Yet, the law is also rooted in an evolutionary process. Because No Child Left Behind builds on and departs from earlier stages of federal education policy-making, the law cannot be fully appreciated without understanding what came before it. By knowing where No Child Left Behind came from, we can also begin to determine where the law is going and what it means for the future of public education.

The administration's No Child Left Behind proposal, the amendments considered in Congress, the deliberations in both houses of Congress, and the votes were a political and ideological potpourri. Many issues were debated at length, and politicians of all stripes raised numerous—and at times surprising—arguments in favor of and against the proposal's different provisions. Several of these issues and arguments are treated at length in this chapter: accountability, testing, funding, private-school vouchers, and federal control. In addition to analyzing the ideological and political significance of these issues, I examine the ideological shifts that had occurred by the time No Child Left Behind passed. The question guiding this chapter—indeed, the entire book—is how radical a departure is No Child Left Behind from the tradition of limited federal involvement in schools?

By the time the No Child Left Behind Act became law, ideological values and beliefs with respect to federal involvement in education had evolved in unusual directions. These transformations led legislators in Congress to pass a law that departed from past traditions in federal education policy. Even though they still espoused recognizable ideological positions, many conservative and liberal legislators were influenced by the views and opinions of each other. For example, liberals in the No Child Left Behind debate were more likely than they had been in past episodes to reconcile their advocacy for more money with "conservative" demands for fiscal accountability. Similarly, conservatives consented to an expansion of the federal role in schools of a magnitude formerly supported only by liberals. The interaction between new and traditional ideological positions accounts for why No Child Left Behind looks like it does and for the direction in which the new law is taking federal education policy.

Provisions of the No Child Left Behind Act

As in past reauthorizations of the Elementary and Secondary Education Act, Title I is the centerpiece of the No Child Left Behind Act. Most of the legislation's funds and notoriety are concentrated here. Title I lays out a variety of new requirements aimed at "improving the academic achievement of the disadvantaged." States are required to define standards and develop assessments in math and reading for grades 3–8. Although these requirements are consistent with trends in standards-based assessment that predate No Child Left Behind, the new law has turned them into a nationwide high-stakes accountability system for all schools and students. In this regard, No Child Left Behind breaks with past versions of the Elementary and Secondary Education Act quite dramatically.

Schools must demonstrate "adequate yearly progress" (as defined by states and approved by the U.S. Department of Education) for all elementary and secondary students and student subgroups, including "economically disadvantaged students," students from major racial and ethnic groups, students with disabilities, and "students with limited English proficiency" (P.L.107-110, Title I, sec. 1111[b][2][C][v]). Using achievement scores from the 2001–2 school year as the baseline, all students are expected to reach proficient levels on state assessments by the school year 2013–14. In addition, when Title I is fully implemented, schools, districts, and states will have to meet adequate yearly progress criteria for student performance and all teachers will have to be "highly qualified" in the subjects they teach.

Schools that do not make adequate yearly progress in meeting proficiency levels on state assessments are to be identified as being "in need of school improvement." School districts and states can also be flagged for improvement based on aggregate scores. The law includes a few due-process provisions for schools identified for improvement, but there is little flexibility on timelines or consequences. For schools that fail to make progress, a sequence of corrective measures must be taken by the school district, including providing the option for students to transfer from the school in need of improvement to another public school within the district (ibid., Title I, sec. 1116[b][1][E][I]). Consequences for schools that continue to struggle increase over time: supplemental services (for example, subsidized tutors) for students in identified schools and, later, reorganizing the school (or school district) that remains in need of improvement. Finally, Title I also establishes the Reading First and Early Reading First programs to support early literacy activities.

Title II, "Preparing, Training, and Recruiting High Quality Teachers and Principals," includes various teacher training and recruitment programs, along with specialized curriculum programs such as civics education and "teaching of traditional American history." Title II also includes teacher liability protection. Title III covers "language instruction for limited English proficient and immigrant students" and Title IV authorizes or reauthorizes several school-level programs, such as "safe and drug-free schools and communities" and "21st century community learning centers." In addition to the school-choice provisions of Title I, Title V is focused on "promoting informed parental choice" by means of the charter schools program, magnet schools assistance program, and voluntary public-school choice program. Title V also includes more than a dozen "innovative programs," such as character education partnerships; smaller learning communities; community technology centers; and "Educational, Cultural, Apprentice-ship, and Exchange Programs for Alaska Natives, Native Hawaiians, and Their Historical Whaling and Trading Partners in Massachusetts."

Title VI encompasses several programs under the aegis of flexibility and accountability and establishes new mechanisms for state and local flexibility and "transferability" of certain federal funds. Title VII organizes programs for Indian, Native Hawaiian, and Alaska Native education, and Title VIII covers the impact aid program (funds for school systems impacted by the presence of non-taxpaying federal installations). Several miscella-neous provisions and assurances are made throughout the legislation, including "prohibition against federal mandates, direction, or control" (ibid., Title VI, sec. 6301), prohibition on "the Federal Government to mandate . . . a State or any subdivision thereof to spend any funds or incur any costs not paid for under this Act" (Title IX, sec. 9527[a]), "prohi-bition on [federal] endorsement of curriculum" (Title IX, sec. 9527[b]), and "prohibition on federally sponsored testing" (Title IX, sec. 9529).

The No Child Left Behind statute is a lengthy document, perhaps suggesting what a software manual would look like if all the code were included. It is the end product of a long and contentious debate that itself generated a lot of output. The legislative process is a richer source of ideological and political raw material than is the resulting statute. Hence, most of this chapter focuses on the No Child Left Behind debates in the House of Representatives and the Senate. The deliberations show how different ideological factions influenced each other and how they continued to set boundary lines between acceptable and unacceptable federal policies. The No Child Left Behind debate also documents the law's relationship with earlier legislation.

Issues in the No Child Left Behind Debate

Accountability

Accountability was one of the most prominent topics in the No Child Left Behind debate. It tied together virtually all the other key topics: funding—including past federal investments in education—testing, and private-school vouchers. Although the implementation of the resulting legislation is breaking new ground under school accountability, the original debate was influenced by an accountability and assessment movement that predated No Child Left Behind. The contribution of the 2001 law to the accountability movement was to raise the stakes for schools, school districts, and states that do not meet their performance targets and to put the federal government in charge of school accountability processes and consequences nationwide.

The concept of accountability in federal education policy was once as limited as the policies themselves: states and school systems that received federal funds were expected to spend them within the categories that Congress specified. Recall that even this limited definition of accountability was ideologically controversial before the 1950s and 1960s. Some conservatives, such as Senators Raymond E. Baldwin and Barry Goldwater, quoted in the Introduction, equated "accountability to the purposes of the legislation" with "federal control." The narrowness of this definition and the controversy it generated faded after a time. Note, however, that it took several years after the passage of the Elementary and Secondary Education Act to develop a metric for assessing student progress in Title I (the Title I Evaluation and Reporting System—TIERS) and several more years for accountability standards to be applied in a meaningful way (that is, the program improvement requirements for Title I [then called Chapter 1] in the 1988 reauthorization of the Elementary and Secondary Education Act [P.L.100-297]).

While an overview of the school accountability movement is beyond the scope of this book, some of its concepts need to be highlighted. Government agencies are accustomed to monitoring the expenditure of public funds through routine audits and other mechanisms. Traditional accountability procedures track "inputs," such as money and regulations. This form of accountability has been supplemented—but not replaced—by new accountability systems that focus on results and such outcomes as student performance. States and testing companies have done most of the heavy lifting in designing and deploying large-scale student assessment systems. To varying degrees, states and national organizations have also developed content and performance standards. The tests administered in a state are typically aligned with the state's standards, as are state curriculum and textbook guidelines. The accountability movement predates the federal government's interest in it, but now Congress and the Department of Education are key players.

In the Goals 2000 debate (Chapter 6), a few accountability concepts were too controversial for Congress to enact in a meaningful way in 1994. For example, "opportunity-to-learn standards"—gauges for judging the adequacy of resources received by public schools—had to be watered down before Goals 2000 (and the Improving America's Schools Act of 1994) could pass. Although it still does not encompass opportunity-to-learn standards or their equivalent, the concept of accountability has expanded dramatically in the past decade. Without the intense focus on outcomes and results on standardized tests in the larger accountability movement, the accountability provisions of No Child Left Behind might have looked much different.

The coming-of-age of the accountability movement helps explain how it influenced the No Child Left Behind statute. Another major factor was the level of agreement between liberals and conservatives about the need for increased accountability, a consensus that was missing in the Goals 2000 and Improving America's Schools Act debates. Consensus between liberals and conservatives on accountability was also absent during the failed attempt to reauthorize ESEA/IASA during the 1999 and 2000 sessions of the 106th Congress (Congressional Quarterly Inc. 2001, 9-3 and 9-6; McGuinn 2006, 142–43). Of course, the most important development in the movement occurred when the federal government decided to set accountability requirements for every public school in the United States under No Child Left Behind.

During the No Child Left Behind floor debate, Senator Jack Reed (D-RI; 2002 ADA score: 100) referred to the recent accountability tradition that the 2001 bill built on. (Recall from Chapter 6 that Reed did not succeed in getting stronger accountability-for-results provisions into the Goals 2000 law.)

> We are building on previous efforts. As a younger Member of the other body, I served on the conference committee for the Goals 2000 Act and the 1994 reauthorization of the Elementary and Secondary Education Act. It was there that we talked about tougher accountability and stronger insistence that the States step in when schools are failing. We insisted upon higher standards. We met resistance, but we insisted. We did not go as far then as I believe

we could have gone, or should have gone. But today I believe there is vindication of those efforts almost 8 years ago when we talked about insisting that schools be held accountable and that real money flow to schools so that children can learn. (*Congressional Record* 2001, 26371)

Much of the congressional deliberations on the No Child Left Behind proposal portrayed its increased accountability requirements as a necessary response to lagging student performance. Public schools were cast in a negative light, and most previous federal actions to support them were condemned. Several conservatives, for example, argued that past federal investments had not improved school performance and that it was time to hold the public education system to a substantially higher standard. This logic underlies the shift away from the ideology of limited federal involvement made by many conservatives during this period. Senator Judd Gregg (R-NH; 2002 ADA score: 10) made the following claim during the Senate floor debate of No Child Left Behind: "We have spent $120 billion in the last 35 years on Title I, directed at trying to help low-income kids. The result of those expenditures has been that low-income kids are reading two grade levels below their peers and are graduating from high school at half the rate of their peers. There has been absolutely no academic improvement in those kids over this 35-year period. In the last 10 years, when we spent the most amount of money, the academic improvement also has not increased at all" (ibid., 10401–2).

Senator Gregg and other legislators used this argument to justify No Child Left Behind's new accountability requirements. Federal aid had been in place for so long that many conservatives were able to spin the mixed track record of Title I into a broader indictment of public schools. Many liberals, especially New Democrats, joined conservatives in demanding increased accountability requirements as a precondition for additional funding. Senator Thomas Carper (D-DE; 2002 ADA score: 80) captured the sentiments of many of his liberal colleagues in his remarks: "[W]e have agreed with the President . . . that, while we will provide . . . more money with greater flexibility, we will demand results. We will not throw good money after bad. We want results. There will be consequences for those schools that do well and consequences for those that do not" (ibid., 26362). Even legislators who believed more strongly in the positive achievements and future potential of state and local education agencies were inclined to hold schools more accountable. There may not have been agreement on the reasons for increased accountability—or for other

components of the proposed law—but the broad consensus on accountability in Congress contributed to the increased reach of the federal government into schools. In the No Child Left Behind debate, traditionally liberal
demands for increased resources were eclipsed by widespread bipartisan
calls for schools to be held responsible for past federal investments.

Nevertheless, support for No Child Left Behind accountability requirements was not unanimous. Disagreements occurred at the boundaries
of the larger accountability discussion. For example, there was a lot of
controversy where the general desire for accountability bumped up against
specific testing requirements or private-school vouchers. Several conservatives (and liberals) also worried about the overall intrusiveness of the new
provisions. In the following remark made on the House floor, Representative Peter Hoekstra (R-MI; 2002 ADA score: 5) also draws the connection
between Goals 2000 and No Child Left Behind, although with none of
the approval voiced by Senator Reed above. "We are now going to tell
States and local school districts how to spend their money as well as
the results they are going to get. What we are left with is Goals 2001,
after we fought Goals 2000; and accountability putting us on the road
to national testing and spending that only President Clinton could
have dreamed of" (ibid., 8853). Hoekstra, a vocal conservative, believed
that Congress would be spending too much on No Child Left Behind.
As we shall see below, many liberals did not think that Congress was
spending enough.

There were other disagreements. One of them concerned the accountability expectations for public schools versus private schools under the
administration's ill-fated proposal for private-school vouchers. The George W.
Bush administration wanted to provide vouchers for students in failing
public schools to use to pay tuition at private schools. The fact that the
administration's voucher plan did not impose the same testing or accountability requirements on private schools receiving vouchers as it did on
public schools provoked many negative reactions. The following exchange
between Representative Robert E. Andrews (D-NJ; 2002 ADA score: 90)
and Kenneth L. Connor, President of the pro-voucher Family Research
Council occurred during hearings before the House Committee on Education
and the Workforce.

> Rep. Andrews: Now, I think I heard you say earlier that once these
> children, however many, choose to go to the private school, that you
> do not favor any sort of standardized testing of them once they get
> there. Is that right?

Mr. Connor: Well, look, we do not favor federal mandates for standardized testing for public schools, and even less so for private schools. . . . We don't favor mandating the particular test. We agree with the notion that the state and local school officials ought to be able to select the assessment that they use, and we would favor the same principle for the private school as well.

Rep. Andrews: So you would support the idea of the state and local officials having the right to require these children to take the test once they get to the private school?

Mr. Connor: Well, in the final analysis I would say that I think parents are the ones who have the biggest stake in the outcome of their children's education.

Rep. Andrews. Well, is the answer yes or no? If the state of Florida were to decide to impose its standardized tests on children that have left the public school under the Bush plan to go to a private school, do you think the Florida test should be administered to those children in a private school?

Mr. Connor: We have not taken a position on that. My initial reaction is that we would not favor a state-imposed test on a private school.

Rep. Andrews: I have to tell you, I find your position completely disingenuous. You just said that based upon the results of standardized tests, we should permit parents to take public money and spend it in a private school. That is a valid position. I don't agree with it, but it is a valid position.

You then say once they get there, the same standardized test that would be used to determine their lack of achievement in a public school cannot be used to measure their achievement or lack of achievement in a private school. Why don't we apply it to the same school?

Mr. Connor: Well, the position is not disingenuous. The position revolves around . . . government intrusion into private organizations, where we think in the final analysis that parents are the best judge of the results being achieved.

I think there is a legitimate concern for ensuring that children measure up, that they perform to certain levels of performance. I just think that once government begins to mandate particular tests, whether that mandate comes from the state or Federal Government, on private institutions, that there are real concerns that need to be addressed.

Rep. Andrews: So, and I will close this; so it is your position that taking the public money is okay, but taking the responsibility that comes with it is not?

Mr. Connor: No, that is not my position. I think the demonstrated history is that children do well in these schools. (U.S. House of Representatives 2001c, 38–39)

Kenneth Connor talked about schools being accountable to parents, a type of accountability that is especially familiar to private schools. Connor elevates it to the most important form of accountability, thereby suggesting that government accountability rules are unnecessary as well as intrusive for private schools. Representative Hoekstra reinforced this point on the floor of the House during the debate on an amendment to restore private-school vouchers to the No Child Left Behind bill. "This [voucher amendment] is empowering parents and will force schools to be accountable not to a bureaucrat in Washington, not to a bureaucrat in the Department of Education, and not to a bureaucratic test that is mandated out of Washington" (*Congressional Record* 2001, 9241). For many conservatives, a private school's market-based accountability to parents is the competitive force that is needed in public schools. Therefore, it was logically consistent to support private-school vouchers and increased accountability requirements for public schools. (Note, however, that Hoekstra was opposed to new testing requirements for public schools on the grounds of federal interference.)

The mismatch between the accountability requirements for public and private schools was an innovative argument against the private-school voucher concept. It is noteworthy that an argument rooted in accountability was added to the considerable arsenal of political, ideological, and economic arguments leveled against vouchers by liberals. Representative Jim Langevin (D-RI; 2002 ADA score: 85) summarized the views of voucher critics in a written statement appended to the House hearings volume. "Private and parochial schools are not required to administer the annual tests that are the cornerstone of the President's plan. Therefore, we will never know whether the alternative school is any better or worse than the one he or she left. This system simply assumes that private or parochial schools are better than public schools, and in many cases that assumption may not be valid" (U.S. House of Representatives 2001b, 68).

Again, the accountability requirements of the bills provoked more controversy when they intersected with private-school vouchers and testing (or both).

Testing

Most legislators participating in the No Child Left Behind debate did not dwell on the use of test scores as the basis for the proposal's vast accountability apparatus. It appears that most lawmakers approved broadening the concept of accountability to include student outcomes. They were not picky about how these outcomes would be measured. This is a reasonable stance: members of the House and Senate are politicians, not educational psychologists. Nevertheless, there were some fairly specialized remarks during the deliberations. Representative Ted Strickland (D-OH; 2002 ADA score: 90) provided a concise description of how test scores should and should not be used:

> In my judgment, educational testing should be used diagnostically to determine what learning impediments might exist and prescriptively to determine what methods might be best to help a particular student learn better.
>
> Educational testing is not intended to be a measure of accountability or a factor in decisions about how much money a school district wins as a bonus or loses as a sanction. The use of a statewide test to make high-stakes decisions about individual students, teachers or schools is in my judgment a misuse of standardized testing and has had a predictably negative result in my state of Ohio. (Ibid., 12)

Strickland went on to highlight a widely held view within the education establishment and decried the negative impact of intensive test preparation: "Test scores reflect more than the quality of education being provided by the school and the teacher. Test scores reflect a whole host of factors including socioeconomic status, parental involvement, the educational background of the parents, and the level of economic investment in the student. Yet, this bill assumes that test scores are always valid and reliable indicators of educational quality" (ibid., 13).

Again, most of the remarks about testing in Congress did not attain Representative Strickland's sophistication. Nevertheless, many liberal and conservative legislators expressed concerns about the implications of No Child Left Behind's detailed testing requirements. (For a brief summary of these implications, see Elmore 2002. For a more technical critique of state testing systems, see Hanushek and Raymond 2003.) Criticisms from liberals tended to reflect their traditional aversion to testing. Conservative critics relied on their opposition to *national* testing. Conservative Representative Ron Paul (R-TX; 2002 ADA score: 30) was one of the few voices in Congress in 2001 that still questioned the constitutionality of federal regulations for education. He added written comments to the

Congressional Record after the oral debate, a common practice among legislators in Congress:

> It is time Congress stopped trying to circumvent the constitutional limitations on its authority by using the people's own money to bribe them into complying with unconstitutional federal dictates.
>
> Mr. Chairman, H.R.1 [the House NCLB bill] will lead to de facto, if not de jure, national testing.
>
> National testing will inevitably lead to a national curriculum as teachers will teach what their students need to know in order to pass their mandated "assessment." After all, federal funding depends on how students perform on these tests! Proponents of this approach dismiss these concerns by saying "there is only one way to read and do math." Well then what are the battles about phonics versus whole language or new math versus old math about? There are continuing disputes about teaching all subjects as well as how to measure mastery of a subject matter. Once federal mandatory testing is in place, however, those arguments will be settled by the beliefs of whatever regime currently holds sway in DC. Mr. Chairman, I would like my colleagues to consider how comfortable they would feel supporting this bill if they knew that in five years proponents of fuzzy math and whole language could be writing the [National Assessment of Educational Progress]? (*Congressional Record* 2001, 8872)

Representative Paul was joined by another unreconstructed conservative, Representative Mark Souder (R-IN; 2002 ADA score: 10). "[W]hen we pass things that mandate national testing, we are taking a risk that the next president will not be George W. Bush and, instead, we may have someone who is going to ram this stuff down our throat, and we may regret and rue the day that we passed a bill with less flexibility, more money, more bureaucracy, and now national testing" (ibid., 9008). In other remarks, Souder worried that national testing requirements would eventually lead to the control of curriculum in private schools and for home schoolers (ibid., 8301).

Testing was a good litmus test for differentiating conservatives who supported new authority for the federal government from those who did not. Although some liberals echoed these concerns, they were more likely to criticize testing as an "unfunded mandate"—a relatively less ideological argument and one with a history in federal education policy dating to the

Education for All Handicapped Children Act of 1975 (P.L.94-142). Liberal legislator Representative Tom Allen (D-ME; 2002 ADA score: 95)—and many others—used the concept of unfunded mandates to link No Child Left Behind and special education. (Note that by 2001, P.L.94-142 had been renamed the Individuals with Disabilities Education Act [IDEA].) "Requiring yearly tests imposes a new mandate on our already fiscally troubled state budgets. The President has said, albeit without much detail, that the Federal Government would provide the necessary financial assistance. . . . This would force yet another unfunded mandate upon the states, the most prominent of which is the Individuals with Disabilities Education Act" (U.S. House of Representatives 2001b, 38).

In addition to the question about who would pay for the new testing requirements, there was debate about how test results might influence a school's eligibility for federal funds. Recall Representative Strickland's comments about test validity and reliability above. These concerns were supplemented by objections that the basis for identifying failing schools was invalid or at least too narrow in light of the high-stakes consequences these schools would face. Senator Patrick Leahy (D-VT; 2002 ADA score: 95) expressed these sentiments during the floor debate. "I am concerned about the extensive Federal control exerted in this bill over the evaluation of whether a school is failing. I am particularly concerned about the definition of what constitutes a failing school, especially because this is a determination that could ultimately lead to the elimination of Federal funds for that school" (*Congressional Record* 2001, 26591).

The final law imposed financial consequences on struggling schools gradually and, for the most part, indirectly. There was a much greater volume of debate about funding levels generally. Although most legislators agreed that accountability and testing requirements were appropriate, opinions were sharply divided about whether Title I schools were receiving enough money to succeed. This divide was discernible even among those who voted for No Child Left Behind, and it separated liberals and conservatives in ways that were not revealed in the final votes.

Funding

I believe that a principal reason that conservatives in Congress were willing to expand federal authority for education was their widespread belief that past federal investments had been misdirected. Even Secretary of Education Roderick Paige made this assertion (U.S. Senate 2001, 5). If the representative of a conservative, albeit activist, administration urges Congress to overhaul federal education policy before spending more money, it is a good bet that conservative legislators will listen. Funding levels was one of the topics in the No Child Left Behind debate where conservatives and liberals resembled their earlier selves. However, the conceptual relationship between funding and accountability brought many of these legislators together in a new way.

No Child Left Behind is a distinct evolutionary stage in conservative thinking about education. Instead of advocating a limited federal role in schools, the majority of conservatives—and liberals—in Congress endorsed the view that the transfer of public funds to schools entitled the federal government to define the results that schools would be required to achieve. As in the case of P.L.94-142, the Education for All Handicapped Children Act of 1975, these requirements would remain in place even if funding levels did not meet the cost of fulfilling them. In crafting a national blueprint for high-stakes accountability, conservatives were also able to criticize the track record of federal spending under earlier policies.

I do not attempt to judge the veracity of conservative claims that the quality of American public schools was declining or that previous investments were squandered. However, it is worth noting that both conservatives and liberals supported increased funding and increased accountability. This implied an agreement that schools needed to improve and that the federal government could play a role in improving them. Senator Edward Kennedy (D-MA; 2002 ADA score: 100) put it well: "Investment without accountability is a waste of money, but accountability without investment is a waste of time" (*Congressional Record* 2001, 6025).

Likewise, Senator Orrin Hatch (R-UT; 2002 ADA score: 5) emphasized the importance of money, flexibility, and accountability—apparently in that order: "I have been a longtime advocate of federal support for education, and I will continue to make that a top priority. . . . We need additional resources, plain and simple. But, resources with so many strings attached bog us down. Give us the flexibility to manage these resources and apply them to the areas of greatest need in our State. Measure our children's educational progress. We will meet the challenge" (ibid., 6263).

No Child Left Behind was a large-scale compromise between liberals and conservatives on questions about federal support and high-stakes accountability. The compromise prevailed because most conservatives in Congress recognized the long-standing liberal assertion that federal investments in schools were legitimate. For their part, many liberals embraced typically—but not exclusively—conservative demands that schools produce results for the money they received. (For a summary of the party politics underlying this compromise, see McGuinn 2006, chap. 10.) Of course, there was a competing, more liberal view. Many liberals (and a few conservatives) were concerned about persistently inadequate funding levels for Title I and warned that schools could not meet their student performance targets without adequate—or at least additional—resources. The most readily identifiable liberal argument in the debate was the claim that No Child Left Behind funding levels were too low.

During the floor debate, Senator Patty Murray (D-WA; 2002 ADA score: 90) was irritated by comments about Title I's shortcomings:

> But these glib statements about Title I having failed our disadvantaged students are perhaps most disingenuous and frustrating when one considers the chronic underfunding of Title I. . . .
>
> Let's assume that Congress decides we must build a bridge from the House to the Senate side of the Capitol; after building a third of that bridge, we begin sending people over that bridge. Not surprisingly, no one makes it to the other side. Some Senators come to the floor and express shock and dismay that no one has crossed the incomplete bridge. After years of this kind of folly, we finally declare on the floor of the Senate that the bridge is clearly a failure and it has to be torn down.
>
> That is what we have done with Title I. We have determined that a need exists. We have developed a solution. We have failed to implement that solution. And then we have declared that the solution is not a good one. (Ibid., 10178–79)

Senator Jack Reed had an opportunity to remind Secretary (and former Houston Superintendent) Rod Paige of the important relationship between school performance and resources: "I would suggest that without additional resources, the chances of a failing school becoming a successful school are very remote. Part of the experience in Texas was not just testing but was a significant reorientation of funding in which, in the case of Houston, historically, your funding went up dramatically because of court cases and because of legislative reform. Yet, you do not seem to be making that connection in the President's proposal" (U.S. Senate 2001, 26).

Throughout the debate, the bills' funding levels incurred the wrath of many conservatives who thought they were too high and liberals who thought they were too low. The administration's proposal included a modest increase in funds for federal education programs, although the increase was not large enough to satisfy liberals who wanted more money for Title I.

Even though most conservatives agreed that federal aid to schools was legitimate, they did not necessarily agree on how much money ought to be spent. Legislators from different ideological quarters voiced concerns about No Child Left Behind's new, unfunded mandates. President George W. Bush's proposed tax cut also caused a fair amount of confusion at the beginning of the No Child Left Behind debate, leading many liberals to question the depth of the administration's commitment to education. Moreover, the appropriations in the administration's bill did not match the education line items in the new administration's first budget.

It is interesting that the Reagan administration began in a similar manner: with a large tax cut and an ambitious plan to reorganize the federal role in schools. President Reagan, however, matched his tax cut with a systematic plan to cut spending on domestic programs, including education. President George W. Bush, on the other hand, increased education spending while cutting taxes. The federal education reforms of both eras were portrayed as corrections that were overdue. The respective policy proposals included tradeoffs designed to make them more palatable. In 1981, turning numerous federal programs into a single block grant was designed to increase state and local flexibility; under the original No Child Left Behind plan, increased accountability requirements were accompanied by a slight increase in funds and by declarations that local flexibility would be increased by means of a block grant. (President Reagan's block grant fared better in 1981 than the block grant requested by President George W. Bush twenty years later.)

Block grants, which allow flexible spending, are an ideological paradox. A second strategy, categorical aid (that is, money earmarked for specific purposes), has been exploited since the 1950s to defuse controversy about a third type of assistance, unrestricted aid to schools. Unrestricted aid (or "general aid") has never been politically viable, in part because legislators worry that there is no accountability to the federal government for how the funds are used. Categorical aid has not proven to be a bulletproof concept, however. By the late 1970s, categorical programs were seen as examples of government interference and irrelevance, targeting funds to activities that might not address state and local needs. Block grants grew out of this shift in perception. The shift became a cycle by 1988. Reports of unfocused state and local spending (for example, Henderson 1983) led Congress to specify broad program areas for the second iteration of the education block grant. Both categorical aid and block grants provoked negative reactions, but the former has proved more durable than the latter. By 2001, block grants had become too controversial to survive Congress when the final version of No Child Left Behind was approved. For this reason, No Child Left Behind programs employ categorical funding mechanisms.

Again, the debate about No Child Left Behind spending levels highlighted traditional ideological differences between liberals and conservatives. While some liberals were renewing their long-standing demands for the federal government to cover one-third of the cost of public schools (for example, Senator Dodd [D-CT; 2002 ADA score: 80], *Congressional Record* 2001, 6017), some conservatives believed that spending proposed in the bill was out of control. Indeed, lingering concerns about the high funding levels in the bill demonstrated that some conservatives stayed true to their traditional principles. Senator Jon Kyl (R-AZ; 2002 ADA score: 0) believed that the bill relied on an "old model" of federal involvement that gauged commitment to education "by how many taxpayer dollars were spent" (ibid., 6531). Despite his reservations, Kyl, along with most other conservatives in Congress, eventually voted to enact No Child Left Behind. One of the three conservatives in the Senate who did not go along with the final bill was Senator Robert Bennett (R-UT; 2002 ADA score: 5). He believed that the law would cost too much. Bennett's exasperation about funding—and his president's ideological inconsistency—was expressed well during the Senate floor debate. "President Bush wants to spend more money on education. A lot of people say, boy, that is unusual for a Republican. The Democrat reaction is, we want to spend even more money than President Bush wants to spend, and we are back in the same Washington trap, which is, if it is a good program, spend more money on it; if it is a bad program, fix it by spending more money on it" (ibid., 6720).

Senator Bennett and other conservatives were also distressed that the president's private-school voucher proposal did not make it into the final bill. I have already discussed the accountability mismatch between public and private schools. The private-school voucher proposal triggered many other debates, some of which recalled issues from earlier episodes.

Private-School Vouchers

Debates about federal involvement in elementary and secondary education have included private schools since the 1960s. (Private institutions of higher education were eligible to receive funds through the G.I. Bill after World War II and the National Defense Education Act in the late 1950s.) The managers of the bills and debates leading to the Elementary and Secondary Education Act in 1965 had to meet private-school demands for a share of federal funds. However, direct or indirect federal aid to private schools has always been controversial, both for members of Congress and for recipients of such aid. Religious private schools, for example, are extremely wary of the strings attached to tax dollars and are far more likely than public schools to decline federal support.

The administration's proposal for No Child Left Behind included a large private-school voucher component. It was added to the Title I program to help students leave public schools that were repeatedly identified as being in need of improvement. Like private-school vouchers generally, the proposal was a lightning rod for almost everyone in the debate. It was promptly removed by the House and Senate committees before they "reported out" their bills. Legislators in both chambers offered amendments to restore the voucher provision and reduce its overall cost and per voucher dollar value, but the amendments did not pass. Nevertheless, the voucher controversy was an important part of the overall No Child Left Behind debate because it exposed remaining ideological divisions on education.

Like Senator Bennett, some conservatives in the House cited the voucher defeat as one of their reasons for opposing the final bill. Representative Mike Pence (R-IN; 2002 ADA score: 5) was among the "no" voters in the House, and he offered a historical aside in his remarks during the House floor debate: "This debate, Mr. Chairman, between the status quo and the needs of largely minority students is not new. Decades ago, the defenders of the status quo stood in the schoolhouse door and said to some, you may not come in. Now, the defenders of the status quo stand in the schoolhouse door and say to the grandchildren of many of those same Americans, you may not come out" (*Congressional Record* 2001, 9241).

Even though some conservatives were troubled by the omission of vouchers from the final bill, far more liberals would have abandoned the bill if vouchers had been retained. School-choice and privatization advocates had to settle for the law's within-district transfer compromise and private-tutoring option (known as "supplemental services" in the law). The defeat of the voucher plan makes No Child Left Behind resemble Goals 2000: some of the most controversial aspects of the Clinton administration's original proposal, such as opportunity-to-learn standards, were weakened or rejected. In other words, private-school vouchers were still "out-of-bounds" ideologically in 2001.

As in certain past episodes (for example, the bruising tuition tax-credit debates in the late 1970s and early 1980s), liberals charged supporters of proposals that benefited private schools with attempting to undermine public education. Representative John Tierney (D-MA; 2002 ADA score: 100) regarded money for vouchers as resources that would not be used to help public schools. His colleagues who supported vouchers, he said, "are unwilling to make the commitment in our public schools. . . . They would rather privatize education" (ibid., 9250). The administration remained committed to private-school vouchers, even after their removal from the No Child Left Behind bills. President Bush's budget blueprint for the next year (2003), which he submitted to Congress on the same day he signed No Child Left Behind into law, included a request for $4 billion for private-school vouchers while making cuts in other education programs (U.S. Senate 2002, 2 and 20). The budget Congress passed for fiscal year 2003 did not include funds for the president's voucher request.

Ideological Shifts

The overwhelming support of the final No Child Left Behind conference report in Congress makes it easy to forget that the debate exposed far more viewpoints than did the final votes. However, the votes confirm some of the ideological shifts revealed in the debate. For example, the measure received overwhelming support from Republicans and conservatives in both chambers. Past measures sometimes alienated these groups, most recently in the votes on Goals 2000. In general, conservative opposition to No Child Left Behind was more pronounced in the House than in the Senate, and liberal opposition was more pronounced in the Senate than in the House. The main story, however, is that conservatives had moved further than liberals on the ideological continuum by 2001. They were under political pressure from President George W. Bush to pass No Child Left Behind, but the conservative drift in favor of an expanded federal role was already under way.

Recall also that liberals and conservatives were influencing each other's viewpoints during this episode. This mutual influence contributed to the narrowing of the ideological differences among most legislators and also helps explain why the federal role in schools expanded so dramatically under No Child Left Behind. Several members of the House of Representatives and the Senate commented on the shifts that were occurring, usually with disapproval. Nevertheless, the ideological transformations were palpable and explain why the law passed.

Representative Mark Souder was among several legislators in both chambers who referred explicitly to the political pressure conservatives felt to support No Child Left Behind: "I know there are not going to be many conservatives who are going to stand up under the pressures that we are under, and against the polls, and oppose this bill. . . . but there are some of us who are going to say that there are still Republicans who are conservative on the education issue, as on other issues" (*Congressional Record* 2001, 8864).

Liberal Senator Paul Wellstone (D-MN; 2002 ADA score: 100) was puzzled about the ideological shifts on both sides inasmuch as both sides seemed to have completely abandoned even the pretense of limited federal involvement in schools: "I must say that I think this oversteps, if not the authority, the sort of boundaries of congressional decision-making on education. Here I am, a liberal Senator from Minnesota, but this is my honest-to-God belief. I am just amazed that so many Senators have voted for this, especially my conservative friends" (ibid., 26579).

The "boundaries of congressional decision-making" referred to by Senator Wellstone are important. In addition to his concerns about too much testing and too little funding, Wellstone sensed that No Child Left Behind was crossing the tacit boundaries that had usually limited the reach of the federal government into schools. The fact that this expansion of federal authority was being done with the active consent of his "conservative friends" was, to him, a shocking development. Troubled by the boundaries that were being "overstepped," Wellstone cast a "no" vote on the No Child Left Behind conference report.

Perhaps the boundaries were being moved rather than crossed or ignored. Certain components of No Child Left Behind that were dear to conservatives—along with other features that liberals hoped for—were rejected, suggesting that certain boundaries were still in place. The majority of legislators were not prepared to authorize private-school vouchers or other initiatives (for example, class-size reduction, a favorite of liberals). The domain encompassed within the "ideological space" of acceptable federal education policies had been expanding since the late 1950s. Rather than violating these boundaries, No Child Left Behind can be interpreted as legally annexing territory that used to lie beyond them.

However one chooses to deploy the boundaries metaphor, we need to consider one concept that no legislator has ever been willing to embrace by name: federal control of education. For this reason, federal control is the most serious political and ideological charge one can level against a federal policy. Legislators take great pains to deny or avoid accusations that they favor federal control, or that the policies they embrace today will lead to federal control in the future. As we have seen in previous chapters, the federal-control threat has to be confronted whenever Congress takes up the question of inserting itself into the nation's schools.

Federal Control

Conservatives have a history of distrusting the federal government, especially when they do not control Congress. The reason for this distrust is
their fear of federal interference in policy domains that tradition or the
constitution says ought to be controlled by states or smaller units. Even
liberals give lip service to the desirability of limited government, but they
have a history of being less averse to using the federal government as an
instrument for expanding and institutionalizing ideologically and politically
liberal values.

Even though internal conditions like inequality or poor school quality
or external events like the Cold War may be used to justify federal action,
nothing ever justifies federal control. Until recently, most conservatives
could usually be relied on to make the federal-control charge against proposals to increase federal authority or support for schools. Likewise, liberals
simply denied the federal-control implications of the policies they endorsed.
Although conservatives and liberals altered their ideological stances during
the No Child Left Behind episode, "federal control" remained controversial.

"Federal control" is a serious accusation. It is also a vague one. Those
who make the charge sometimes refer to the immediate consequences of
a national education policy, but they almost always refer to the policy's
future effects. In addition, control or authority over schools is a zero-sum
game in education-policy discourse. For the federal government to expand
its authority, states, districts, and schools must lose some of theirs. One's
opinion of the trustworthiness of different intergovernmental levels often
reveals larger views about the federal-control threat.

Several traditionally conservative views about federal involvement were
expressed by Senator George Voinovich (R-OH; 2002 ADA score: 5). He
was another of the three hard-line conservatives to vote against No Child
Left Behind in the Senate:

> By seeking to abolish the role that State and local governments,
> specifically locally elected school boards, have in our children's
> education, I fear will put us on the slippery slope to the eventual
> federalization of all education in this country. . . .
>
> None of these provisions are, on their face, bad for education.
> What is troubling is the direction in which these measures lead
> us. Make no mistake, with this bill we take a giant leap forward
> toward federalizing our education system. We should not let Federal

bureaucrats become the national school board. (*Congressional Record* 2001, 26594–95)

Voinovich expresses a suspicion of the federal government on principle and an equally principled preference for state and local authority for schools. Sounding similarly conservative, liberal Representative Lynn Rivers (D-MI; 2002 ADA score: 95) said the following in the House. "What we have before us is a huge Federal intrusion into the jurisdiction of State legislatures and local school boards. . . . This is a power grab by the Federal Government, pure and simple. It represents an attempt to leverage only 7 percent of the funding for American schools into control of the entire K-12 system. Such action flies in the face of our long-standing tradition of local control of education" (ibid., 8859).

Representative Wayne T. Gilchrest (R-MD; 2002 ADA score: 10), a conservative colleague of Representative Rivers, went even further. He sided with teachers against the federal government in terms of smarts and wisdom. "Teachers receive degrees. They are licensed to teach in a State. They are professionals. They represent the broad diversity of the country. Now we summarily assume that the aristocracy of Washington and the State capitals are smarter and wiser" (ibid., 8987).

Bashing the Department of Education is a popular pastime in Washington, D.C. and some of the hostility about the federal role was directed at it. During the House hearings, for example, Representative John Thune (R-SD; 2002 ADA score: 10) accused "the Washington education bureaucracy" of "waste, fraud, and abuse" and a "few federal bureaucrats" of "malfeasance" in connection with missing funds for rural districts in South Dakota and other states (U.S. House of Representatives 2001b, 35).

Education Secretary Rod Paige was probably the only participant in the No Child Left Behind debate who openly maligned each level of the system in his remarks. Recall his belief that past federal spending had been unsuccessful. Secretary Paige also believed that the "bewildering array of Federal programs . . . gets in the way of promising reform at the State and local levels" (U.S. Senate 2001, 5). At the same time, he also had faith that the federal government could provide valuable leadership, but only if it had the legal authority to ensure accountability for results. During the House committee hearings on the administration's No Child Left Behind bill, Secretary Paige believed that state and local education governance systems were "in many cases incoherent" (U.S. House of Representatives 2001a, 33–34).

Legislators were more likely to criticize federal actions and motives than the actions and motives of state and local education agencies during the

No Child Left Behind debate. Liberal Senator Patrick Leahy (D-VT; 2002 ADA score: 95), for example, was concerned that No Child Left Behind requirements would forcibly replace Vermont's "home-grown" efforts to aid struggling schools with an accountability package designed for urban schools (*Congressional Record* 2001, 26590–91). (Conservative Senator Orrin Hatch had similar concerns about Utah's autonomy [ibid., 6263].) Senator Hillary Rodham Clinton (D-NY; 2002 ADA score: 95) took a dimmer view of states, despite having been the first lady of one. She argued against block grants because she believed that funds "get siphoned off in the bureaucracy of the State capitol" (ibid., 6027). Recall that one of Senator Clinton's predecessors from New York, Senator Robert F. Kennedy, did not trust local boards of education to address the needs of their "educationally deprived" students (see Chapter 3).

Again, several liberal legislators expressed concerns about the potential for abuse of federal power (for example, Representative Patsy Mink [D-HI; 2002 ADA score: 88] and Senator Paul Wellstone), invoking what had previously been ideological concerns for conservatives. Indeed, it is important to acknowledge the relative paucity of conservatives raising traditionally conservative objections to the federal-control threat embodied in No Child Left Behind. At the same time, legislators did not abandon their principles on this or other federal involvement questions. Liberals were still more interested than conservatives in inputs like money; conservatives were more interested than liberals in schools being held accountable for the funds they received. Moreover, most conservatives—including those who supported the law—still wanted to save taxpayer dollars. The votes on No Child Left Behind confirm traditional ideological divisions while indicating many interesting departures.

The No Child Left Behind Votes in Congress

The No Child Left Behind Act passed both houses of Congress by large margins. The data displayed in Table 7 confirm the political and ideological trends suggested in the debate. Support for No Child Left Behind was overwhelming among both parties and across the conservative-liberal continuum, as measured by ADA scores. Analyzed in this way, the votes reveal important departures from the tradition of liberal support and conservative opposition to federal involvement in schools. As shown in the table, opponents of No Child Left Behind in the House of Representatives tended to be more conservative than the law's supporters. Opponents in

Table 7   2001 No Child Left Behind Votes with 2002 ADA Statistics

2001 NCLB votes with 2002 ADA scores	House December 13, 2001	Senate December 18, 2001
Final vote on H.R.1	381–41	87–10
(NCLB conference report)	(87.8% yes)	(89.7% yes)
Democrats	198–6	43–6
	(97.1% yes)	(86% yes)
Republicans	183–33	44–3
	(84.7% yes)	(93.6% yes)
Independents	0–2	0–1
ADA Score Analyses		
Mean ADA of "yes" voters	46.6 (n=381)	47.1 (n=87)
Mean ADA of "no" voters	18.8 (n=41)	63.0 (n=10)
Mean ADA score of Democrat "yes" voters	84.7 (n=198)	83.1 (n=43)
Mean ADA score of Republican "yes" voters	5.5 (n=183)	11.9 (n=44)
Mean ADA score of Democrat "no" voters	90 (n=6)	85.8 (n=6)
Mean ADA score of Republican "no" voters	3.9 (n=33)	6.7 (n=3)
Mean Democrat ADA score (whole chamber)	85.2 (n=211)	83.4 (n=50)
Mean Republican ADA score (whole chamber)	5.3 (n=221)	11.1 (n=49)
Mean ADA of whole chamber (2002)	44.4 (n=434)	48.1 (n=100)

NOTE: NCLB = No Child Left Behind; ADA = Americans for Democratic Action; n = the number of legislators in each cell with 2002 ADA scores. ADA figures in the "whole chamber" cells include all legislators, regardless of whether they participated in the final vote on NCLB. In three cases in the House, scores were taken from 2000 because these representatives did not have 2002 scores. The House had one vacancy when the NCLB vote took place.
SOURCES: Congressional Quarterly Inc. 2002, S-76 and H-170–H-177 for the votes on NCLB and Americans for Democratic Action website for ADA scores. (Scores downloaded March 9, 2004, from http://www.adaction.org/2002voting.html and http://www.adaction.org/2000voting. html.)

the Senate, on the other hand, tended to be *less* conservative than supporters. This comparison must be interpreted with care because of the relatively small number of "no" votes in the Senate (n=10). Nevertheless, these "no" voters, which included liberals like Senator Paul Wellstone (D-MN) and conservatives like Senator Robert Bennett (R-UT), made their ideological objections known during the debate and remind us that legislators who voted the same way on the bill may have had different reasons for doing so. Other opponents of No Child Left Behind may have been moved by politics as well as ideology.

The Ideological Meaning of No Child Left Behind

The No Child Left Behind Act both built on and departed from previous federal education policies and principles. No Child Left Behind injected federal regulations into more schools and districts than did earlier laws, in addition to setting high expectations for students and teachers. It did this by putting the federal government at the center of the movement for standards-based accountability. Although federal involvement in education and high-stakes accountability were not new ideas, they were combined in No Child Left Behind in important new ways.

Even though No Child Left Behind, like all laws, was the result of a political process, it has rich ideological meaning for the evolution of federal education policy. Changes to ideological viewpoints, like all evolutionary processes, need to be assessed over time. By understanding the modern origins of federal support and regulation of schools, we can evaluate our present position and what it means for the future of education in the United States.

Over time, there has been a gradual weakening of the traditional ideological divisions between liberals and conservatives in Congress with regard to federal education aid. The weakening of these divisions has both obvious and not so obvious implications for No Child Left Behind. Consider, for example, the similarities between P.L.94-142 and No Child Left Behind. Both laws passed by huge margins, and with the support of legislators in both parties. A related but subtler fact is that few conservative legislators opposed either law. That is, both laws represented significant expansions of federal authority for education, yet they were not widely opposed on ideological grounds.

Now consider the bruising debate of President Carter's proposal to establish the Department of Education. Several liberal legislators opposed its creation, and at least one conservative registered his enthusiastic support for the measure. Taken together, the bipartisan roster of the Department of Education foes demonstrates that both liberals and conservatives can argue against excessive federal involvement in schools. Similarly, conservatives can support the expansion of federal action, as demonstrated by the votes on P.L.94-142 and No Child Left Behind.

Finally, notice a few things about No Child Left Behind. A handful of prominent liberals (for example, Senator James Jeffords [I-VT]; 2002 ADA score: 95) opposed NCLB for political reasons. Another handful of conservatives (for example, Representative Tom DeLay [R-TX]; 2002 ADA score: 0) opposed the law on ideological grounds. Nevertheless, the strong support by conservatives for No Child Left Behind is powerful evidence that the rhetorical truism of limited federal involvement in schools has been permanently overturned. A generation earlier, both liberals and conservatives would have been much more likely to emphasize the need for limits to the federal presence in schools. Moreover, conservative support for a law like No Child Left Behind would have been inconceivable.

Traditional ideological positions on federal education questions had weakened by the time No Child Left Behind was introduced. In particular, conservative support for the measure disrupted the balance between the federal government involving itself too much or too little in the nation's schools. The ideological tension between conservative support for limited federal involvement and liberal support for certain types of federal action in schools was a constructive force. No Child Left Behind's rapid expansion of federal authority for education is due, in part, to the earlier success of liberals in expanding the scope of federal action in schools *and* to the gradual acquiescence of conservatives to this expansion. Although no less insistent about the need for increased aid to education, liberals joined conservatives in demanding fiscal accountability from schools during the No Child Left Behind debate. Legislators of all ideological and political persuasions agreed that schools ought to improve student achievement in exchange for receiving federal dollars.

Of course, there are still types of federal action that are ideologically "out-of-bounds." No Child Left Behind sponsors, for example, were unable to pass the private-school voucher and block-grant components of the original bill. (Both vouchers and block grants are quite appealing to conservatives.) Likewise, liberals were unable to obtain federal funds for school construction projects and class-size reduction. The long-term viability of the controversial features of No Child Left Behind is still being determined, and the Department of Education has already loosened certain regulations relating to "highly qualified teachers" in rural areas, testing participation rates for students, and the participation of English-language learners in mandated testing.

Does conservative support for the expansion of federal influence over schools mean that conservatives have abandoned their principles? No, it does not. In response to several decades of steadily increasing federal aid to schools, conservatives have supplemented their earlier warnings of federal control with other principles. In the case of No Child Left Behind, these principles included fiscal conservatism generally and "not throwing good money after bad." Once the National Defense Education Act of 1958 and the Elementary and Secondary Education Act of 1965 breached the ramparts of effective opposition to federal aid, conservatives could (and did) invoke the track record of federal spending in later debates. Conservatives and Republicans portrayed the results of the decades of spending under the Elementary and Secondary Education Act in an extremely negative light as a justification for adding an unprecedented high-stakes accountability component to No Child Left Behind. A newer conservative principle—giving taxpayers at all levels their money's worth—has replaced the nostalgic preference for limited federal involvement.

Liberals did not move as far on the ideological continuum as conservatives, but they did some acquiescing of their own. Again, a growing number of liberals embraced conservative-sounding demands for fiscal accountability. Liberals did not abandon their calls for additional resources for schools, but they did buy into conservatives' perceptions that schools were failing and allowed the law's accountability requirements to outstrip its funding levels. President Ford's 1975 warning about P.L.94-142 also applies to No Child Left Behind: "[The law's] requirements will remain in effect even though the Congress appropriates . . . less than the amounts contemplated in [the conference report]" (Ford 1975, 1335).

In sum, a bipartisan agenda for school accountability has replaced the long-standing liberal agenda for increased federal education funding. In recent years, conservatives have come to accept expanded federal involvement in schools after strenuously objecting to it in earlier debates. Liberals helped persuade conservatives that there was a legitimate federal role in schools. Similarly, conservatives, with their evolving beliefs, blazed the fiscal accountability trail now traveled by liberals. This convergence of viewpoints has resulted in a law that dramatically increases federal authority for public education.

Why are conservatives and liberals in Congress more likely to agree now than they were in past episodes? Today, both sides acknowledge the financial needs of schools and the national economic consequences of uneven public-school quality. This agreement has led to an activist federal agenda for education. Note, however, that this agreement has not filtered down to the state and local levels. In addition to removing the practical and ideological constraints provided by the rhetoric of limited federal involvement, No Child Left Behind has provoked discontent in states and school districts that are accustomed to a much different relationship with Washington, D.C. Ideological agreement in Congress is exacerbating intergovernmental disagreement about the appropriate role of the national government in the affairs of local schools. A large-scale revolt by state and local policy-makers and educators against federal authority may be the most significant, albeit unintended consequence of No Child Left Behind. The intended consequence of the law—federal domination of public-school accountability—is also provocative. This new level of federal authority would never have occurred without the gradual evolution and narrowing of ideological viewpoints on education in Congress over the past five decades.

8

where is federal education policy taking us?

Is there something magic about the Federal Government that it can do things better than the man that is right close to the problem next door to him? Or have we got to hire somebody down here in Washington to set up certain standards and rules and so forth and so on because they are appropriating money for it?

—U.S. Representative Donald W. Nicholson (R-MA) (1958)

For more than 220 years, the government of the United States has encouraged and supported education in America. Initially, the federal government provided indirect subsidies to schools. Later, direct assistance to schools came in the form of programs to meet specific needs. For the past five decades, the share of education revenues supplied by the federal government has grown steadily, along with the federal government's regulatory presence in schools. Indeed, with the passage of the No Child Left Behind Act a previously uncrossable ideological divide between a strictly limited federal role and the expansion of that role has been bridged. The bridge was conceived by liberals. Conservatives opposed the bridge at first, but then offered input on its design and ultimately insisted that its regulatory span be more sweeping. The bridge may be extended across other divides, such as private-school vouchers and the content of school curriculums. It is also possible that the bridge will be scaled back or dismantled, although this course seems unlikely at the moment.

The episodes covered in this book illustrate how conservative and liberal legislators influenced federal education policy and one another over time. Ideologically acceptable modes of federal involvement were brokered through the interaction of conservative and liberal values and beliefs. An evolving level of agreement on limited but gradually increasing levels of federal support and regulation was disrupted by No Child Left Behind. Under No

Child Left Behind, dramatically increased federal regulation of schools has replaced the tradition of limited federal involvement. If politicians ever rediscover and reembrace limits on federal authority over schools, they may retreat from the far-reaching accountability provisions of No Child Left Behind. On the other hand, values and beliefs of legislators sometimes undergo permanent shifts—such as political and ideological views on race—leading to permanent policy changes. Because it builds on such a deliberately negotiated and gradually developed array of earlier laws, No Child Left Behind appears to represent a permanent transformation of dominant views about limited federal involvement in schools.

The values and beliefs that underlie political transactions on education are my main interest in this book and each of the legislative episodes treated in the preceding chapters has been analyzed from the perspective of ideological politics. Congressional debates on federal education policy are rich sources of information about competing ideologies. The rhetoric reveals the values and beliefs that underlie contrasting views on proposed and existing policies. Because I treat the interaction of various ideologies over time rather than seeking a dominant or prevailing ideology, I find it useful to focus on how the competing ideologies are reflected in legislative proposals and final statutes. All of the laws in this study were shaped by competing, overlapping, and dynamic liberal and conservative arguments and ideologies.

We are left with a key question about the future: Where will future federal education policies take us? I have selected a few possibilities for discussion below. Of course, predicting the future is usually futile. The future that actually occurs may not even be foreseen. For example, would anyone have predicted the expansive No Child Left Behind just five years before it was enacted? Nevertheless, the following possible directions illustrate how the past may help us understand the future.

Possibilities for the Future

• Continued emphasis on high-stakes accountability

High-stakes accountability—financial and organizational consequences for schools based on student test scores—is here to stay. The movement that gave rise to it predates No Child Left Behind, and test-based accountability will continue with or without federal aid to schools. Test scores and other student outcomes have replaced older, input-based indicators in the minds of most politicians and the public at large. The criticisms leveled at No Child Left Behind testing mandates suggest to some leaders that the law is right on target: schools and teachers do not want to be shamed into improving, but improve they will if (and only if) their feet are kept to the fire. Public scrutiny of their performance and, perhaps, competition with private schools, will lead to measurable improvements in student learning, according to this thinking.

Note, however, that the testing requirements in the No Child Left Behind statute expose a wide divide between the knowledge of politicians and the knowledge of testing experts. Politics and education, two oft-maligned fields, are presently dominated by conflicting views on what is possible and desirable with respect to educational assessments. The political declaration that all students be proficient on state assessments by the 2013–14 school year flies in the face of decades of research about student performance on standardized tests. For starters, these assessments were designed to formally quantify the different performance levels of students (that is, the bell curve) and identify the needs of those who were struggling. Most of the tests that states administer to satisfy the requirements of No Child Left Behind are not suitable for large-scale judgments about school success and failure.

Notwithstanding the mismatch between the political and educational purposes of testing, supporters of No Child Left Behind should be commended for having high expectations for all students. The law's focus on student subgroups, for example, is an important continuation of the federal government's long-standing interest in civil rights. (No Child Left Behind's subgroup accountability requirements were originally introduced by Representative George Miller [D-CA; 2002 ADA score: 100] as part of the ill-fated ESEA reauthorization in 1999–2000 [Rudalevige 2003, 32–33].) I believe that many critics of No Child Left Behind have underestimated the civil rights significance of its subgroup accountability and reporting requirements.

The fact remains, however, that not all students will be able to meet these expectations in their current form. Special-education students and English-language learners, in particular, may find the performance standards very challenging. No Child Left Behind will brand many students and their schools as failures because they have not met proficiency targets set for them by noneducators in Congress. Not all these schools will "fail" in the same way. Yet, No Child Left Behind does not distinguish between schools that require major intervention and schools identified for improvement because test scores or participation rates were too low for one student subgroup. (For a technical but accessible discussion of the pitfalls of subgroup accountability reporting, see Kane and Staiger 2003.) There are not enough resources at the state and federal level to intervene in each of the growing number of schools identified as being in need of improvement. Moreover, it is a waste of time, money, and morale to overhaul a school that is not actually "failing."

Even if critics of the accountability movement do not buy all the arguments in favor of it, they should acknowledge the importance of gathering meaningful data on the effectiveness of educational programs receiving federal funds. The focus of No Child Left Behind on outcomes builds on earlier efforts by liberals and conservatives to understand the effects of, and improve on, federal education policies. As the consequences of No Child Left Behind are realized in more and more schools, it is possible that Congress will authorize more funds to pay the costs incurred by the law.

- Additional federal funds for assessments and corrective actions (including private-school vouchers)

Two proposals made during the original deliberations on No Child Left Behind did not make it into the final law: (1) additional funding for the law's testing requirements and (2) private-school vouchers as an option for students in persistently failing schools. The administration's limited acknowledgment of the cost of the law's testing provisions was a victory for conservatives; the removal of vouchers from the No Child Left Behind proposal was a victory for liberals. Neither faction abandoned its goals, however, and these debates are likely to replay when No Child Left Behind is reauthorized in 2007.

With respect to testing, we are already familiar with the unfunded mandate charge against the testing requirements of No Child Left Behind. I believe that most politicians are sensitive to this charge and want to avoid it. At the same time, politicians seem to accept the inevitability of unfunded mandates when federal regulations are imposed on education and other policy domains. Helping to pay for the law's testing provisions was part of the George W. Bush administration's rationale for requesting a modest Title I funding increase. Lingering concerns about the assessment costs facing states and school districts are likely to lead to increased federal funds for testing, along with reminders that some of these costs ought to be borne by state and local education agencies as a reasonable exchange for federal funds. At least one state is unconvinced. Connecticut has filed suit against the federal government, charging that No Child Left Behind unlawfully imposes testing costs that are not paid for by the federal government. (No Child Left Behind prohibits unfunded mandates, including unfunded assessment requirements [P.L.107-110, Title IX, sec. 9527(a)].)

Predictions about private-school vouchers are more problematic than predictions about testing subsidies. Once a congressional mandate (for example, annual assessments in grades 3–8) is on the books, its costs are on a sliding scale from completely funded to completely unfunded. Reasonable minds can disagree on how much of the bill is actually paid by Congress and on how much of it *ought* to be. Private-school vouchers are "out-of-bounds" at present; they are a clear-cut instance of a program that currently rests outside the ideological boundaries of acceptable educational policies. It is possible that these boundaries will shift, as they did when federal testing requirements stopped being out-of-bounds. Note, however, that vouchers are more controversial than test-based account-ability. The two ideas may be related, however. Some No Child Left Behind critics fear that as more schools are deemed failures, public support for vouchers and other privatization schemes will increase (Reeves 2005).

If federally supported vouchers do come to pass, a lot of legislative log-rolling will have had to occur. In past legislative episodes, neither conservatives nor liberals have gotten what they wanted without concessions and compromises. In exchange for a voucher program, for example, conservatives might have to agree to higher levels of Title I funding than they have consented to in the past. Voucher demonstration projects may precede a full-blown initiative. If evaluations of these projects are negative or mixed, liberals might be armed with the data they need to forestall a larger program. (In response to the hurricanes of 2005, a onetime voucher program for the Gulf Coast was enacted.) The voucher debate is interesting because it demonstrates that certain ideological divisions on education policy have not lessened over time.

- Additional federal funds for operations in schools identified for improvement (for example, teacher salaries and school facilities)

In addition to objecting to the cost and prescriptiveness of No Child Left Behind testing requirements, states and school districts are also concerned about the costs of assisting schools identified for improvement. State-level politicians and educators will continue to press Congress and the Department of Education to relax the accountability consequences in No Child Left Behind or, alternatively, to appropriate more money to help pay for them. The possibility of new, voucher-like interventions aside, compromises and concessions may be needed to retain the consequences for failing schools that No Child Left Behind already imposes, such as school reorganization or closure. If education advocates are successful in arguing for substantial new federal investments in the name of meaningful reform, activities that were formerly "out-of-bounds" may start to receive federal dollars: salaries (and salary increases) for teachers who work in high poverty, low-achieving schools; facility upgrades for aging schools; class-size reduction.

In the past, conservatives argued that increased federal funding for schools would lead to federal control of education. Liberals took pains to refute these accusations when they proposed school-aid programs. Today it appears that conservatives' warnings were correct. Federal control of schools—leveraged by past and current payments to schools—is coming at the expense of state and local autonomy. We are back on the sliding scale of perceptions about funding and authority for schools, but I believe that the proportion of federal regulation of and funding for public education will increase as No Child Left Behind is fully implemented. In addition, the variety of school expenses paid for with federal funds will also increase. (Of course, this growth may not occur if federal budget deficits or other government commitments threaten federal education spending.)

- Eroding political support for public schools identified as
  failing under No Child Left Behind

There is a provocative conspiracy theory about No Child Left Behind. Recall that federal requirements for "adequate yearly progress" (AYP) demand that all schools, regardless of baseline performance, keep improving until every student reaches proficiency on standardized tests. The theory holds that this definition of adequate performance is unrealistic and that, as a result, the database of "failing" schools will eventually consist of virtually every public school and school district in the nation. In the face of such "decisive" evidence that its schools have failed, the public will finally demand the private-school vouchers and tuition tax credits. Because they have been seeking these results for years, conservatives will find this scenario very appealing, according to the conspiracy theory. By redirecting tax dollars away from the public-school "monopoly"—another desire of conservatives—families will enjoy a wider range of public and private options for their children's education. In the process, increased competition from the private sector will impel public schools to improve.

This theory is as farfetched as it is intriguing. I believe that most Americans have faith in their public schools. They may not be willing to support them adequately—the sliding scale again—but they do favor them. Americans tend to be skeptical about schemes that enrich private schools—or the parents of the children who attend them—at the expense of public schools. When voucher programs are on state ballots, for example, they have usually been defeated. At the same time, Americans embrace school choice and endorse the rights of families to send their children to private schools at their own expense. Both belief systems are deeply rooted in American social and religious history. What most Americans seem to reject is the advisability of using public funds to merge these public- and private-school traditions.

Nevertheless, I believe that No Child Left Behind may contribute to a gradual erosion of support for public schools in a less dramatic and more indirect way. By not correctly distinguishing between schools that are truly struggling and those that are not, No Child Left Behind may divert our concern from high-poverty schools that need immediate help to the public education system as a whole (Hochschild 2003, 110–11). Skepticism about the quality of public schools relies on *perceptions* of low quality as well as on actual evidence. This makes the school-improvement designations under No Child Left Behind problematic because schools that are not actually failing will be told that they are. A supposedly objective, systematic, and comprehensive method that identifies large numbers of "failing" schools fuels the nagging perception that public schools are no longer working. The cumulative effect of these perceptions may be to foster the belief that public schools need constant federal monitoring more than they need tax dollars. Even if private-school vouchers do not result from No Child Left Behind's database of unsuccessful schools, erosion of public support is likely if schools are presumed to have failed simply because the bar for success is set unrealistically high.

Two Remaining Questions

• Will Congress retreat from some or all of No Child Left Behind?

We know that Congress has rejected a number of education proposals during its long history: funding for general aid and a national school system in the nineteenth century; school construction, tuition tax credits, and school prayer in the twentieth. Retreats from existing policies are rarer events, but they do happen. When federal education laws are perceived as doing too much too fast, they are sometimes modified or overturned by later actions. The formation and subsequent elimination of the Department of Education in the 1860s is a good example of such a retreat, as is the weakening of the Goals 2000 law after the 1994 midterm elections.

Will a similar fate befall No Child Left Behind? Will some or all of its controversial aspects be overturned or allowed to expire without being reauthorized? So far, the evidence does not suggest that it will. Even though the accountability requirements of No Child Left Behind go further than those of Goals 2000, No Child Left Behind does not seem to have overplayed its support in Congress. The main reason for this is the strong endorsement the latter law received from conservatives. Advocates of Goals 2000 did overplay the law's congressional support, and were forced to relax the law's requirements for state accountability two years after it was first enacted. The state accountability plans that were voluntary under Goals 2000 were more controversial than the mandatory plans under No Child Left Behind.

Nevertheless, the Department of Education has had to do quite a bit of public relations to persuade states and school districts that the provisions of No Child Left Behind are workable. The Education Department has also made some important concessions, especially under Education Secretary Margaret Spellings. For example, it has offered some flexibility on the implementation of "highly qualified teacher" requirements for rural teachers, science teachers, and multiple-subject teachers (U.S. Department of Education 2005a). The department has given states and school districts some leeway in calculating the testing participation rates for students with disabilities (U.S. Department of Education 2005b), flexibility in the timing of assessments for students who are English-language learners (ELL), and flexibility on the calculation of "adequate yearly progress" for ELL subgroups (U.S. Department of Education 2004).

At the same time, the Department of Education has held the line on the core accountability requirements of No Child Left Behind and was not able to prevent Connecticut's legal challenge to the law. This kind of court challenge to the unfunded mandates of No Child Left Behind might accelerate the allocation of additional federal funds to defray testing costs. The fact that the lawsuit was filed also indicates that there are requirements that the Department of Education does not intend to loosen. By comparison, the Department of Education and Congress made a rapid and decisive retreat on Goals 2000. The Department's minor concessions on

No Child Left Behind have been slower to come and do not reveal any equivocation about the purposes of the law. The Department of Education and Congress have signaled that they intend to stay the course on No Child Left Behind, despite concessions made by the Department of Education so far. Continued resistance by state and local policy-makers and educators may test the resolve of the Department of Education and Congress when No Child Left Behind is reauthorized, but a federal retreat from the law's high-stakes accountability requirements appears unlikely.

- Has the federal government done too much or too little for public education?

There are conflicting conservative and liberal answers to this question, and different answers at different times. Until recently, conservatives regularly claimed that the government was doing too much. The billions of dollars in aid was leading—per their earlier warnings—to too much regulatory control of schools. Liberals have reliably and successfully fought for increased financial support and today would like to see still more. Until public education receives substantially larger investments from the U.S. Treasury, the federal government will have done too little, according to the liberal view.

These ideological views have evolved in the past decade or so, and conservatives and liberals are now fairly similar in their calls for increased accountability. Conservatives believe that the mixed record of past federal investments justifies these demands. Conservatives are also more sympathetic to long-standing liberal demands for equality of educational opportunity. As we know from earlier episodes, liberals were demanding accountability for results long before conservatives were. In addition, liberals are making conservative-sounding arguments for fiscal accountability as they press for more school aid.

Not everyone's views have evolved, however. No Child Left Behind makes no sense to unreconstructed conservatives who favor a smaller federal government. The federal role in schools has expanded so dramatically under No Child Left Behind that even some liberals question the wisdom of placing the national government at the center of public-school accountability. The 2001 law attempts to do too much according to conservative ideological standards of yesterday. According to the liberal political standards of today, the law is also doing too much because its regulations overshadow the resources it provides.

No Child Left Behind is the eighth reauthorization of the Elementary and Secondary Education Act of 1965. The original law supported contrasting interpretations of the scope and meaning of federal involvement in education. That is, it permitted different answers to the question about the government doing too much or too little for U.S. schools. It did this by merging key ideological and political factors. Recall that the backers of the 1965 law simultaneously deployed an ideologically persuasive categorical-aid strategy and a politically necessary general-aid strategy. The law passed because most legislators believed that it was legitimate to target federal aid to economically disadvantaged students. Yet, congressional support also depended on spreading these funds as widely as possible. The two-pronged strategy of the Elementary and Secondary Education Act has had political and ideological repercussions for more than forty years.

If we go with a strict reading of the Elementary and Secondary Education Act's rationale for serving poor students and their schools, the federal government has not done enough to equalize funds within and across different states. Funding equalization, in turn, might help narrow the achievement gap between richer and poorer schools. Even with subsequent adjustments to the original 1965 Title I distribution formula, the neediest schools have not received enough money to narrow the funding and achievement gaps that separate them from wealthier schools.

The flip side of the categorical-aid rationale for the Elementary and Secondary Education Act is the general-aid argument that made expanded federal aid to schools politically possible. I would argue that, as a de facto general-aid program, the Elementary and Secondary Education Act has done too much. Through the ESEA, the federal government has given too much money to school districts and schools that do not need it. Hence, the *politically* motivated funding formula entails a different kind of intervention than the *ideologically* persuasive argument for delivering funds to economically disadvantaged students. The promise of Title I was compromised by the very design that made the program possible.

The original paradox of Title I has been supplemented by a new one in No Child Left Behind. The accountability provisions of the newer law will result in the punitive mislabeling of many schools as failing that, by most educational standards, are not. It may have been a Faustian bargain: by continually receiving funds they did not truly need, schools may find themselves with labels for ineffectiveness they do not deserve. Neither the Elementary and Secondary Education Act nor No Child Left Behind delivered resources and assistance to the schools that really needed them.

Differing views about the wisdom of expanding federal aid and authority for schools invites us to examine another assumption that underlies liberal and, later, conservative education activism. The assumption is that the federal government can actually do the job that Congress assigns it when legislators pass increasingly prescriptive school laws. Why does anyone—members of Congress, educators, or citizens—think the federal government can do a good job understanding or meeting local needs? State governments and local school districts are remarkably resistant to directives imposed from the outside. No matter how well conceived a federal policy may be or how well intentioned the Congress that enacts it, educators and schools have their own way of doing business. This does not mean that federal efforts to improve schools are doomed, but it does tell us that we need to understand what schools require to succeed and what success really looks like. Conservatives and liberals are now willing to indict public schools—and past federal efforts on behalf of schools—without understanding or acknowledging what is necessary to bring about true reform.

references

Alexander, Lamar. 1993. What we were doing when we were interrupted. In Jennings, John F., ed., *National issues in education: The past is prologue.* Bloomington, IN: Phi Delta Kappa International; and Washington, DC: Institute for Educational Leadership, 3–18.

Aly, Bower, ed. 1934. *Equalizing educational opportunity by means of federal aid to education.* Columbia, MO: Debate Handbook, Committee on Debate Materials and Interstate Cooperation.

Anderson, Lee W. 1997. *Ideology and the politics of federal aid to education, 1958–1996.* Unpublished doctoral dissertation, Stanford University (UMI/ProQuest no. AAT 9723318).

Atkin, J. Myron. 1980. The government in the classroom. *Daedalus* 109, no. 3 (Summer), 85–97.

Bailey, Stephen K., and Edith K. Mosher. 1968. ESEA: *The Office of Education administers a law.* Syracuse, NY: Syracuse University Press.

Bell, Terrel E. 1988. *The thirteenth man: A Reagan cabinet memoir.* New York: Free Press.

Bennett, William J. 1992. *The de-valuing of America: The fight for our culture and our children.* New York: Summit Books.

Carlson, Theodora E. 1959. *Guide to the National Defense Education Act of 1958.* U.S. Department of Health, Education, and Welfare circular no. 553. Washington, DC: U.S. Government Printing Office.

Carmines, Edward C., and James A. Stimson. 1989. *Issue evolution: Race and the transformation of American politics.* Princeton: Princeton University Press.

Clark, Duncan Ellsworth. 1930. *Nationalism in education, revealed in Congressional action, to 1862.* Unpublished doctorial dissertation, Stanford University.

Clowse, Barbara Barksdale. 1981. *Brainpower for the Cold War: The Sputnik crisis and the National Defense Education Act of 1958.* Westport, CT: Greenwood Press.

Cohodas, Nadine. 1993. *Strom Thurmond and the politics of southern change.* New York: Simon & Schuster.

Commission on Chapter 1. 1992. *Making schools work for children in poverty.* Washington, DC: American Association for Higher Education.

Congressional Quarterly Inc. 1959. *Congressional quarterly almanac* XIV (85th Cong., 2d sess., 1958). Washington, DC: Author.

Congressional Quarterly Inc. 1966. *Congressional quarterly almanac* XXI (89th Cong., 1st sess., 1965). Washington, DC: Author.

Congressional Quarterly Inc. 1976. *Congressional quarterly almanac* XXXI (94th Cong., 1st sess., 1975). Washington, DC: Author.

Congressional Quarterly Inc. 1980. *Congressional quarterly almanac* XXXV (96th Cong., 1st sess., 1979). Washington, DC: Author.

Congressional Quarterly Inc. 1982. *Congressional quarterly almanac* XXXVII (97th Cong., 1st sess., 1981). Washington, DC: Author.

Congressional Quarterly Inc. 1985. *Congressional quarterly almanac* XL (98th Cong., 2d sess., 1984). Washington, DC: Author.

Congressional Quarterly Inc. 1989. *Congressional quarterly almanac* XLIV (100th Cong., 2d sess., 1988). Washington, DC: Author.

Congressional Quarterly Inc. 1993. *Congressional quarterly almanac* XLVIII (102d Cong., 2d sess., 1992). Washington, DC: Author.

Congressional Quarterly Inc. 1995. *Congressional quarterly almanac* XL (103d Cong., 2d sess., 1994). Washington, DC: Author.

Congressional Quarterly Inc. 2001. *Congressional quarterly almanac* LVI (106th Cong., 2d sess., 2000). Washington, DC: Author.

Congressional Quarterly Inc. 2002. *Congressional quarterly almanac* LVII (107th Cong., 1st sess., 2001). Washington, DC: Author.

Congressional Record. 1948. 80th Cong., 2d sess. (94, pt. 3). Washington, DC: U.S. Government Printing Office.

Congressional Record. 1950. 81st Cong., 2d sess. (96, pt. 8). Washington, DC: U.S. Government Printing Office.

Congressional Record. 1958. 85th Cong., 2d sess. (104, pt. 13). Washington, DC: U.S. Government Printing Office.

Congressional Record. 1965. 89th Cong., 1st sess. (111, pts. 5, 6, 17). Washington, DC: U.S. Government Printing Office.

Congressional Record. 1975. 94th Cong., 1st sess. (121, pts. 20, 29). Washington, DC: U.S. Government Printing Office.

Congressional Record. 1978. 95th Cong., 2d sess. (124). Washington, DC: U.S. Government Printing Office. (Reprinted in U.S. Senate, 1980, *Legislative history of Public Law 96–88: Department of Education Organization Act.* 96th Cong., 2d sess., pt. 1. Committee on Governmental Affairs. Washington, DC: U.S. Government Printing Office. Page numbers in citations refer to *Legislative history.*)

Congressional Record. 1979. 96th Cong., 1st sess. (125). Washington, DC: U.S. Government Printing Office. (Reprinted in U.S. Senate, 1980, *Legislative history of Public Law 96–88: Department of Education Organization Act.* 96th Cong., 2d sess., pts. 1, 2. Committee on Governmental Affairs. Washington, DC: U.S. Government Printing Office. Page numbers in citations refer to *Legislative history.*)

Congressional Record. 1993. 103rd Cong., 1st sess. (139, pt. 17). Washington, DC: U.S. Government Printing Office.

Congressional Record. 1994a. 103rd Cong., 2d sess. (140, pts 1, 2, 5, 20). Washington, DC: U.S. Government Printing Office.

Congressional Record. 1994b. 103rd Cong., 2d sess. (140, pt 17 [unbound {February 24}]). Washington, DC: U.S. Government Printing Office.

Congressional Record. 2001. 107th Cong., 1st sess. (147, pts. 5, 6, 7, 8, 19). Washington, DC: U.S. Government Printing Office.

Cross, Christopher T. 2004. *Political education: National policy comes of age.* New York: Teachers College Press.

Cuban, Larry. 1982. Enduring resiliency: Enacting and implementing federal vocational education legislation. In Kantor, Harvey, and David B. Tyack, eds., *Work, youth, and schooling: Historical perspectives on vocationalism in American education.* Stanford, CA: Stanford University Press, 45–78.

Doak, E. Dale. 1968. Public money for parochial schools? *Educational Leadership* 26, no. 3 (December), 246–49.

Duffy, Cathy. 1995. *Government nannies: The cradle-to-grave agenda of Goals 2000 and outcome based education.* Gresham, OR: Noble Publishing Associates.

Dumenil, Lynn. 1990. "The insatiable maw of bureaucracy": Antistatism and education reform in the 1920s. *Journal of American History* 77, no. 2 (September), 499–524.

Eidenberg, Eugene, and Roy D. Morey. 1969. *An act of Congress: The legislative process and the making of educational policy.* New York: W. W. Norton.

Elam, Stanley M., ed. 1978. *A decade of Gallup Polls of attitudes toward education, 1969–1978.* Bloomington, IN: Phi Delta Kappa Inc.

Elazar, Daniel J. 1962. *The American partnership: Intergovernmental co-operation in the nineteenth-century United States.* Chicago: University of Chicago Press.

Elmore, Richard F. 2002. Unwarranted intrusion. *Education Next* 2, no. 1 (Spring), 30–35.

Elmore, Richard F., and Susan H. Fuhrman. 1995. Opportunity-to-learn standards and the state role in education. *Teachers College Record* 96, no. 3 (Spring), 432–57.

Elmore, Richard F., and Milbrey Wallin McLaughlin. 1988. *Steady work: Policy, practice, and reform of American education.* Santa Monica: RAND Corporation.

Encarnation, Dennis J. 1982. *Why create a separate Department of Education? A budgetary analysis.* Program report no. 82-B5. Stanford, CA: Institute for Research on Educational Finance and Governance.

Ford, Gerald R. 1975. Education for All Handicapped Children Act of 1975: Statement by the President upon signing the bill into law, while expressing reservations about certain of its provisions. In *Weekly compilation of Presidential documents* 11, no. 49 (December 2), 1335. Washington, DC: Office of the Federal Register, National Archives and Records Service, General Services Administration.

Goldwater, Barry. 1960. *The conscience of a conservative.* Shepherdsville, KY: Victor Publishing Company Inc.

Graham, Hugh Davis. 1984. *The uncertain triumph: Federal education policy in the Kennedy and Johnson years.* Chapel Hill: University of North Carolina Press.

Guthrie, James W. 1982. The future of federal education policy. *Education and Urban Society* 14, no. 4 (August), 511–30.

Guthrie, James W., and Julia Koppich. 1987. Exploring the political economy of national education reform. In Boyd, William Lowe, and Charles Taylor Kerchner, eds., *The politics of excellence and choice in education (1987 Yearbook of the Politics of Education Association).* New York: Falmer Press, 25–47.

Gutmann, Amy. 1999. *Democratic education.* Princeton: Princeton University Press.

Halperin, Samuel. 1978. *Some diagnoses and prescriptions.* In Cross, Christopher T., et al., *Education policy in the Carter years.* Washington, DC: Institute for Educational Leadership, George Washington University, 57–71.

Hanushek, Eric A., and Margaret E. Raymond. 2003. Lessons about the design of state accountability systems. In Peterson, Paul E., and Martin R. West, eds., *No Child Left Behind? The politics and practice of school accountability.* Washington, DC: Brookings Institution Press, 127–51.

Henderson, Anne, ed. 1983. *No strings attached: An interim report on the education block grant.* Columbia, MD: National Committee for Citizens in Education Inc.

Hochschild, Jennifer. 2003. Rethinking accountability politics. In Peterson, Paul E., and Martin R. West, eds., *No Child Left Behind? The politics and practice of school accountability.* Washington, DC: Brookings Institution Press, 107–23.

Holt, W. Stull. 1922. *The federal board for vocational education: Its history, activities, and organization.* New York: Institute for Government Research / D. Appleton & Company.

James, Edmund J. 1910. The origin of the Land Grant Act of 1862 (the so-called Morrill Act). *University Studies* 4, no. 1 (November). Urbana-Champaign, IL: University Press.

Jeffrey, Julie Roy. 1978. *Education for children of the poor: A study of the origins and implementation of the Elementary and Secondary Education Act of 1965.* Columbus: Ohio State University Press.

Jennings, Frank G. 1967. It didn't start with Sputnik. *Saturday Review,* September 16, 77–79 and 95–97.

· Kaestle, Carl F. 1983. *Pillars of the republic: Common schools and American society, 1780–1860.* New York: Hill & Wang / Farrar, Straus & Giroux.

Kaestle, Carl F., and Marshall S. Smith. 1982. The federal role in elementary and secondary education, 1940–1980. *Harvard Educational Review* 52, no. 4 (November), 384–408.

Kane, Thomas J., and Douglas O. Staiger. 2003. Unintended consequences of racial subgroup rules. In Paul E. Peterson and Martin R. West, eds., *No Child Left Behind? The politics and practice of school accountability.* Washington, DC: Brookings Institution Press, 152–76.

Kantor, Harvey. 1982. Vocationalism in American education: The economic and political context, 1880–1930. In Kantor, Harvey, and Tyack, David B., eds., *Work, youth, and schooling: Historical perspectives on vocationalism in American education.* Stanford, CA: Stanford University Press, 14–44.

Kantor, Harvey, and Robert Lowe. 1995. Class, race, and the emergence of federal education policy: From the New Deal to the Great Society. *Educational Researcher* 24, no. 3 (April), 4–11, 21.

Lee, Gordon Canfield. 1949. *The struggle for federal aid, first phase, A history of the attempts to obtain federal aid for the common schools, 1870–1890.* Contributions to Education series, no. 957. New York: Teachers College, Columbia University, Bureau of Publications.

Majone, Giandomenico. 1989. *Evidence, argument, and persuasion in the policy process.* New Haven: Yale University Press.

Manna, Paul. 2006. *School's in: Federalism and the national education agenda.* Washington, DC: Georgetown University Press.

Marsh, Paul E., and Ross A. Gortner. 1963. *Federal aid to science education: Two programs,* Syracuse, NY: Syracuse University Press.

Martin, Ruby, and Phyllis McClure. 1969. *Title I of ESEA: Is it helping poor children?* Washington, DC: Washington Research Project and NAACP Legal Defense and Education Fund Inc.

McGuinn, Patrick J. 2006. *No Child Left Behind and the transformation of federal education policy, 1965–2005.* Lawrence: University Press of Kansas.

Meranto, Philip. 1967. *The politics of federal aid to education in 1965.* Syracuse, NY: Syracuse University Press.

Moynihan, Daniel Patrick. 1988. Federal aid to education: A zero-sum game? In Daniel Patrick Moynihan, *Came the revolution: Argument in the Reagan era.* San Diego: Harcourt Brace Jovanovich, 42–50.

Muller, Helen M., ed. 1934. *Federal aid for the equalization of educational opportunity.* New York: H. W. Wilson Company.

Munger, Frank J., and Richard F. Fenno, Jr. 1962. *National politics and federal aid to education*. Syracuse, NY: Syracuse University Press.

National Assessment of Chapter 1 Independent Review Panel. 1993. *Reinventing chapter 1: The current chapter 1 program and new directions*. Washington, DC: U.S. Department of Education, Office of Policy and Planning, Planning and Evaluation Service.

National Commission on Excellence in Education. 1983. *A nation at risk: The imperative for educational reform*. Washington, DC: U.S. Government Printing Office.

Neal, David, and David L. Kirp. 1986. The allure of legalization reconsidered: The case of special education. In Kirp, David L. and Donald N. Jensen, eds., *School days, rule days*. Philadelphia: Falmer Press, 343–65.

Nichols, Egbert Ray, ed. 1948. *Selected readings on federal aid to education: A handbook on the 1948–49 college subject*. Redlands, CA: Nichols Publishing House.

Peskin, Allan. 1973. The short, unhappy life of the federal Department of Education. *Public Administration Review* 33, no. 6 (November/December), 572–75.

Peterson, Paul E. 1976. *School politics Chicago style*. Chicago: University of Chicago Press.

Pitsch, Mark. 1995. "Goals 2000 Fails to Gain Firm Foothold," *Education Week*, June 7, 1 and 18.

Powell, Theodore. 1960. *The school bus law: A case study in education, religion, and politics*. Middletown, CT: Wesleyan University Press.

Price, Hugh Douglas. 1962. Race, religion, and the Rules Committee: The Kennedy aid-to-education bills. In Westin, Alan F., ed., *The uses of power*. New York: Harcourt, Brace & World, 1–71.

Public Law 88-352 (Civil Rights Act of 1964). *United States Statutes at Large* 78 (88th Cong., 2d sess., July 2, 1964), 241–68.

Public Law 89-10 (Elementary and Secondary Education Act of 1965). *United States Statutes at Large* 79 (89th Cong., 1st sess., April 11, 1965), 27–58.

Public Law 94-142 (Education for All Handicapped Children Act of 1975). *United States Statutes at Large* 89 (94th Cong., 1st sess., November 29, 1975), 773–96.

Public Law 100-297 (Augustus F. Hawkins—Robert T. Stafford Elementary and Secondary School Improvement Amendments of 1988). *United States Statutes at Large* 102 (pt. 1) (100th Cong., 2d sess., April 28, 1988), 130–431.

Public Law 103-227 (Goals 2000: Educate America Act). *United States Statutes at Large* 108 (pt. 1) 103rd Cong., 2d sess., March 31, 1994), 125–280.

Public Law 103-382 (Improving America's Schools Act of 1994). *United States Statutes at Large* 108 (pt. 5) 103rd Cong., 2d sess., October 20, 1994), 3518–4062.

Public Law 107-110 (No Child Left Behind Act of 2001). *United States Statutes at Large* 115 (pt. 2) (107th Cong., 1st sess., January 8, 2002), 1425–2094.

Radin, Beryl A., and Willis D. Hawley. 1988. *The politics of federal reorganization: Creating the U.S. Department of Education*. Elmsford, NY: Pergamon Press.

Reeves, Douglas B. 2005. "Education, not litigation: Four keys to a mediated solution of the 'No Child' debate." *Education Week*. October 12, 40.

Report of the President's Task Force on Education. 1964. Unpublished final report (November 14). Source: Papers of John W. Gardner, Green Special Collections, Stanford University Libraries.

Riker, William H. 1986. Exploiting the Powell amendment. In Riker, William H., *The art of political manipulation*. New Haven: Yale University Press, 114–28.

Riley, Richard W. 1995. Reflections on Goals 2000. *Teachers College Record* 96, no. 3 (Spring), 380–88.

Rose, Mark H. 1979. *Interstate: Express highway politics, 1941–1956.* Lawrence, KS: Regents Press of Kansas.

Rudalevige Andrew. 2003. No Child Left Behind: Forging a congressional compromise. In Peterson, Paul E., and Martin R. West, eds., *No Child Left Behind? The politics and practice of school accountability.* Washington, DC: Brookings Institution Press, 23–55.

Scott, Robert L. 1997. Cold War and rhetoric: Conceptually and critically. In Medhurst, Martin J., et al., eds., *Cold War rhetoric: Strategy, metaphor, and ideology,* rev. ed. East Lansing: Michigan State University Press, 1–16.

Sharp, J. Michael. 1988. *The directory of congressional voting scores and interest group ratings.* New York: Facts on File Publications.

Smith, Gilbert E. 1982. *The limits of reform: Politics and federal aid to education, 1937–1950.* New York: Garland Publishing.

Stoner, Floyd Eugene. 1976. *Implementation of ambiguous legislative language: Title I of the Elementary and Secondary Education Act.* Unpublished doctoral dissertation, University of Wisconsin–Madison.

Sufrin, Sidney C. 1963. *Administering the National Defense Education Act.* Syracuse, NY: Syracuse University Press.

Swift, Fletcher Harper. 1931. *Federal and state policies in public school finance in the United States.* Boston: Ginn & Company.

Tigert, J. J. 1934. The real peril of federal subsidies: A calm examination of a stormy issue. *The Nation's Schools,* July, 12–15. Reprinted in Quattlebaum, Charles A., *Federal aid to elementary and secondary education* (Chicago: Public Administration Service, 1948), 132–33.

Tyack, David; Thomas James; and Aaron Benavot. 1987. *Law and the shaping of public education, 1785–1954.* Madison: University of Wisconsin Press.

U.S. Department of Education. 1996. *Goals 2000: Increasing student achievement through state and local initiatives.* Report to Congress. April 30. Washington, DC: Author.

U.S. Department of Education. 2004. *New policies provide states with increased flexibility to help English language learners.* February 20. Retrieved November 8, 2005, from http://www.ed.gov/print/news/newsletters/extracredit/2004/02/0220.html.

U.S. Department of Education. 2005a. *New No Child Left Behind flexibility: Highly qualified teachers.* March 15. Retrieved November 8, 2005, from http://www.ed.gov/print/nclb/methods/teachers/hqtflexibility.html.

U.S. Department of Education. 2005b. *No Child Left Behind provision gives schools new flexibility and ensures accountability for students with disabilities.* May 5. Retrieved November 8, 2005, from http://www.ed.gov/print/news/pressreleases/2005/05/05102005.html.

U.S. House of Representatives. 1958a. *National Defense Education Act of 1958.* Report of the Committee on Education and Labor (House report no. 2157). 85th Cong., 2d sess. In U.S. House of Representatives, *House miscellaneous reports on public bills* IV. Washington, DC: U.S. Government Printing Office.

U.S. House of Representatives. 1958b. *Scholarship and Loan Program.* Hearings before a Subcommittee [Subcommittee on Special Education and Subcommittee on General Education] of the Committee on Education and Labor (pts. 1–3). 85th Cong., 1st sess. Washington, DC: U.S. Government Printing Office.

U.S. House of Representatives. 1965a. *Aid to Elementary and Secondary Education.* Hearings before the General Subcommittee on Education of the Committee on Education and Labor on H.R.2361 and H.R.2362 (pts. 1 and 2). 89th Cong., 1st sess. Washington, DC: U.S. Government Printing Office.

U.S. House of Representatives. 1965b. *Elementary and Secondary Education Act of 1965*. Report of the Committee on Education and Labor to accompany H.R.2362 (House report no. 143). 89th Cong., 1st sess. In U.S. House of Representatives, *House miscellaneous reports on public bills* I. Washington, DC: U.S. Government Printing Office.

U.S. House of Representatives. 1975. *Education For All Handicapped Children Act of 1975*. Report of the Committee on Education and Labor to accompany H.R. 7217 (House report no. 94-332). 94th Cong., 1st sess. In U.S. House of Representatives, *House miscellaneous reports on public bills* VI. Washington, DC: U.S. Government Printing Office.

U.S. House of Representatives. 1978a. Department of Education Organization Act. Report of the Committee on Government Operations on H.R.13778 (House report no. 95-1531). 95th Cong., 2d sess. In U.S. Senate, 1980, *Legislative history of Public Law 96-88: Department of Education Organization Act*. 96th Cong., 2d sess., pt. 2. Committee on Governmental Affairs. Washington, DC: U.S. Government Printing Office, 1004–77.

U.S. House of Representatives. 1978b. *Establishing a Department of Education*. Hearings before a Subcommittee [the Legislation and National Security Subcommittee] of the Committee on Government Operations on H.R.13778. 95th Cong., 2d sess. Washington, DC: U.S. Government Printing Office.

U.S. House of Representatives. 1979a. *Department of Education Organization Act*. Hearings before a Subcommittee [the Legislation and National Security Subcommittee] of the Committee on Government Operations on H.R.2444. 96th Cong., 1st sess. Washington, DC: U.S. Government Printing Office.

U.S. House of Representatives. 1979b. Department of Education Organization Act. Report of the Committee on Government Operations to accompany H.R. 2444 (House report no. 96-143). 96th Cong., 1st sess. In U.S. Senate, 1980, *Legislative history of Public Law 96-88: Department of Education Organization Act*. 96th Cong., 2d sess., pt. 2. Committee on Governmental Affairs. Washington, DC: U.S. Government Printing Office, 1103–205.

U.S. House of Representatives. 1981. *Field hearings on the Education for All Handicapped Children Act*. Hearings before the Subcommittee on Select Education, Committee on Education and Labor. 96th Cong., 2d sess. Washington, DC: U.S. Government Printing Office.

U.S. House of Representatives. 1993a. *Goals 2000: Educate America Act*. Report of the Committee on Education and Labor to accompany H.R.1804 (House report no. 103-168). 103rd Cong., 1st sess. Washington, DC: U.S. Government Printing Office.

U.S. House of Representatives. 1993b. *Hearings on H.R.1804—Goals 2000: Educate America Act*. Hearings before the Subcommittee on Elementary, Secondary, and Vocational Education of the Committee on Education and Labor. 103rd Cong., 1st sess. Washington, DC: U.S. Government Printing Office.

U.S. House of Representatives. 1998. *H.R.3130, The Improving America's Schools Act of 1993: The implications for urban districts*. Hearing before the Human Resources and Intergovernmental Relations Subcommittee of the Committee on Government Operations. 103rd Cong., 1st sess. Washington, DC: U.S. Government Printing Office.

U.S. House of Representatives. 2001a. *Leave no child behind.* Hearing before the Committee on Education and the Workforce. 107th Cong., 1st sess. (serial no. 107-5). Washington, DC: U.S. Government Printing Office.

U.S. House of Representatives. 2001b. *No Child Left Behind.* Hearing on H.R.1. Committee on Education and the Workforce. 107th Cong., 1st sess. (serial no. 107-9). Washington, DC: U.S. Government Printing Office.

U.S. House of Representatives. 2001c. *Transforming the federal role in education for the 21st century.* Hearing on H.R.1, H.R.340, and H.R 345. Committee on Education and the Workforce. 107th Cong., 1st sess. (serial no. 107-10). Washington, DC: U.S. Government Printing Office.

U.S. Senate. 1958a. *National Defense Education Act of 1958.* Report of the Committee on Labor and Public Welfare (Senate report no. 2242). 85th Cong., 2d sess. In U.S. Senate, *Senate miscellaneous reports on public bills* IV. Washington, DC: U.S. Government Printing Office.

U.S. Senate. 1958b. *Science and education for national defense.* Hearings before the Committee on Labor and Public Welfare. 85th Cong., 2d sess. Washington, DC: U.S. Government Printing Office.

U.S. Senate. 1965a. *Elementary and Secondary Education Act of 1965.* Hearings before the Subcommittee on Education of the Committee on Labor and Public Welfare on S.370. 89th Cong., 1st sess. Washington, DC: U.S. Government Printing Office.

U.S. Senate. 1965b. *Elementary and Secondary Education Act of 1965.* Report of the Committee on Labor and Public Welfare to accompany H.R.2362 (Senate report no. 146). 89th Cong., 1st sess. In U.S. Senate, 1965, *Senate Miscellaneous Reports on Public Bills* I. Washington, DC: U.S. Government Printing Office.

U.S. Senate. 1973. *Education for all handicapped children, 1973–74.* Hearings before the Subcommittee on the Handicapped of the Committee on Labor and Public Welfare on S.6. 93rd Cong., 1st sess. Washington, DC: U.S. Government Printing Office.

U.S. Senate. 1975. *Education for all handicapped children, 1975.* Hearings before the Subcommittee on the Handicapped of the Committee on Labor and Public Welfare on S.6. 94th Cong., 1st sess. Washington, DC: U.S. Government Printing Office.

U.S. Senate. 1977. *Department of Education Act of 1977.* Hearings before the Committee on Governmental Affairs on S.991, S.255, S.300, S.894, and S.1685. 95th Cong., 1st sess., pt. 1. Washington, DC: U.S. Government Printing Office.

U.S. Senate. 1978a. *Department of Education Act.* Hearings before the Committee on Governmental Affairs on S.991, S.255, S.300, S.894, and S.1685. 95th Cong., 2d sess., pt. 2. Washington, DC: U.S. Government Printing Office.

U.S. Senate. 1978b. *Department of Education Organization Act of 1978.* Report from the Committee on Governmental Affairs to accompany S.991 (Senate report no. 95-1078). 95th Cong., 2d sess. In U.S. Senate, 1980, *Legislative history of Public Law 96-88: Department of Education Organization Act.* 96th Cong., 2d sess., pt. 1. Committee on Governmental Affairs. Washington, DC: U.S. Government Printing Office, 64–225.

U.S. Senate. 1979. *Department of Education Organization Act of 1979.* Hearings before the Committee on Governmental Affairs on S.210 and S.510. 96th Cong., 1st sess. Washington, DC: U.S. Government Printing Office.

U.S. Senate. 1993a. *Goals 2000: Educate America Act.* Hearing before the Committee on Labor and Human Resources on S.846. 103rd Cong., 1st sess. Washington, DC: U.S. Government Printing Office.

U.S. Senate. 1993b. *Goals 2000: Educate America Act.* Report of the Committee on Labor and Human Resources to accompany S.1150 (Senate report no. 103-85). Washington, DC: U.S. Government Printing Office.

U.S. Senate. 2001. *President Bush's educational proposals.* Hearing of the Committee on Health, Education, Labor, and Pensions. 107th Cong., 1st Sess (S.Hrg.107-8). Washington, DC: U.S. Government Printing Office.

U.S. Senate. 2002. *Implementation of the No Child Left Behind Act.* Hearing before the Committee on Health, Education, Labor, and Pensions. 107th Cong., 2d sess. (S.Hrg.107-423). Washington, DC: U.S. Government Printing Office.

Wirt, Frederick M., and Michael W. Kirst. 1975. ESEA and intergovernmental relations. In Wirt, Frederick M., and Michael W. Kirst, *Political and social foundations of education.* Berkeley, CA: McCutchan Publishing Corporation, 153–72.

Zirkel, Perry A., and Richardson, Sharon Nalbone. 1988. *A digest of Supreme Court decisions affecting education.* 2d ed. Bloomington, IN: Phi Delta Kappa Educational Foundation.

index